7-50

RYAN

# PUBLISHED

Jane Austen: *Emma*  DAVID LODGE
Jane Austen: *'Northanger Abbey' & 'Persuasion'*  B.C. SOUTHAM
Jane Austen: *'Sense and Sensibility', 'Pride and Prejudice' & 'Mansfield Park'*
  B.C. SOUTHAM
Beckett: *Waiting for Godot*  RUBY COHN
William Blake: *Songs of Innocence and Experience*  MARGARET BOTTRALL
Charlotte Brontë: *'Jane Eyre' & 'Villette'*  MIRIAM ALLOTT
Emily Brontë: *Wuthering Heights*  MIRIAM ALLOTT
Browning: *'Men and Women' & Other Poems*  J.R. WATSON
Bunyan: *The Pilgrim's Progress*  ROGER SHARROCK
Chaucer: *Canterbury Tales*  J.J. ANDERSON
Coleridge: *'The Ancient Mariner' & Other Poems*  ALUN R. JONES & WILLIAM TYDEMAN
Congreve: *Comedies*  PATRICK LYONS
Conrad: *'Heart of Darkness', 'Nostromo' & 'Under Western Eyes'*  C.B. COX
Conrad: *The Secret Agent*  IAN WATT
Dickens: *Bleak House*  A.E. DYSON
Dickens: *'Hard Times', 'Great Expectations' & 'Our Mutual Friend'*  NORMAN PAGE
Dickens: *'Dombey and Son' & 'Little Dorrit'*  ALAN SHELSTON
Donne: *Songs and Sonets*  JULIAN LOVELOCK
George Eliot: *Middlemarch*  PATRICK SWINDEN
George Eliot: *'The Mill on the Floss' & 'Silas Marner'*  R.P. DRAPER
T.S. Eliot: *Four Quartets*  BERNARD BERGONZI
T.S. Eliot: *'Prufrock', 'Gerontion', 'Ash W̶e̶d̶n̶e̶s̶d̶a̶y̶' & Other Shorter P̶o̶e̶m̶s̶*
  B.C. SOUTHAM
T.S. Eliot: *The Waste Land*  C.B. COX
T.S. Eliot: *Plays*  ARNOLD P. HINCHLI̶F̶F̶E̶
Henry Fielding: *Tom Jones*  NEIL COM̶P̶T̶O̶N̶
E.M. Forster: *A Passage to India*  MAL̶C̶O̶L̶M̶
William Golding: *Novels 1954-64*  NO̶R̶M̶A̶N̶
Hardy: *The Tragic Novels*  R.P. DRAPER̶
Hardy: *Poems*  JAMES GIBSON & TREVOR JOHNSON
Hardy: *Three Pastoral Novels*  R.P. DRAPER
Gerard Manley Hopkins:  MARGARET BOTTRALL
Henry James: *'Washington Square' & 'The Portrait of a Lady'*  ALAN SHELSTON
Jonson: *Volpone*  JONAS A. BARISH
Jonson: *'Every Man in his Humour' & 'The Alchemist'*  R.V. HOLDSWORTH
James Joyce: *'Dubliners' & 'A Portrait of the Artist as a Young Man'*  MORRIS BEJA
Keats: *Odes*  G.S. FRASER
Keats: *Narrative Poems*  JOHN SPENCER HILL
D.H. Lawrence: *Sons and Lovers*  GAMINI SALGADO
D.H. Lawrence: *'The Rainbow' & 'Women in Love'*  COLIN CLARKE
Lowry: *Under the Volcano*  GORDON BOWKER
Marlowe: *Doctor Faustus*  JOHN JUMP
Marlowe: *'Tamburlaine the Great', 'Edward the Second' & 'The Jew of Malta'*
  JOHN RUSSELL BROWN
Marvell: *Poems*  ARTHUR POLLARD
Milton: *Paradise Lost*  A.E. DYSON & JULIAN LOVELOCK
O'Casey: *'Juno and the Paycock', 'The Plough and the Stars' & 'The Shadow of a
  Gunman'*  RONALD AYLING
John Osborne: *Look Back in Anger*  JOHN RUSSELL TAYLOR

OTHER CASEBOOKS ARE IN PREPARATION

# Shakespeare
## *The Tempest*

A CASEBOOK

EDITED BY

D. J. PALMER

MACMILLAN
EDUCATION

First published 1968
11th reprint 1988

Published by
MACMILLAN EDUCATION LTD
Houndmills, Basingstoke, Hampshire RG21 2XS
and London
Companies and representatives
throughout the world

Printed in Hong Kong

ISBN 0-333-01375-1

# CONTENTS

## Part 2: *Recent Studies*

# SOURCES
# AND ACKNOWLEDGEMENTS

PART I

The John Dryden and Sir William Davenant version of *The Tempest* (1670); John Dryden's Preface to *Troilus and Cressida* (1679); Nicholas Rowe, *Some Account of the Life &c. of Mr. William Shakespeare* (1709); Joseph Warton, from *The Adventurer*, no. 93 and no. 97 (1753); Dr Johnson's Note on *The Tempest*, Act I, scene iv, from *The Works of William Shakespeare* (1765); S. T. Coleridge's Ninth Lecture from *Lectures on Shakespeare and Milton* (1811) and an extract from *Literary Remains* (pub. 1836); William Hazlitt, *Characters of Shakespeare's Plays* (1817); Edward Dowden, *Shakspere – His Mind and Art* (1875); Henry James's Introduction to *The Tempest*, first published in *The Complete Works of William Shakespeare*, vol. XVI of the Renaissance Edition (1907); extract from 'Caliban to the Audience', from *The Sea and the Mirror* in *For the Time Being* (Faber & Faber Ltd, Random House Inc., 1945).

PART 2

John Middleton Murry, *Shakespeare* (Jonathan Cape Ltd and The Society of Authors); E. M. W. Tillyard, *Shakespeare's Last Plays* (Miss Angela Tillyard and Chatto & Windus Ltd); G. Wilson Knight, *The Crown of Life* (Methuen & Co. Ltd, Barnes & Noble Inc.); Reuben A. Brower, *The Fields of Light* (Oxford University Press Inc., New York; © Oxford University Press Inc. 1951); Frank Kermode (ed.), *The Tempest* (1954) in *The Arden Edition of the Works of William Shakespeare* (Methuen & Co. Ltd, Harvard University Press); John P. Cutts,

'Music and the Supernatural in *The Tempest*', from *Music and Letters*, XXXVI (Oct 1958) 2 (The Editor); Frank Davidson, '*The Tempest*: An Interpretation', in *Journal of English and Germanic Philology*, 62 (1963) (The University of Illinois Press); 'Form and Disorder in *The Tempest*', from *Shakespeare Quarterly* (Dr Rose Zimbardo and The Shakespeare Association of America Inc.); Jan Kott, *Shakespeare Our Contemporary* (Methuen & Co. Ltd, Doubleday & Co. Inc.; © Panstwowe Wydawnictwo Naukowe 1964).

# GENERAL EDITOR'S PREFACE

EACH of this series of Casebooks concerns either one well-known and influential work of literature or two or three closely linked works. The main section consists of critical readings, mostly modern, brought together from journals and books. A selection of reviews and comments by the author's contemporaries is also included, and sometimes comments from the author himself. The Editor's Introduction charts the reputation of the work from its first appearance until the present time.

What is the purpose of such a collection? Chiefly, to assist reading. Our first response to literature may be, or seem to be, 'personal'. Certain qualities of vigour, profundity, beauty or 'truth to experience' strike us, and the work gains a foothold in our mind. Later, an isolated phrase or passage may return to haunt or illuminate. Where did we hear that? we wonder – it could scarcely be better put.

In these and similar ways appreciation begins, but major literature prompts to very much more. There are certain facts we need to know if we are to understand properly. Who were the author's original readers, and what assumptions did he share with them? What was his theory of literature? Was he committed to a particular historical situation, or to a set of beliefs? We need historians as well as critics to help us with this. But there are also more purely literary factors to take account of: the work's structure and rhetoric; its symbols and archetypes; its tone, genre and texture; its use of language; the words on the page. In all these matters critics can inform and enrich our individual responses by offering imaginative recreations of their own.

For the life of a book is not, after all, merely 'personal'; it is more like a tripartite dialogue, between a writer living 'then', a reader living 'now', and whatever forces of survival and honour link the two. Criticism is the public manifestation of this dialogue, a witness to the continuing power of literature to arouse and excite. It illuminates the possibilities and regards of the dialogue, pushing 'interpretation' as far forward as it can go.

And here, indeed, is the rub: how far can it go? Where does 'interpretation' end and nonsense begin? Why is one interpretation superior to another, and why does each age need to interpret for itself? The critic knows that his insights have value only in so far as they serve the text, and that he must take account of views differing sharply from his own. He knows that his own writing will be judged as well as the work he writes about, so that he cannot simply assert inner illumination or a differing taste.

The critical forum is a place of vigorous conflict and disagreement, but there is nothing in this to cause dismay. What is attested is the complexity of human experience and the richness of literature, not any chaos or relativity of taste. A critic is better seen, no doubt, as an explorer than as an 'authority', but explorers ought to be, and usually are, well equipped. The effect of good criticism is to convince us of what C. S. Lewis called 'the enormous extension of our being which we owe to authors'. A Casebook will be justified only if it helps to promote the same end.

A single volume can represent no more than a small selection of critical opinions. Some critics have been excluded for reasons of space, and it is hoped that readers will follow up the further suggestions in the Select Bibliography. Other contributions have been severed from their original context, to which some readers may wish to return. Indeed, if they take a hint from the critics represented here, they certainly will.

A. E. DYSON

# INTRODUCTION

## I

*The Tempest* was Shakespeare's last play, excluding his contributions to *Henry VIII* and *The Two Noble Kinsmen*. The first recorded performance took place at Court on 1 November 1611: 'Hallomas nyght was presented att Whithall before y^e kinges Maiestie, a play Called the Tempest.' From Shakespeare's use in the play of certain documents relating to the Virginia Company, published in the previous autumn, it seems likely that *The Tempest* was written during 1611. It was not printed during Shakespeare's lifetime and first appeared in the Folio of 1623, where the text shows signs of careful editorial preparation. Although we have no direct evidence about its contemporary popularity, the fact that Shakespeare's fellows, in collecting his dramatic work for publication, thought *The Tempest* worthy to stand as the first play in the Folio, suggests that as qualified judges they held a high opinion of its merits and of its appeal to current taste.

Theories that *The Tempest* was an earlier play revived and refurbished for some Court occasion are no longer widely believed. Such hypotheses usually involve the suspicion that the masque in Act IV was not an integral part of the play, but an interlude inserted into the main structure in order to celebrate a Court wedding or betrothal. E. K. Chambers convincingly disposed of these arguments in his essay 'The Integrity of *The Tempest*'; and other critics have since shown how the betrothal masque relates directly to the main dramatic interests of the play. *The Tempest* was performed again at Court in the winter of 1612–13 as part of the entertainments celebrating the marriage of Princess Elizabeth to the Elector Palatine, which took place on 14 February 1613; but it was one of several plays presented for these festivities, and there are no grounds for supposing the masque of Act IV to have been more than a happy coincidence in its appropriateness to that occasion.

*The Tempest* as a whole shows the influence on Shakespeare's dramatic techniques of the Court Masque, a form of private entertainment which reached new heights of splendour and lavishness under James I, who was more extravagant, and whose queen was more enthusiastic, than his predecessor in promoting such shows at royal expense. The emphasis of the masques upon music and spectacle, and their use of improbable settings and supernatural figures, are reflected in Shakespeare's play. The acting company of which he was a leading member had strengthened its links with the Court since Elizabeth's day, first by receiving the patronage of the new monarch (signified by the title of the King's Men, which had been theirs since 1603), and later by their acquisition in 1608 of the 'private' indoor theatre at Blackfriars, frequented by a more exclusive, courtly audience.

Thus by 1611, although the King's Men still occupied the larger public playhouse at the Globe for most of the year, they were also catering to a narrower social élite in Blackfriars and with performances at Court. It has been argued that the romantic plays written by Shakespeare at the close of his career reflect these changing circumstances and illustrate Shakespeare's readiness, as ever, to exploit new trends in dramatic taste and fashion. Similarities of a general kind have been observed between these plays and the Italianate tragi-comedies of Beaumont and Fletcher, who also wrote for the King's Men, and whose work in these same years was enjoying great success among those who considered themselves sophisticated and refined. Nevertheless it is possible to exaggerate the importance of the courtly audience in searching for an explanation of Shakespeare's last plays; the fact remains that the first references we have to performances of *Cymbeline* and *The Winter's Tale* relate them to the Globe, and therefore we should not assume that Shakespeare was incapable of pleasing both popular and courtly tastes with the same play, or that *The Tempest* was 'caviare to the general'.

## II

While the dramatic form of *The Tempest* can be shown to reflect theatrical innovations of its day, no source has been found for the plot of the play. Analogies to the story abound in folk-tale and romance, and the central situations have been compared with certain *scenari* written for the contemporary *commedia dell' arte* in Italy. No direct relationship between *The Tempest* and any of such analogues has been established, however, and, reluctant as critics are to credit Shakespeare's inventive powers in this respect, it seems as though we must suppose that on this occasion Shakespeare composed his own version of a story whose elements are conventional and familar enough to be regarded as the common property of romance. The only 'sources' of the play (if we mean something more specific than influences of a general kind) are three documents in the Virginia Company's papers relating to a shipwreck on the Bermudas in 1609; Montaigne's essay 'Of the Caniballes'; and, for Prospero's speech renouncing his magic arts, the *Metamorphoses* of Ovid. Of these, the papers concerning the Bermudas shipwreck are perhaps the most important, because they may well have been the true 'occasion' of Shakespeare's play. The three documents are Sylvester Jourdain's *A Discovery of the Bermudas* (1610), the London Council of Virginia's *A True Declaration of the Estate of the Colonie in Virginia* (1610), and a letter from William Strachey to the Council, dated 1609, later published in 1625 as *A True Reportory of the Wracke and Redemption of Sir Thomas Gates, Knight*. Each of these papers tells of the expedition which left England in May 1609 under the command of Sir Thomas Gates and Sir George Summers, carrying five hundred colonists bound for Virginia. The ship bearing both Gates and Summers was separated from the others in a storm and was wrecked on the coast of the Bermudas. All on board reached shore safely and stayed on the island until May 1610, when they left to continue their voyage to Virginia. News of their survival, and of the beauty and fertility of the island, was reported to the Company by Jourdain and Strachey, each of whom had shared the fate of the shipwrecked colonists. The adventure was seen as a miraculous deliverance from disaster, and the island discovered seemed a new Paradise. The Virginia Company published Jourdain's account, together with its own *True Declaration*, which also related a recent uprising in Virginia and its successful quelling by the governor. Shakespeare seems to have made more use of Strachey's then unpublished account, however, and he might well have had access to this private communication through his acquaintance with leading members of the Company, such as the Earl of Southampton and Sir Dudley Digges (whose brother Leonard was to write commemorative verses for the 1623 Folio).

The narratives of the Bermudas shipwreck and of mutiny in the colony probably lie behind several details and 'authentic' touches in Shakespeare's play, but the most interesting link between them and *The Tempest* is the way in which the colonists interpreted their adventures in pious terms illustrating the goodness of divine providence. It may at first seem a far cry from the realism of the Virginia Company's publicity to the fantasy world of romance, but Professor Kermode, in his Introduction to the New Arden edition of the play, has shown how attitudes to the New World were conditioned by the ideas of the Old World. Marvell's poem 'The Bermudas', written in the 1650s, expresses the same tendency to assimilate the modern experiences of colonisation to the ancient biblical or classical beliefs concerning providential voyages, primitive mankind, and unspoiled nature. Consequently Montaigne's essay 'Of the Caniballes' is not very remote from the preoccupations of Jourdain and Strachey in their reports. For Montaigne is reflecting upon such travellers' tales about the savages of the New World, and the theme of his essay is the moral superiority of uncivilised man. Shakespeare's use of Montaigne in *The Tempest* is not confined to the close verbal parallels between the essay and Gonzalo's speech on the ideal commonwealth, for the ideas of Montaigne's primitivism permeate many aspects of the play. Caliban may derive his name from a simple anagram of 'cannibal', and the contrasts with the drunken sailors and with the corrupt Antonio, which reflect so favourably upon him, are in line with Montaigne's attitude. Some of the nobility and generosity attributed by Montaigne to primitive chieftains in war also seems to have rubbed off on Prospero. But in other respects Shakespeare's point of view is more complex than that of the essay: Gonzalo's raptures are treated ironically, and Caliban, in his brutality and cunning, is scarcely an idealised representation of the savage. To Montaigne's comparisons between the virtues of primitivism and the vices of civilisation Shakespeare adds a series of contrasts between the baser instincts of untutored nature and the higher values of a life ordered by reason and honour.

In Renaissance literature these ideas were particularly associated with the pastoral convention, and Professor Kermode has argued convincingly that *The Tempest* is primarily a pastoral play, composed on the theme of Nature and Art. In this context 'Art' embraces all aspects of man's endeavour to improve on Nature, not competing with her, but co-operating in order to sustain a life worthy of his rational and moral nature. Civilisation, government, and the values of society, breeding, education, and virtue, are achieved by Art. Thus Prospero's magic powers, which Miranda calls his 'art', are seen as the human improvement of nature, raised to its highest level; his control over the spirits of earth, air, and water is derived from his learning and virtue, unlike that of the witch Sycorax, whose powers were diabolical. Thus, too, Miranda and Ferdinand are contrasted with Caliban, since their royal blood gives them an innate nobility lacking in the monstrous offspring of a witch and a demon; while, on the other hand, Antonio and Sebastian show how noble birth may be betrayed by unnatural vices. Caliban is ineducable, as Prospero realises, but Antonio's breeding makes him the more dangerous enemy; Caliban will sue for mercy, but Antonio remains unreconciled. By means of parallels and contrasts of this kind the carefully balanced structure of *The Tempest* expresses the traditional concern of pastoral with the antithesis of primitive and sophisticated planes of existence. The pastoral convention itself is a product of this duality, being essentially a highly artificial image of an ideal simplicity.

*The Tempest* is consequently a very subtle composition of realism and fantasy. From one point of view it is a topical play closely related to the discovery of the New World and to the literature of colonisation. At the same time it derives from the world of folk-tale and make-believe, being a romantic story of a magician and his daughter the princess, with the inevitable happy ending. It is both a charming entertainment, full of music and stage-spectacle, and a serious philosophical drama employing the concepts of its day in distinguishing virtue's true simplicity from baseness and deception. Yet again, it is a play of severely restricted compass and symmetrical form, although so comprehensive that it ranges through the scale of creation from a sub-human brute to the spirits of the air, between which extremes the mechanicals, the courtiers, the members of royalty, children and their fathers, each occupies an appropriate station. Such seeming contradictions pay tribute to the artistry with which Shakespeare has blended the elements of his work. The complexity of Shakespeare's pattern is illustrated by Caliban. In that he cannot respond to Prospero's attempts to teach him, he is a foil to Miranda; in that he resents the tasks imposed upon him by Prospero, he is a foil to Ferdinand; in that he plots with Trinculo and Stephano, he is a foil to Antonio; in that he urges his fellow conspirators to ignore the flashy clothes left by Prospero to distract them, he is a foil to Stephano and Trinculo. He is both villain and clown – in one respect an unnatural hybrid monster, in another sense the savage man of pastoral tradition; and he might even be claimed as the only American in Shakespeare. The whole is greater than the sum of its parts.

### III

It is this sensitive poise of *The Tempest* – between sheer enchantment and the issues of the real world – which makes the play a great work of art, and yet which is most difficult to analyse or represent. The particular balance and tone of the work have almost always eluded critics, and the history of *Tem-*

*pest* criticism chiefly reveals the changes of emphasis upon this or that aspect of the play.

Even within the half-century that separated Shakespeare's play from the version composed by Dryden and Davenant in 1667, the cultural climate had changed so sharply that while Dryden was able to feel the Shakespearean harmony, he was unable to reproduce it. This quality in the original *Tempest* receives its tribute from Dryden in his Prologue to the new version:

> But *Shakespear's* Magick could not copy'd be;
> Within that Circle none durst walk but he.

Perhaps Dryden's witty metaphorical identification of Shakespeare with Prospero in this famous couplet anticipates the later romantic interpretations of *The Tempest* as an autobiographical work. The fact remains that the Dryden and Davenant adaptation is a poor thing compared with Shakespeare's play, as Dryden half-confesses. Milton's *Comus* (1634) is much closer to the spirit of *The Tempest* than this crude piece of work, though the comparison between the Dryden and Davenant version and the original is instructive. To please the tastes of the Restoration the spectacular elements were elaborated and the comic potentialities of Miranda's ignorance of the opposite sex exploited to the full. Indeed, as the excerpts included in this volume show, Dryden and Davenant completely recast the play by multiplying the sexual partnerships, giving Miranda a sister, Dorinda, who has similarly never seen a man other than her father, and balancing this situation by introducing Hippolito as Prospero's young ward, who has never set eyes on a woman. In addition Ariel and Caliban each have female counterparts. Shakespeare's main action involving the confrontation of Prospero with his enemies is thus rendered subordinate to a farce, in which dramatic conflict is generated by sexual jealousy, and amusement, if that is the right word, is chiefly dependent on *doubles entendres* at the expense of sexual naivety. The only element which strikes a less frivolous note is the political satire provided by the quarrels between Trinculo, Stephano, Mustacho and Ventoso, in their attempts to set up a rival régime to that of Prospero. Dryden and Davenant's version is not only a much simpler and more superficial play than Shakespeare's, it represents a marked coarsening and vulgarising of the original. The solemnity with which Shakespeare treats conceptions of chastity and honour has been replaced by some rather cheap sniggers about virginity. The differences between the two plays reveal that profounder changes than literary fashions separated Shakespeare from the Restoration.

Neo-classical critics of the later seventeenth and the eighteenth centuries showed little awareness of the philosophical themes in *The Tempest*, but recognised its appeal as a charming fantasy. Since so many of the conceptions and attitudes underlying Shakespeare's work belong to a view of the world which had become outmoded and forgotten, Ben Jonson's strictures on Shakespeare's want of learning gained currency, and the author of *The Tempest* was regarded as an untutored genius of prodigious imaginative power, whose natural abilities compensated for an assumed deficiency in book-learning. Dryden's admiration for *The Tempest*, acknowledged in the Preface to *Troilus and Cressida*, was based on a view of the play as a triumph of sheer poetic invention. According to this view, Shakespeare had succeeded precisely because he needed no learning, but only his imagination, to create such an original and fanciful romance. In particular, Dryden singled out for praise the character of Caliban, as a creature of an entirely new species, not to be found in nature, and one whom Shakespeare had appropriately endowed with a new language. Dryden's encomium was echoed throughout the Augustan period in virtually the same terms; we find it reiterated by Addison, that reliable index to contemporary taste, in *The Spectator* for 19 January 1712:

It shews a greater Genius in *Shakespear* to have drawn his *Calyban*, than his *Hotspur* or *Julius Caesar*: The one was to be supplied out of his own Imagination, whereas the other might have been formed upon Tradition, History and Observation.

Dr Johnson did his best to crush what must have been quite a cliché by his time (1765), asserting rather testily that there was nothing peculiar to Caliban's language which anyone of similar sentiments and in similar circumstances would not utter. The fact that *The Tempest* obeys the unities of action, place and time gratified neo-classical tastes, but it was thought to spring more from accident than design on Shakespeare's part.

Joseph Warton's essays on the play in 1753 mainly elaborate the familiar eighteenth-century response, although there is a distinctively new emphasis, and a relatively new word, in his observation that 'He has there given the reins to his boundless imagination, and has carried the romantic, the wonderful, and the wild, to the most pleasing extravagance'. We seem with Warton to be on the verge of Romanticism; nevertheless the critics of the Romantic generation show less interest in the fanciful extravagance of the play than in its harmony of design and in the ideal truths apprehended by poetic vision.

Coleridge's affirmation that *The Tempest* 'addresses itself entirely to the imagination' bears only a superficial resemblance to the emphasis of eighteenth-century commentaries, for the word 'imagination' itself has developed new implications, and his lectures on the play explore deeper significances than the older critics were aware of. Like Coleridge, Lamb thought the play too profound, too exalted, for its effects to be properly conveyed by the crudities of theatrical performance:

Much has been said, and deservedly, in reprobation of the vile mixture which Dryden has thrown into the Tempest: doubtless without some such vicious alloy, the impure ears of that age would never have sate out to hear so much innocence of love as is contained in the sweet courtship of Ferdinand and Miranda. But is the Tempest of Shakespeare at all a subject for stage representation? It is one thing to read of an enchanter, and to believe the wondrous tale while we are reading it; but to have a conjuror brought before us in his conjuring-gown, with his spirits about him, which none but himself and some hundred of favoured spectators before the curtain are supposed to see, involves such a quantity of the *hateful incredible*, that all our reverence for the author cannot hinder us from perceiving

such gross attempts upon the senses to be in the highest degree
childish and inefficient. Spirits and fairies cannot be represented,
they cannot even be painted, – they can only be believed. But
the elaborate and anxious provision of scenery, which the luxury
of the age demands, in these cases works a quite contrary effect
to what is intended. That which in comedy, or plays of familiar
life, adds so much to the life of the imitation, in plays which
appeal to the higher faculties, positively destroys the illusion
which it is introduced to aid.[1]

We shall be less astonished at this failure to appreciate the
eminent stageworthiness of *The Tempest* when we recall that in
Lamb's day – and throughout the nineteenth century – methods
of production were dominated by a concern for gross literalism
and decorative detail on the grandest scale. The encumbrances
of the naturalistic stage, in terms of which Lamb was thinking,
were quite inappropriate to Shakespeare. Charles Kean's production of *The Tempest* in 1857 was just such a travesty, to
judge from his self-congratulatory programme-note:

> The scenic appliances of the play are of more extensive and
> complicated nature than ever has been attempted in any theatre
> in Europe, requiring the aid of one hundred and forty operatives
> nightly, who, unseen by the audience, are engaged in working
> the machinery and carrying out the various effects.

The fabric of this vision must have been an unwieldy parody of
that presented to Ferdinand and Miranda. It was not until the
end of the nineteenth century, when William Poel made his
audiences begin to realise the advantages of the kind of open
stage for which Shakespeare had originally written, and so rid
Shakespearean productions of extravagant scenic distractions,
that the poetic quality of the plays could be shown as theatrically
effective.

Meanwhile the Romantic conception of *The Tempest* as a
dramatic poem reflects a more philosophical interest in its structure and meaning. From Coleridge onwards, interpretation has
been an important part of the critic's approach to the play. In

---

[1] Charles Lamb, *On the Tragedies of Shakespeare, considered with
reference to their fitness for Stage Representation* (1811).

this respect Coleridge is justly called the father of modern Shakespeare criticism, although it was the development of historicism later in the nineteenth century which led to the first attempts to relate *The Tempest* to its contemporary context. The New Shakspere Society, founded in 1873, was strongly influenced by German scholarship and sought to establish the chronology of the plays as the basis for understanding them. Victorian critics betray their Romantic heritage, however, in their use of chronology to interpret Shakespeare's work as spiritual autobiography. Thus Edward Dowden, who associates *The Tempest* with the other romances of Shakespeare's last years in the theatre, studies them not as examples of a dramatic genre, but as the serene and idealised dreams of contented old age. While it contains some perceptive criticism and recognises the idyllic charm of the play, Dowden's rather sentimental treatment of *The Tempest* really signifies the fading of the high Romantic vision. The Victorian image of *The Tempest* is less substantial, less powerful, and fundamentally less serious than the work of genius celebrated in Coleridge's lectures.

Impatience with Dowden's interpretation provoked Lytton Strachey's famous essay of 1906 on 'Shakespeare's Final Period', which roundly asserted that the author of *The Tempest* was 'bored with people, bored with real life, bored with drama, bored, in fact, with everything except poetry and poetical dreams'. Such a view of course still implies that Shakespeare's work can be read as a direct expression of his personal state of mind, but Strachey's emphasis upon disillusion and cynicism announces a characteristically twentieth-century response to the play.

It may at first seem odd to cite Lytton Strachey as typical of the modern approach, since so much later criticism has taken as its point of departure the need to show that far from boredom, *The Tempest* displays a profound and lively interest in 'people', 'real life', and 'drama', as well as in poetry. Far from revealing the decline of a flagging genius, the last plays are now commonly regarded as among Shakespeare's supreme achievements, as a group second only to the major tragedies. Nevertheless Strachey is the prophet of the anti-sentimental, anti-Romantic, 'realist' school of interpretation which has done so much to shape twentieth-century attitudes to Shakespeare. As it emerges from the great variety of modern criticism, *The Tempest* is a play of disenchantment as much as an enchanting romance.

As the essays in this volume show, the prevailing emphasis of critics during the last thirty years has been upon the seriousness of the play. From different points of view they have found in *The Tempest* profounder and more complex meanings beneath the idyllic charm. G. Wilson Knight, for instance, invites us to see the play as a final distillation and summary of Shakespeare's life-work, embodying echoes of his deepest concerns throughout his entire career. E. M. W. Tillyard relates *The Tempest*, and the other final romances, to the tragedies, and regards them as completing a cycle of action from tragic disaster to renewal and restoration of order and happiness.

More recent critics, exploring the background of Renaissance ideas underlying the play, offer to us a learned and philosophical drama, the work of a conscious and sophisticated artist who is very different both from the Romantic image of an intuitive but unschooled genius and also from the more prosaic early-twentieth-century conception of Shakespeare as a craftsman skilled in the use of theatrical convention if in little else. Thus Frank Kermode's discussion of the significance of Art and Nature as controlling concepts in the play (anticipated in general terms by Middleton Murry) has established itself as a standard approach to *The Tempest*. Other commentators of recent years who have interpreted the play according to orthodox Renaissance doctrines and beliefs reflect Kermode's stress upon the antitheses of its thematic structure. John P. Cutts examines the philosophical and symbolic importance of music as it contributes to the dramatic meaning in its use of harmony and discord; Frank Davidson explores the conflict between reason and the passions in terms of Elizabethan psychology, with particular reference to Prospero, Caliban, and Ariel; and Rose Zimbardo analyses the forces of order and chaos in the play. These studies complement each other, and suggest how rich in meaning, as well as how finely organised, *The Tempest* is despite its lightness of touch.

Reuben Brower's essay on the poetic texture and metaphoric design reinforces this sense of highly wrought art, and in another respect provides a corrective balance to the more philosophical interpretations just referred to. For the play carries its learning lightly, and Brower's analysis brings out for us the intimate relationship between verbal imagery and theatrical effects, between sensuous apprehension and intellectual comprehension. 'The island is a world of fluid, merging states of being and forms of life', he writes, describing that quality of the play by which the poetry, spectacle, and music together create an evanescent world subject to swift transitions and transformations of mood, tempo, and poise. The 'meaning' of *The Tempest* exists in this quality as much as in the metaphysical ideas and moral doctrines it draws upon.

The last item in this collection is taken from the Polish critic Jan Kott's book, *Shakespeare Our Contemporary*, which, as its title implies, seeks to find in Shakespeare's work a reflection of the twentieth-century experience of violence and horror, of political cynicism and social breakdown. Kott writes polemically and provocatively, and his interpretative methods are guaranteed to arouse an equally vigorous disagreement in many of his readers. But as a man of the theatre he is a rarity among Shakespearean critics, and for this reason at least his approach to the plays should be of considerable interest. In fact, despite Kott's allegation that 'for most commentators the island in *The Tempest* is a utopia', when his grim conception of *The Tempest* is put alongside that of the academic critics, it seems that he is really intensifying the characteristic modern emphasis upon the darker, profounder conflicts in the play. 'The questions raised by *The Tempest* are philosophical and bitter,' writes Kott, and, as we have seen, to the first part of this proposition, at least, most of the play's recent interpreters would agree. To some extent, therefore, Kott is fighting a battle against the sentimentalist's view of *The Tempest* as merely an enchanting day-dream: a battle which was won in the field of literary criticism many years ago, even though apparently it may still need to be fought in the

theatre. But one cannot help feeling that if Kott finds no genuine
charm or beauty to admire in Prospero's island, he is as im-
pervious and unfortunate as those partners in misanthropy,
Antonio and Sebastian.

Good criticism, of course, has a permanent value transcending
its interest as a reflection of the age in which it was written, and
the most helpful criticism is not always that which endorses our
own judgement. The essays chosen for this collection will, it is
hoped, by their individual quality enhance the reader's enjoyment and understanding of *The Tempest*, and also by their
collective variety remind him that no single key fits all the doors
to be opened.

# PART ONE

# Adaptations, and Extracts from Earlier Critics, 1670-1945

# John Dryden
# and Sir William Davenant

## THE TEMPEST (1670)

### Act II Scene ii

*Cypress trees and a Cave*

*Enter* PROSPERO *alone*

*Prosp.* 'Tis not yet fit to let my daughters know,
  I keep the infant duke of Mantua
  So near them in this isle;
  Whose father, dying, bequeathed him to my care;
  Till my false brother (when he designed to usurp
  My dukedom from me) exposed him to that fate,
  He meant for me.
  By calculation of his birth, I saw
  Death threat'ning him, if, till some time were past,
  He should behold the face of any woman:
  And now the danger's nigh. – Hippolito!

*Enter* HIPPOLITO

*Hip.* Sir, I attend your pleasure.
*Prosp.* How I have loved thee, from thy infancy,
  Heaven knows, and thou thyself canst bear me witness;
  Therefore accuse not me of thy restraint.
*Hip.* Since I knew life, you've kept me in a rock;
  And you, this day, have hurried me from thence,
  Only to change my prison, not to free me.
  I murmur not, but I may wonder at it.

*Prosp.* O, gentle youth! fate waits for thee abroad;
A black star threatens thee; and death, unseen,
Stands ready to devour thee.

*Hip.* You taught me
Not to fear him in any of his shapes: —
Let me meet death rather than be a prisoner.

*Prosp.* 'Tis pity he should seize thy tender youth.

*Hip.* Sir, I have often heard you say, no creature
Lived in this isle, but those which man was lord of.
Why, then, should I fear?

*Prosp.* But here are creatures which I named not to thee,
Who share man's sovereignty by nature's laws,
And oft depose him from it.

*Hip.* What are those creatures, sir?

*Prosp.* Those dangerous enemies of men, called women.

*Hip.* Women! I never heard of them before. —
What are women like?

*Prosp.* Imagine something between young men and angels;
Fatally beauteous, and have killing eyes;
Their voices charm beyond the nightingale's;
They are all enchantment: Those, who once behold them,
Are made their slaves for ever.

*Hip.* Then I will wink, and fight with them.

*Prosp.* 'Tis but in vain;
They'll haunt you in your very sleep.

*Hip.* Then I'll revenge it on them when I wake.

*Prosp.* You are without all possibility of revenge;
They are so beautiful, that you can ne'er attempt,
Nor wish, to hurt them.

*Hip.* Are they so beautiful?

*Prosp.* Calm sleep is not so soft, not winter suns,
Nor summer shades, so pleasant.

*Hip.* Can they be fairer than the plumes of swans?
Or more delightful than the peacock's feathers?
Or than the gloss upon the necks of doves?
Or have more various beauty than the rainbow? —
These I have seen, and, without danger, wondered at.

*Prosp.* All these are far below them: Nature made
    Nothing but woman dangerous and fair.
    Therefore if you should chance to see them,
    Avoid them straight, I charge you.
*Hip.* Well, since you say they are so dangerous,
    I'll so far shun them, as I may with safety
    Of the unblemished honour, which you taught me.
    But let them not provoke me, for I'm sure
    I shall not then forbear them.
*Prosp.* Go in, and read the book I gave you last.
    To-morrow I may bring you better news.
*Hip.* I shall obey you, sir.            [*Exit* Hip.
*Prosp.* So, so; I hope this lesson has secured him,
    For I have been constrained to change his lodging
    From yonder rock, where first I bred him up,
    And here have brought him home to my own cell,
    Because the shipwreck happened near his mansion.
    I hope he will not stir beyond his limits,
    For hitherto he hath been all obedience:
    The planets seem to smile on my designs,
    And yet there is one sullen cloud behind:
    I would it were dispersed!

*Enter* Miranda *and* Dorinda

    How, my daughters!
    I thought I had instructed them enough:
    Children! retire; why do you walk this way?
*Mir.* It is within our bounds, sir.
*Prosp.* But both take heed, that path is very dangerous;
        remember what I told you.
*Dor.* Is the man that way, sir?
*Prosp.* All that you can imagine ill is there,
    The curled lion, and the rugged bear,
    Are not so dreadful as that man.
*Mir.* Oh me, why stay we here then?
*Dor.* I'll keep far enough from his den, I warrant him.

*Mir.* But you have told me, sir, you are a man;
　　And yet you are not dreadful.
*Prosp.* Ay, child; but I
　　Am a tame man; old men are tame by nature,
　　But all the danger lies in a wild young man.
*Dor.* Do they run wild about the woods?
*Prosp.* No, they are wild within doors, in chambers, and in
　　closets.
*Dor.* But, father, I would stroak them, and make them gentle;
　　then sure they would not hurt me.
*Prosp.* You must not trust them, child: No woman can come
　　near them, but she feels a pain, full nine months.
　　Well, I must in; for new affairs require my presence:
　　Be you, Miranda, your sister's guardian.
　　　　　　　　　　　　　　　　　　　　[*Exit* Pros.
*Dor.* Come, sister, shall we walk the other way?
　　The man will catch us else: We have but two legs,
　　And he, perhaps, has four.
*Mir.* Well, sister, though he have; yet look about you.
*Dor.* Come back! that way is towards his den.
*Mir.* Let me alone; I'll venture first, for sure he can
　　Devour but one of us at once.
*Dor.* How dare you venture?
*Mir.* We'll find him sitting like a hare in's form,
　　And he shall not see us.
*Dor.* Ay, but you know my father charged us both.
*Mir.* But who shall tell him on't? we'll keep each other's
　　counsel.
*Dor.* I dare not, for the world.
*Mir.* But how shall we hereafter shun him, if we do not know
　　him first?
*Dor.* Nay, I confess I would fain see him too. I find it in my
　　nature, because my father has forbidden me.
*Mir.* Ay, there's it; sister; if he had said nothing, I had been
　　quiet. Go softly, and if you see him first, be quick,
　　and beckon me away.
*Dor.* Well, if he does catch me, I'll humble myself to him, and

ask him pardon, as I do my father, when I have done
a fault.

*Mir.* And if I can but escape with life, I had rather be in pain
nine months, as my father threatened, than lose my
longing.                                              [*Exeunt.*

## Scene iii

### *Enter* HIPPOLITO

*Hip.* Prospero has often said, that nature makes
Nothing in vain: Why then are women made?
Are they to suck the poison of the earth,
As gaudy coloured serpents are? I'll ask
That question, when next I see him here.

### *Enter* MIRANDA *and* DORINDA *peeping*

*Dor.* O sister, there it is! it walks about
Like one of us.

*Mir.* Ay, just so, and has legs as we have too.

*Hip.* It strangely puzzles me: Yet 'tis most likely,
Women are somewhat between men and spirits.

*Dor.* Hark! it talks: – sure this is not it my father meant,
For this is just like one of us: Methinks,
I am not half so much afraid on't as
I was; see, now it turns this way.

*Mir.* Heaven! what a goodly thing it is!

*Dor.* I'll go nearer it.

*Mir.* O no, 'tis dangerous, sister! I'll go to it.
I would not for the world that you should venture.
My father charged me to secure you from it.

*Dor.* I warrant you this is a tame man; dear sister,
He'll not hurt me, I see it by his looks.

*Mir.* Indeed he will! but go back, and he shall eat me first: Fie,
are you not ashamed to be so inquisitive?

*Dor.* You chide me for it, and would give him yourself.

*Mir.* Come back, or I will tell my father.

Observe how he begins to stare already!

I'll meet the danger first, and then call you.

*Dor.* Nay, sister, you shall never vanquish me in kindness. I'll
venture you no more than you will me.

*Prosp.* [*within*] Miranda, child, where are you?

*Mir.* Do you not hear my father call? Go in.

*Dor.* 'Twas you he named, not me; I will but say my prayers,
and follow you immediately.

*Mir.* Well, sister, you'll repent it.                    [*Exit* MIR.

*Dor.* Though I die for it, I must have the other peep.

*Hip.* What thing is that? [*Seeing her.*] Sure 'tis some infant of
The sun, dressed in his father's gayest beams,
And comes to play with birds: My sight is dazzled,
And yet I find I'm loth to shut my eyes:
I must go nearer it; — but stay a while;
May it not be that beauteous murderer, woman,
Which I was charged to shun? Speak, what art thou,
Thou shining vision!

*Dor.* Alas, I know not; but I'm told I am
A woman; do not hurt me, pray, fair thing.

*Hip.* I'd sooner tear my eyes out, than consent
To do you any harm; though I was told,
A woman was my enemy.

*Dor.* I never knew
What 'twas to be an enemy, nor can I e'er
Prove so to that, which looks like you: For though
I've been charged by him (whom yet I ne'er disobeyed,)
To shun your presence, yet I'd rather die
Than lose it; therefore, I hope you will not have the heart
To hurt me: Though I fear you are a man,
The dangerous thing of which I have been warned.
Pray, tell me what you are?

*Hip.* I must confess, I was informed I am a man;
But if I fright you, I shall wish I were some other creature.
I was bid to fear you too.

*Dor.* Ah me! Heaven grant we be not poison to
    Each other! Alas, can we not meet, but we must die?
*Hip.* I hope not so! for, when two poisonous creatures,
    Both of the same kind, meet, yet neither dies.
    I've seen two serpents harmless to each other,
    Though they have twined into a mutual knot:
    If we have any venom in us, sure, we cannot be
    More poisonous, when we meet, than serpents are.
    You have a hand like mine – may I not gently touch it?
                     *[Takes her hand.*
*Dor.* I've touched my father's and my sister's hands,
    And felt no pain; but now, alas! there's something,
    When I touch yours, which makes me sigh: Just so
    I've seen two turtles mourning when they met:
    Yet mine's a pleasing grief; and so, methought,
    Was theirs: For still they mourned, and still they seemed
    To murmur too, and yet they often met.
*Hip.* Oh heavens! I have the same sense too: your hand,
    Methinks, goes through me; I feel it at my heart,
    And find it pleases, though it pains me.
*Prosp.* [*within*] Dorinda!
*Dor.* My father calls again; ah, I must leave you.
*Hip.* Alas, I'm subject to the same command.
*Dor.* This is my first offence against my father,
    Which he, by severing us, too cruelly does punish.
*Hip.* And this is my first trespass too: But he
    Hath more offended truth, than we have him:
    He said our meeting would destructive be,
    But I no death, but in our parting, see. [*Exeunt severally.*

*John Dryden*

# THE CHARACTER OF CALIBAN
## (1679)

To return once more to Shakespeare; no man ever drew so many characters, or generally distinguished them better from one another, excepting only Jonson. I will instance but in one, to show the copiousness of his invention; it is that of Caliban, or the monster, in *The Tempest*. He seems there to have created a person which was not in nature, a boldness which, at first sight, would appear intolerable; for he makes him a species of himself, begotten by an incubus on a witch; but this, as I have elsewhere proved, is not wholly beyond the bounds of credibility, at least the vulgar still believe it. We have the separated notions of a spirit, and of a witch; (and spirits, according to Plato, are vested with a subtle body; according to some of his followers, have different sexes;) therefore, as from the distinct apprehensions of a horse, and of a man, imagination has formed a centaur; so, from those of an incubus and a sorceress, Shakespeare has produced his monster. Whether or no his generation can be defended, I leave to philosophy; but of this I am certain, that the poet has most judiciously furnished him with a person, a language, and a character, which will suit him, both by father's and mother's side: he has all the discontents, and malice of a witch, and of a devil, besides a convenient proportion of the deadly sins; gluttony, sloth, and lust, are manifest; the dejectedness of a slave is likewise given him, and the ignorance of one bred up in a desert island. His person is monstrous, and he is the product of unnatural lust; and his language is as hobgoblin as his person; in all things he is distinguished from other mortals.

# Nicholas Rowe

## SOLEMN AND POETICAL MAGIC
### (1709)

BUT certainly the greatness of this Author's Genius do's no
where so much appear, as where he gives his Imagination an
entire Loose, and raises his Fancy to a flight above Mankind
and the Limits of the visible World. Such are his Attempts in
*The Tempest, Midsummer-Night's Dream, Macbeth* and *Hamlet.*
Of these, *The Tempest,* however it comes to be plac'd the first by
the former Publishers of his Works, can never have been the first
written by him: It seems to me as perfect in its Kind, as almost
any thing we have of his. One may observe, that the Unities are
kept here with an Exactness uncommon to the Liberties of his
Writing: Tho' that was what, I suppose, he valu'd himself least
upon, since his Excellencies were all of another Kind. I am very
sensible that he do's, in this Play, depart too much from that
likeness to Truth which ought to be observ'd in these sort of
Writings; yet he do's it so very finely, that one is easily drawn
in to have more Faith for his sake, than Reason does well allow
of. His Magick has something in it very Solemn and very Poetical:
And that extravagant Character of *Caliban* is mighty well sustain'd, shews a wonderful Invention in the Author, who could
strike out such a particular wild Image, and is certainly one of the
finest and most uncommon Grotesques that was ever seen. The
Observation, which I have been inform'd* three very great Men
concurr'd in making upon this Part, was extremely just. *That*
Shakespear *had not only found out a new Character in his* Caliban,
*but had also devis'd and adapted a new manner of Language for that*
*Character.* Among the particular Beauties of this Piece, I think
one may be allow'd to point out the Tale of *Prospero* in the First
Act; his Speech to *Ferdinand* in the Fourth, upon the breaking up

* *Ld.* Falkland, *Ld. C. J.* Vaughan, *and Mr.* Selden.

the Masque of *Juno* and *Ceres*; and that in the Fifth, where he
dissolves his Charms, and resolves to break his Magick Rod.
This Play has been alter'd by Sir *William D'Avenant* and Mr.
*Dryden*; and tho' I won't Arraign the Judgment of those two
great Men, yet I think I may be allow'd to say, that there are
some things left out by them, that might, and even ought to have
been kept in. Mr. *Dryden* was an Admirer of our Author, and,
indeed, he owed him a great deal, as those who have read them
both may very easily observe.

# Joseph Warton

## 'AMAZING WILDNESS OF FANCY'
## (1753)

As Shakespeare is sometimes blameable for the conduct of his
fables, which have no unity; and sometimes for his diction,
which is obscure and turgid; so his characteristical excellencies
may possibly be reduced to these three general heads: 'his
lively creative imagination; his strokes of nature and passion;
and his preservation of the consistency of his characters'. These
excellencies, particularly the last, are of so much importance in
the drama, that they amply compensate for his transgressions
against the rules of Time and Place, which being of a more
mechanical nature, are often strictly observed by a genius of
the lowest order; but to portray characters naturally, and to
preserve them uniformly, requires such an intimate knowledge
of the heart of man, and is so rare a portion of felicity, as to
have been enjoyed, perhaps, only by two writers, Homer and
Shakespeare.

Of all the plays of Shakespeare, *The Tempest* is the most
striking instance of his creative power. He has there given the
reins to his boundless imagination, and has carried the romantic,
the wonderful, and the wild, to the most pleasing extravagance.
The scene is a desolate island; and the characters the most new
and singular that can well be conceived: a prince who practises
magic, an attendant spirit, a monster the son of a witch, and a
young lady who had been brought to this solitude in her
infancy, and had never beheld a man except her father.

As I have affirmed that Shakespeare's chief excellence is the
consistency of his characters, I will exemplify the truth of this
remark, by pointing out some master-strokes of this nature in
the drama before us.

The poet artfully acquaints us that Prospero is a magician,

by the first words which his daughter Miranda speaks to him:

> If by your art, my dearest father, you have
> Put the wild waters in this roar, allay them:

which intimate that the tempest described in the preceding
scene, was the effect of Prospero's power. The manner in which
he was driven from his dukedom of Milan, and landed afterwards
on this solitary island, accompanied only by his daughter, is
immediately introduced in a short and natural narration.

The offices of his attendant Spirit, Ariel, are enumerated
with amazing wildness of fancy, and yet with equal propriety:
his employment is said to be,

> ――――To tread the ooze
> Of the salt deep;
> To run upon the sharp wind of the north;
> To do me business in the veins o' th' earth,
> When it is bak'd with frost;
> ――――to dive into the fire; to ride
> On the curl'd clouds.

In describing the place in which he has concealed the Neapoli-
tan ship, Ariel expresses the secrecy of its situation by the
following circumstance, which artfully glances at another of his
services;

> ――――In the deep nook, where once
> Thou call'st me up at midnight, to fetch dew
> From the still-vext Bermudas.

Ariel, being one of those elves or spirits, 'whose pastime is to
make midnight mushrooms, and who rejoice to listen to the
solemn curfew'; by whose assistance Prospero has bedimm'd
the sun at noon-tide,

> And 'twixt the green sea and the azur'd vault,
> Set roaring war;

has a set of ideas and images peculiar to his station and office;
a beauty of the same kind with that which is so justly admired
in the Adam of Milton, whose manners and sentiments are all
Paradisaical. How delightfully and how suitably to his character,

are the habitations and pastimes of this invisible being pointed out in the following exquisite song!

> Where the bee sucks, there suck I:
> In a cowslip's bell I lie;
> There I couch when owls do cry.
> On the bat's back I do fly,
> After sun-set, merrily.
> Merrily merrily shall I live now,
> Under the blossom that hangs on the bough.

Mr. Pope, whose imagination has been thought by some the least of his excellencies, has, doubtless, conceived and carried on the machinery in his 'Rape of the Lock', with vast exuberance of fancy. The images, customs, and employments of his Sylphs, are exactly adapted to their natures, are peculiar and appropriated, are all, if I may be allowed the expression, Sylphish. The enumeration of the punishments they were to undergo, if they neglected their charge, would, on account of its poetry and propriety, and especially the mixture of oblique satire, be superior to any circumstances in Shakespeare's Ariel, if we could suppose Pope to have been unacquainted with *The Tempest*, when he wrote this part of his accomplished poem.

> ——She did confine thee
> Into a cloven pine; within which rift
> Imprison'd, thou didst painfully remain
> A dozen years: within which space she dy'd,
> And left thee there; where thou dist vent thy
>     groans,
> As fast as mill-wheels strike.

> If thou more murmur'st, I will rend an oak,
> And peg thee in his knotty entrails, 'till
> Thou'st howl'd away twelve winters.

> For this, be sure, to-night thou shalt have cramps,
> Side-stitches that shall pen thy breath up: urchins
> Shall, for that vast of night that they may work,
> All exercise on thee; thou shalt be pinch'd
> As thick as honey-combs, each pinch more stinging
> Than bees that made 'em.

If thou neglect'st or dost unwillingly
What I command, I'll rack thee with old cramps;
Fill all thy bones with aches: make thee roar,
That beasts shall tremble at thy din.

                                              Shakespeare

Whatever spirit, careless of his charge,
Forsakes his post or leaves the Fair at large,
Shall feel sharp vengeance soon o'ertake his sins,
Be stopp'd in vials, or transfix'd with pins;
Or plung'd in lakes of bitter washes lie,
Or wedg'd whole ages in a bodkin's eye:
Gums and pomatums shall his flight restrain,
While clog'd he beats his silken wings in vain;
Or allum styptics with contracting pow'r,
Shrink his thin essence like a shrivell'd flow'r:
Or as Ixion fix'd, the wretch shall feel
The giddy motion of the whirling wheel;
In fumes of burning chocolate shall glow,
And tremble at the sea that froths below!

                                                     Pope

The method which is taken to induce Ferdinand to believe
that his father was drown'd in the late tempest, is exceedingly
solemn and striking. He is sitting upon a solitary rock, and
weeping over-against the place where he imagined his father
was wrecked, when he suddenly hears with astonishment aërial
music creep by him upon the waters, and the Spirit gives him
the following information in words not proper for any but a
Spirit to utter:

Full fathom five thy father lies:
     Of his bones are coral made:
Those are pearls that were his eyes:
     Nothing of him that doth fade,
But doth suffer a sea-change,
Into something rich and strange.

And then follows a most lively circumstance;

Sea-nymphs hourly ring his knell.
Hark! now I hear them – Ding-dong-bell!

This is so truly poetical, that one can scarce forbear exclaiming with Ferdinand,

> There is no mortal business, nor no sound
> That the earth owns! –

The happy versatility of Shakespeare's genius enables him to excel in lyric as well as in dramatic poesy.

But the poet rises still higher in his management of this character of Ariel, by making a moral use of it, that is, I think, incomparable, and the greatest effort of his art. Ariel informs Prospero, that he has fulfilled his orders, and punished his brother and companions so severely, that if he himself was now to behold their sufferings, he would greatly compassionate them. To which Prospero answers,

> – Dost thou think so, Spirit?
> *Ariel.*  Mine would, Sir, were I human.
> *Prospero.*  And mine shall.

He then takes occasion, with wonderful dexterity and humanity, to draw an argument from the incorporeality of Ariel, for the justice and necessity of pity and forgiveness:

> Hast thou, which art but air, a touch, a feeling
> Of their afflictions; and shall not myself,
> One of their kind, that relish all as sharply,
> Passion'd as they, be kindlier mov'd than thou art?

The poet is a more powerful magician than his own Prospero: we are transported into fairy land; we are rapt in a delicious dream, from which it is misery to be disturbed; all around is enchantment!

# Joseph Warton

## REMARKS ON THE CREATION OF CHARACTER (1753)

Χρὴ δὲ χαὶ ἐν τοῖς ἤθεσιν ὥσπερ χαὶ ἐν τῇ τῶν ὦραγμάτων
συστάσει, ἀεὶ ζητεῖν, ἢ τὲ ἀναγχαῖον, ἢ τὸ εἰχος.
ARISTOTLE, *Poetics*

As well in the conduct of the manners as in the constitution of the
fable, we must always endeavour to produce either what is necessary or
what is probable.

'WHOEVER ventures,' says Horace, 'to form a character totally
original, let him endeavour to preserve it with uniformity and
consistency; but the formation of an original character is a
work of great difficulty and hazard.' In this arduous and uncommon task, however, Shakespeare has wonderfully succeeded
in his *Tempest*: the monster Calyban is the creature of his own
imagination, in the formation of which he could derive no
assistance from observation or experience.

Calyban is the son of a witch, begotten by a demon: the
sorceries of his mother were so terrible, that her countrymen
banished her into this desart island as unfit for human society:
in conformity, therefore, to this diabolical propagation, he is
represented as a prodigy of cruelty, malice, pride, ignorance,
idleness, gluttony, and lust. He is introduced with great propriety,
cursing Prospero and Miranda whom he had endeavoured to
defile; and his execrations are artfully contrived to have reference
to the occupation of his mother:

> As wicked dew, as e'er my mother brush'd
> With raven's feather from unwholesome fen,
> Drop on you both!——
> ——All the charms
> Of Sycorax, toads, beetles, bats, light on you!

His kindness is, afterwards, expressed as much in character, as his hatred, by an enumeration of offices, that could be of value only in a desolate island, and in the estimation of a savage:

> I pr'ythee, let me bring thee where crabs grow;
> And I with my long nails will dig the pig-nuts;
> Shew thee a jay's nest; and instruct thee how
> To snare the nimble marmazet. I'll bring thee
> To clust'ring filberds; and sometimes I'll get thee
> Young sea-malls from the rock——
> I'll shew thee the best springs; I'll pluck thee berries;
> I'll fish for thee, and get thee wood enough.

Which last is, indeed, a circumstance of great use in a place, where to be defended from the cold was neither easy nor usual; and it has a farther peculiar beauty, because the gathering wood was the occupation to which Calyban was subjected by Prospero, who, therefore, deemed it a service of high importance.

The gross ignorance of this monster is represented with delicate judgment; he knew not the names of the sun and moon, which he calls the bigger light and the less; and he believes that Stephano was the man in the moon, whom his mistress had often shewn him: and when Prospero reminds him that he first taught him to pronounce articulately, his answer is full of malevolence and rage:

> You taught me language; and my profit on't
> Is, I know how to curse:——

the properest return for such a fiend to make for such a favour. The spirits whom he supposes to be employed by Prospero perpetually to torment him, and the many forms and different methods they take for this purpose, are described with the utmost liveliness and force of fancy:

> Sometimes like apes, that moe and chatter at me,
> And after bite me; then like hedge hogs, which
> Lie tumbling in my bare-foot way, and mount
> Their pricks at my foot-fall: sometimes am I
> All wound with adders, who with cloven tongues
> Do hiss me into madness.

It is scarcely possible for any speech to be more expressive of
the manners and sentiments, than that in which our poet has
painted the brutal barbarity and unfeeling savageness of this son
of Sycorax, by making him enumerate, with a kind of horrible
delight, the various ways in which it was possible for the
drunken sailors to surprize and kill his master:

> ——There thou may'st brain him,
> Having first seiz'd his books; or with a log
> Batter his skull; or paunch him with a stake;
> Or cut his wezand with thy knife——

He adds, in allusion to his own abominable attempt, 'above all
be sure to secure the daughter; whose beauty, he tells them, is
incomparable'. The charms of Miranda could not be more
exalted, than by extorting this testimony from so insensible a
monster.

Shakespeare seems to be the only poet who possesses the
power of uniting poetry with propriety of character; of which I
know not an instance more striking, than the image Calyban
makes use of to express silence, which is at once highly poetical,
and exactly suited to the wildness of the speaker:

> Pray you tread softly, that the blind mole may not
> Hear a foot-fall.——

I always lament that our author has not preserved this fierce
and implacable spirit in Calyban, to the end of the play; instead
of which, he has, I think, injudiciously put into his mouth,
words that imply repentance and understanding:

> ——I'll be wise hereafter
> And seek for grace. What a thrice double ass
> Was I, to take this drunkard for a God,
> And worship this dull fool?

It must not be forgotten, that Shakespeare has artfully taken
occasion from this extraordinary character, which is finely
contrasted to the mildness and obedience of Ariel, obliquely to
satirize the prevailing passion for new and wonderful sights,
which has rendered the English so ridiculous. 'Were I in England

now,' says Trinculo, on first discovering Calyban, 'and had but this fish painted, not an holiday fool there but would give a piece of silver. – When they will not give a doit to relieve a lame beggar, they will lay out ten to see a dead Indian.'

Such is the inexhaustible plenty of our poet's invention, that he has exhibited another character in this play, entirely his own; that of the lovely and innocent Miranda.

When Prospero first gives her a sight of prince Ferdinand, she eagerly exclaims,

> ——What is't? a spirit?
> Lord, how it looks about! Believe me, Sir,
> It carries a brave form. But 'tis a spirit.

Her imagining that as he was so beautiful he must necessarily be one of her father's aërial agents, is a stroke of nature worthy admiration: as are likewise her intreaties to her father not to use him harshly, by the power of his art;

> Why speaks my father so ungently? This
> Is the third man that e'er I saw; the first
> That e'er I sigh'd for!——

Here we perceive the beginning of that passion, which Prospero was desirous she should feel for the prince; and which she afterwards more fully expresses upon an occasion which displays at once the tenderness, the innocence, and the simplicity of her character. She discovers her lover employed in the laborious task of carrying wood, which Prospero had enjoined him to perform. 'Would', says she, 'the lightning had burnt up those logs, that you are enjoined to pile!'

> ——If you'll sit down,
> I'll bear your logs the while. Pray give me that,
> I'll carry't to the pile.——
> ——You look wearily.

It is by selecting such little and almost imperceptible circumstances that Shakespeare has more truly painted the passions than any other writer: affection is more powerfully expressed by this simple wish and offer of assistance, than by the unnatural eloquence and witticisms of Dryden, or the amorous declamations of Rowe.

The resentment of Prospero for the matchless cruelty and wicked usurpation of his brother; his parental affection and solicitude for the welfare of his daughter, the heiress of his dukedom; and the awful solemnity of his character, as a skilful magician; are all along preserved with equal consistency, dignity, and decorum. One part of his behaviour deserves to be particularly pointed out: during the exhibition of a mask with which he had ordered Ariel to entertain Ferdinand and Miranda, he starts suddenly from the recollection of the conspiracy of Calyban and his confederates against his life, and dismisses his attendant spirits, who instantly vanish to a hollow and confused noise. He appears to be greatly moved; and suitably to this agitation of mind, which his danger has excited, he takes occasion, from the sudden disappearance of the visionary scene, to moralize on the dissolution of all things:

> ——These our actors
> As I foretold you, were all spirits: and
> Are melted into air, into thin air.
> And, like the baseless fabric of this vision,
> The cloud-capt towers, the gorgeous palaces,
> The solemn temples, the great globe itself,
> Yea, all which it inherit, shall dissolve;
> And, like this unsubstantial pageant faded,
> Leave not a rack behind——

To these noble images he adds a short but comprehensive observation on human life, not excelled by any passage of the moral and sententious Euripides:

> ——We are such stuff
> As dreams are made on; and our little life
> Is rounded with a sleep!——

Thus admirably is an uniformity of character, that leading beauty in dramatic poesy, preserved throughout *The Tempest*. And it may be farther remarked, that the unities of action, of place, and of time, are in this play, though almost constantly violated by Shakespeare, exactly observed. The action is one, great, and entire, the restoration of Prospero to his dukedom; this business is transacted in the compass of a small island, and in or near the cave of Prospero; though, indeed, it had been more artful and regular to have confined it to this single spot; and the time which the action takes up, is only equal to that of the representation; an excellence which ought always to be aimed at in every well-conducted fable, and for the want of which a variety of the most entertaining incidents can scarcely atone.

# Samuel Johnson

## CALIBAN'S LANGUAGE (1765)

It was a tradition, it seems, that Lord *Falkland,* Lord *C. J. Vaughan,* and Mr. *Seldon* concurred in observing, that *Shakespear* had not only found out a new character in his *Caliban,* but had also devised and adapted a *new manner of language* for that character. – WARBURTON

WHENCE these criticks derived the notion of a new language appropriated to *Caliban* I cannot find: They certainly mistook brutality of sentiment for uncouthness of words. *Caliban* had learned to speak of *Prospero* and his daughter, he had no names for the sun and moon before their arrival, and could not have invented a language of his own without more understanding than *Shakespear* has thought it proper to bestow upon him. His diction is indeed somewhat clouded by the gloominess of his temper and the malignity of his purposes; but let any other being entertain the same thoughts and he will find them easily issue in the same expressions.

# S. T. Coleridge

## AN ANALYSIS OF ACT I (1811)

ALTHOUGH I have affirmed that all Shakespeare's characters are ideal, and the result of his own meditation, yet a just separation may be made of those in which the ideal is most prominent – where it is put forward more intensely – where we are made more conscious of the ideal, though in truth they possess no more nor less ideality; and of those which, though equally idealized, the delusion upon the mind is of their being real. The characters in the various plays may be separated into those where the real is disguised in the ideal, and those where the ideal is concealed from us by the real. The difference is made by the different powers of mind employed by the poet in the representation.

At present I shall only speak of dramas where the ideal is predominant; and chiefly for this reason – that those plays have been attacked with the greatest violence. The objections to them are not the growth of our own country, but of France – the judgment of monkeys, by some wonderful phenomenon, put into the mouths of people shaped like men. These creatures have informed us that Shakespeare is a miraculous monster, in whom many heterogeneous components were thrown together, producing a discordant mass of genius – an irregular and ill-assorted structure of gigantic proportions.

Among the ideal plays, I will take *The Tempest*, by way of example. Various others might be mentioned, but it is impossible to go through every drama, and what I remark on *The Tempest* will apply to all Shakespeare's productions of the same class.

In this play Shakespeare has especially appealed to the imagination, and he has constructed a plot well adapted to the purpose. According to his scheme, he did not appeal to any sensuous impression (the word 'sensuous' is authorized by

Milton) of time and place, but to the imagination, and it is to be
borne in mind, that of old, and as regards mere scenery, his
works may be said to have been recited rather than acted – that
is to say, description and narration supplied the place of visual
exhibition: the audience was told to fancy that they saw what
they only heard described; the painting was not in colours, but
in words.

This is particularly to be noted in the first scene – a storm and
its confusion on board the king's ship. The highest and the
lowest characters are brought together, and with what excellence! Much of the genius of Shakespeare is displayed in these
happy combinations – the highest and the lowest, the gayest and
the saddest; he is not droll in one scene and melancholy in
another, but often both the one and the other in the same scene.
Laughter is made to swell the tear of sorrow, and to throw, as it
were, a poetic light upon it, while the tear mingles tenderness
with the laughter. Shakespeare has evinced the power, which
above all other men he possessed, that of introducing the profoundest sentiments of wisdom, where they would be least
expected, yet where they are most truly natural. One admirable
secret of his art is, that separate speeches frequently do not
appear to have been occasioned by those which preceded, and
which are consequent upon each other, but to have arisen out of
the peculiar character of the speaker.

Before I go further, I may take the opportunity of explaining
what is meant by mechanic and organic regularity. In the
former the copy must appear as if it had come out of the same
mould with the original; in the latter there is a law which all the
parts obey, conforming themselves to the outward symbols and
manifestations of the essential principle. If we look to the growth
of trees, for instance, we shall observe that trees of the same
kind vary considerably, according to the circumstances of soil,
air, or position; yet we are able to decide at once whether they
are oaks, elms, or poplars.

So with Shakespeare's characters: he shows us the life and
principle of each being with organic regularity. The Boatswain,
in the first scene of *The Tempest*, when the bonds of reverence

are thrown off as a sense of danger impresses all, gives a loose to his feelings, and thus pours forth his vulgar mind to the old Counsellor: –

'Hence! What care these roarers for the name of King? To cabin: silence! trouble us not.'

Gonzalo replies – 'Good; yet remember whom thou hast aboard.' To which the Boatswain answers – 'None that I more love than myself. You are a counsellor: if you can command these elements to silence, and work the peace of the present, we will not hand a rope more; use your authority: if you cannot, give thanks that you have lived so long, and make yourself ready in your cabin for the mischance of the hour, if it so hap. – Cheerly, good hearts! – Out of our way, I say.'

An ordinary dramatist would, after this speech, have represented Gonzalo as moralizing, or saying something connected with the Boatswain's language; for ordinary dramatists are not men of genius: they combine their ideas by association, or by logical affinity; but the vital writer, who makes men on the stage what they are in nature, in a moment transports himself into the very being of each personage, and, instead of cutting out artificial puppets, he brings before us the men themselves. Therefore, Gonzalo soliloquizes, – 'I have great comfort from this fellow: methinks, he hath no drowning mark upon him; his complexion is perfect gallows. Stand fast, good fate, to his hanging! make the rope of his destiny our cable, for our own doth little advantage. If he be not born to be hanged, our case is miserable.'

In this part of the scene we see the true sailor with his contempt of danger, and the old counsellor with his high feeling, who, instead of condescending to notice the words just addressed to him, turns off, meditating with himself, and drawing some comfort to his own mind, by trifling with the ill expression of the boatswain's face, founding upon it a hope of safety.

Shakespeare had pre-determined to make the plot of this play such as to involve a certain number of low characters, and at the beginning he pitched the note of the whole. The first scene was meant as a lively commencement of the story; the reader is prepared for something that is to be developed, and in

the next scene he brings forward Prospero and Miranda. How
is this done? By giving to his favourite character, Miranda, a
sentence which at once expresses the violence and fury of the
storm, such as it might appear to a witness on the land, and at the
same time displays the tenderness of her feelings – the exquisite
feelings of a female brought up in a desert, but with all the
advantages of education, all that could be communicated by a
wise and affectionate father. She possesses all the delicacy of
innocence, yet with all the powers of her mind unweakened by
the combats of life. Miranda exclaims: –

> O! I have suffered
> With those that I saw suffer: a brave vessel,
> Who had, no doubt, some noble creatures in her,
> Dash'd all to pieces.

The doubt here intimated could have occurred to no mind but
to that of Miranda, who had been bred up in the island with her
father and a monster only: she did not know, as others do, what
sort of creatures were in a ship; others never would have introduced it as a conjecture. This shows, that while Shakespeare is
displaying his vast excellence, he never fails to insert some touch
or other, which is not merely characteristic of the particular
person, but combines two things – the person, and the circumstances acting upon the person. She proceeds: –

> O! the cry did knock
> Against my very heart. Poor souls! they perish'd.
> Had I been any god of power, I would
> Have sunk the sea within the earth, or e'er
> It should the good ship so have swallow'd, and
> The fraughting souls within her.

She still dwells upon that which was most wanting to the
completeness of her nature – these fellow creatures from whom
she appeared banished, with only one relict to keep them alive,
not in her memory, but in her imagination.

Another proof of excellent judgment in the poet, for I am
now principally adverting to that point, is to be found in the
preparation of the reader for what is to follow. Prospero is

introduced, first in his magic robe, which, with the assistance of his daughter, he lays aside, and we then know him to be a being possessed of supernatural powers. He then instructs Miranda in the story of their arrival in the island, and this is conducted in such a manner, that the reader never conjectures the technical use the poet has made of the relation, by informing the auditor of what it is necessary for him to know.

The next step is the warning by Prospero, that he means, for particular purposes, to lull his daughter to sleep; and here he exhibits the earliest and mildest proof of magical power. In ordinary and vulgar plays we should have had some person brought upon the stage, whom nobody knows or cares anything about, to let the audience into the secret. Prospero having cast a sleep upon his daughter, by that sleep stops the narrative at the very moment when it was necessary to break it off, in order to excite curiosity, and yet to give the memory and understanding sufficient to carry on the progress of the history uninterruptedly.

Here I cannot help noticing a fine touch of Shakespeare's knowledge of human nature, and generally of the great laws of the human mind: I mean Miranda's infant remembrance. Prospero asks her –

> Canst thou remember
> A time before we came unto this cell?
> I do not think thou canst, for then thou wast not
> Out three years old.

Miranda answers,

> Certainly, sir, I can.

Prospero inquires,

> By what? by any other house or person?
> Of any thing the image tell me, that
> Hath kept with thy remembrance.

To which Miranda returns,

> 'Tis far off;
> And rather like a dream than an assurance
> That my remembrance warrants. Had I not
> Four or five women once, that tended me?    (I ii)

This is exquisite! In general, our remembrances of early life arise from vivid colours, especially if we have seen them in motion: for instance, persons when grown up will remember a bright green door, seen when they were quite young; but Miranda, who was somewhat older, recollected four or five women who tended her. She might know men from her father, and her remembrance of the past might be worn out by the present object, but women she only knew by herself, by the contemplation of her own figure in the fountain, and she recalled to her mind what had been. It was not, that she had seen such and such grandees, or such and such peeresses, but she remembered to have seen something like the reflection of herself: it was not herself, and it brought back to her mind what she had seen most like herself.

In my opinion the picturesque power displayed by Shakespeare, of all the poets that ever lived, is only equalled, if equalled, by Milton and Dante. The presence of genius is not shown in elaborating a picture: we have had many specimens of this sort of work in modern poems, where all is so dutchified, if I may use the word, by the most minute touches, that the reader naturally asks why words, and not painting, are used? I know a young lady of much taste, who observed, that in reading recent versified accounts of voyages and travels, she, by a sort of instinct, cast her eyes on the opposite page, for coloured prints of what was so patiently and punctually described.

The power of poetry is, by a single word perhaps, to instil that energy into the mind, which compels the imagination to produce the picture. Prospero tells Miranda,

> One midnight,
> Fated to the purpose, did Antonio open
> The gates of Milan; and i' the dead of darkness,
> The ministers for the purpose hurried thence
> Me, and thy crying self.

Here, by introducing a single happy epithet, 'crying', in the last line, a complete picture is presented to the mind, and in the production of such pictures the power of genius consists.

In reference to preparation, it will be observed that the storm, and all that precedes the tale, as well as the tale itself, serve to develop completely the main character of the drama, as well as the design of Prospero. The manner in which the heroine is charmed asleep fits us for what follows, goes beyond our ordinary belief, and gradually leads us to the appearance and disclosure of a being of the most fanciful and delicate texture, like Prospero, preternaturally gifted.

In this way the entrance of Ariel, if not absolutely forethought by the reader, was foreshewn by the writer: in addition, we may remark, that the moral feeling called forth by the sweet words of Miranda,

> Alack, what trouble
> Was I then to you!

in which she considered only the sufferings and sorrows of her father, puts the reader in a frame of mind to exert his imagination in favour of an object so innocent and interesting. The poet makes him wish that, if supernatural agency were to be employed, it should be used for a being so young and lovely. 'The wish is father to the thought', and Ariel is introduced. Here, what is called poetic faith is required and created, and our common notions of philosophy give way before it: this feeling may be said to be much stronger than historic faith, since for the exercise of poetic faith the mind is previously prepared. I make this remark, though somewhat digressive, in order to lead to a future subject of these lectures – the poems of Milton. When adverting to those, I shall have to explain farther the distinction between the two.

Many Scriptural poems have been written with so much of Scripture in them, that what is not Scripture appears to be not true, and like mingling lies with the most sacred revelations. Now Milton, on the other hand, has taken for his subject that one point of Scripture of which we have the mere fact recorded, and upon this he has most judiciously constructed his whole fable. So of Shakespeare's *King Lear*: we have little historic evidence to guide or confine us, and the few facts handed down

to us, and admirably employed by the poet, are sufficient, while
we read, to put an end to all doubt as to the credibility of the
story. It is idle to say that this or that incident is improbable,
because history, as far as it goes, tells us that the fact was so and
so. Four or five lines in the Bible include the whole that is said
of Milton's story, and the Poet has called up that poetic faith, that
conviction of the mind, which is necessary to make that seem
true, which otherwise might have been deemed almost fabulous.

But to return to *The Tempest*, and to the wondrous creation
of Ariel. If a doubt could ever be entertained whether Shakespeare was a great poet, acting upon laws arising out of his own
nature, and not without law, as has sometimes been idly asserted,
that doubt must be removed by the character of Ariel. The
very first words uttered by this being introduce the spirit, not as
an angel, above man; not a gnome, or a fiend, below man; but
while the poet gives him the faculties and the advantages of
reason, he divests him of all mortal character, not positively, it is
true, but negatively. In air he lives, from air he derives his
being, in air he acts; and all his colours and properties seem to
have been obtained from the rainbow and the skies. There is
nothing about Ariel that cannot be conceived to exist either at
sun-rise or at sun-set: hence all that belongs to Ariel belongs to
the delight the mind is capable of receiving from the most lovely
external appearances. His answers to Prospero are directly to
the question, and nothing beyond; or where he expatiates, which
is not unfrequently, it is to himself and upon his own delights,
or upon the unnatural situation in which he is placed, though
under a kindly power and to good ends.

Shakespeare has properly made Ariel's very first speech
characteristic of him. After he has described the manner in
which he had raised the storm and produced its harmless conse-
quences, we find that Ariel is discontented – that he has been
freed, it is true, from a cruel confinement, but still that he is
bound to obey Prospero, and to execute any commands imposed
upon him. We feel that such a state of bondage is almost
unnatural to him, yet we see that it is delightful for him to be so
employed. – It is as if we were to command one of the winds in a

different direction to that which nature dictates, or one of the waves, now rising and now sinking, to recede before it bursts upon the shore: such is the feeling we experience, when we learn that a being like Ariel is commanded to fulfil any mortal behest.

When, however, Shakespeare contrasts the treatment of Ariel by Prospero with that of Sycorax, we are sensible that the liberated spirit ought to be grateful, and Ariel does feel and acknowledge the obligation; he immediately assumes the airy being, with a mind so elastically correspondent, that when once a feeling has passed from it, not a trace is left behind.

Is there anything in nature from which Shakespeare caught the idea of this delicate and delightful being, with such child-like simplicity, yet with such preternatural powers? He is neither born of heaven, nor of earth; but, as it were, between both, like a May-blossom kept suspended in air by the fanning breeze, which prevents it from falling to the ground, and only finally, and by compulsion, touching earth. This reluctance of the Sylph to be under the command even of Prospero is kept up through the whole play, and in the exercise of his admirable judgment Shakespeare has availed himself of it, in order to give Ariel an interest in the event, looking forward to that moment when he was to gain his last and only reward – simple and eternal liberty.

Another instance of admirable judgment and excellent preparation is to be found in the creature contrasted with Ariel – Caliban; who is described in such a manner by Prospero, as to lead us to expect the appearance of a foul, unnatural monster. He is not seen at once: his voice is heard; this is the preparation; he was too offensive to be seen first in all his deformity, and in nature we do not receive so much disgust from sound as from sight. After we have heard Caliban's voice he does not enter, until Ariel has entered like a water-nymph. All the strength of contrast is thus acquired without any of the shock of abruptness, or of that unpleasant sensation, which we experience when the object presented is in any way hateful to our vision.

The character of Caliban is wonderfully conceived: he is a sort of creature of the earth, as Ariel is a sort of creature of the air. He partakes of the qualities of the brute, but is distinguished

from brutes in two ways: – by having mere understanding
without moral reason; and by not possessing the instincts which
pertain to absolute animals. Still, Caliban is in some respects a
noble being: the poet has raised him far above contempt: he is a
man in the sense of the imagination: all the images he uses are
drawn from nature, and are highly poetical; they fit in with the
images of Ariel. Caliban gives us images from the earth, Ariel
images from the air. Caliban talks of the difficulty of finding
fresh water, of the situation of morasses, and of other circumstances which even brute instinct, without reason, could compre-
hend. No mean figure is employed, no mean passion displayed,
beyond animal passion, and repugnance to command.

The manner in which the lovers are introduced is equally
wonderful, and it is the last point I shall now mention in reference
to this, almost miraculous, drama. The same judgment is
observable in every scene, still preparing, still inviting, and still
gratifying, like a finished piece of music. I have omitted to
notice one thing, and you must give me leave to advert to it
before I proceed: I mean the conspiracy against the life of
Alonzo. I want to shew you how well the poet prepares the
feelings of the reader for this plot, which was to execute the most
detestable of all crimes, and which, in another play, Shakespeare
has called 'the murder of sleep'.

Antonio and Sebastian at first had no such intention: it was
suggested by the magical sleep cast on Alonzo and Gonzalo; but
they are previously introduced scoffing and scorning at what was
said by others, without regard to age or situation – without any
sense of admiration for the excellent truths they heard delivered,
but giving themselves up entirely to the malignant and unsocial
feeling, which induced them to listen to everything that was said,
not for the sake of profiting by the learning and experience of
others, but of hearing something that might gratify vanity and
self-love, by making them believe that the person speaking was
inferior to themselves.

This, let me remark, is one of the grand characteristics of a
villain; and it would not be so much a presentiment, as an
anticipation of hell, for men to suppose that all mankind were as

wicked as themselves, or might be so, if they were not too great fools. Pope, you are perhaps aware, objected to this conspiracy; but in my mind, if it could be omitted, the play would lose a charm which nothing could supply.

Many, indeed innumerable, beautiful passages might be quoted from this play, independently of the astonishing scheme of its construction. Every body will call to mind the grandeur of the language of Prospero in that divine speech, where he takes leave of his magic art; and were I to indulge myself by repetitions of the kind, I should descend from the character of a lecturer to that of a mere reciter. Before I terminate, I may particularly recall one short passage, which has fallen under the very severe, but inconsiderate, censure of Pope and Arbuthnot,* who pronounce it a piece of the grossest bombast. Prospero thus addresses his daughter, directing her attention to Ferdinand:

> The fringed curtains of thine eye advance,
> And say what thou seest yond. (1 ii)

Taking these words as a periphrase of – 'Look what is coming yonder,' it certainly may to some appear to border on the ridiculous, and to fall under the rule I formerly laid down, – that whatever, without injury, can be translated into a foreign language in simple terms, ought to be in simple terms in the original language; but it is to be borne in mind, that different modes of expression frequently arise from difference of situation and education: a blackguard would use very different words, to express the same thing, to those a gentleman would employ, yet both would be natural and proper; difference of feeling gives rise to difference of language: a gentleman speaks in polished terms, with due regard to his own rank and position, while a blackguard, a person little better than half a brute, speaks like half a brute, showing no respect for himself, nor for others.

But I am content to try the lines I have just quoted by the introduction to them; and then, I think, you will admit, that nothing could be more fit and appropriate than such language.

---

* *Memoirs of Martinus Scriblerus,* Book II ('The Art of Sinking in Poetry') ch. xii.

How does Prospero introduce them? He has just told Miranda
a wonderful story, which deeply affected her, and filled her with
surprise and astonishment, and for his own purposes he afterwards lulls her to sleep. When she awakes, Shakespeare has
made her wholly inattentive to the present, but wrapped up in
the past. An actress, who understands the character of Miranda,
would have her eyes cast down, and her eyelids almost covering
them, while she was, as it were, living in her dream. At this
moment Prospero sees Ferdinand, and wishes to point him out to
his daughter, not only with great, but with scenic solemnity,
he standing before her, and before the spectator, in the dignified
character of a great magician. Something was to appear to
Miranda on the sudden, and as unexpectedly as if the hero of a
drama were to be on the stage at the instant when the curtain is
elevated. It is under such circumstances that Prospero says, in a
tone calculated at once to arouse his daughter's attention,

> The fringed curtains of thine eye advance,
> And say what thou seest yond.

Turning from the sight of Ferdinand to his thoughtful
daughter, his attention was first struck by the downcast appearance of her eyes and eyelids; and, in my humble opinion, the
solemnity of the phraseology assigned to Prospero is completely
in character, recollecting his preternatural capacity, in which the
most familiar objects in nature present themselves in a mysterious
point of view. It is much easier to find fault with a writer by
reference to former notions and experience, than to sit down and
read him, recollecting his purpose, connecting one feeling with
another, and judging of his words and phrases, in proportion as
they convey the sentiments of the persons represented.

Of Miranda we may say, that she possesses in herself all the
ideal beauties that could be imagined by the greatest poet of any
age or country; but it is not my purpose now, so much to point
out the high poetic powers of Shakespeare, as to illustrate his
exquisite judgment, and it is solely with this design that I have
noticed a passage with which, it seems to me, some critics, and
those among the best, have been unreasonably dissatisfied. If

Shakespeare be the wonder of the ignorant, he is, and ought to be, much more the wonder of the learned: not only from profundity of thought, but from his astonishing and intuitive knowledge of what man must be at all times, and under all circumstances, he is rather to be looked upon as a prophet than as a poet. Yet, with all these unbounded powers, with all this might and majesty of genius, he makes us feel as if he were unconscious of himself, and of his high destiny, disguising the half god in the simplicity of a child.

# S. T. Coleridge

## 'THE MOVED AND SYMPATHETIC IMAGINATION' (pub. 1836)

[*The Tempest*] addresses itself entirely to the imaginative faculty; and although the illusion may be assisted by the effect on the senses of the complicated scenery and decorations of modern times yet this sort of assistance is dangerous. For the principal and only genuine excitement ought to come from within, – from the moved and sympathetic imagination; whereas, where so much is addressed to the mere external senses of seeing and hearing, the spiritual vision is apt to languish, and the attraction from without will withdraw the mind from the proper and only legitimate interest which is intended to spring from within.

The romance opens with a busy scene admirably appropriate to the kind of drama, and giving, as it were, the keynote to the whole harmony. It prepares and initiates the excitement required for the entire piece, and yet does not demand anything from the spectators, which their previous habits had not fitted them to understand. It is the bustle of a tempest, from which the real horrors are abstracted; – therefore it is poetical, though not in strictness natural – (the distinction to which I have so often alluded) – and is purposely restrained from concentering the interest on itself, but used merely as an induction or tuning for what is to follow.

In the second scene, Prospero's speeches, till the entrance of Ariel, contain the finest example I remember of retrospective narration for the purpose of exciting immediate interest, and putting the audience in possession of all the information necessary for the understanding of the plot. Observe, too, the perfect probability of the moment chosen by Prospero (the very Shakspeare himself, as it were, of the tempest) to open out the truth to his daughter, his own romantic bearing, and how completely any thing that might have been disagreeable to us in the magician, is reconciled and shaded in the humanity and natural feelings of the father. In the very first speech of Miranda the simplicity and tenderness of her character are at once laid open; – it would have been lost in direct contact with the agitation of the first scene. The opinion once prevailed, but, happily, is now abandoned, that Fletcher alone wrote for women; – the truth is, that with very few, and those partial, exceptions, the female characters in the plays of Beaumont and Fletcher are, when of the light kind, not decent; when heroic, complete viragos. But in Shakspeare all the elements of womanhood are holy, and there is the sweet, yet dignified feeling of all that *continuates* society, as sense of ancestry and of sex, with a purity unassailable by sophistry, because it rests not in the analytic processes, but in that sane equipoise of the faculties, during which the feelings are representative of all past experience, – not of the individual only, but of all those by whom she has been educated, and their predecessors even up to the first mother that lived. Shakspeare saw that the want of prominence, which Pope notices for sarcasm, was the blessed beauty of the woman's character, and knew that it arose not from any deficiency, but from the more exquisite harmony of all the parts of the moral being constituting one living total of head and heart. He has drawn it, indeed, in all its distinctive energies of faith, patience, constancy, fortitude, – shown in all of them as following the heart, which gives its results by a nice tact and happy intuition, without the intervention of the discursive faculty, – sees all things in and by the light of the affections, and errs, if it ever err, in the exaggerations of love alone. In all the Shakspearian women there is essentially the same foundation and principle; the distinct individuality and variety are merely the result of the modification of circumstances, whether in Miranda the maiden, in Imogen the wife, or in Katharine the queen.

But to return. The appearance and characters of the super or ultra-natural servants are finely contrasted. Ariel has in every thing the airy tint which gives the name; and it is worthy of remark that Miranda is never directly brought into comparison

with Ariel, lest the natural and human of the one and the supernatural of the other should tend to neutralize each other;
Caliban, on the other hand, is all earth, all condensed and gross
in feelings and images; he has the dawnings of understanding
without reason or the moral sense, and in him, as in some brute
animals, this advance to the intellectual faculties, without the
moral sense, is marked by the appearance of vice. For it is in
the primacy of the moral being only that man is truly human; in
his intellectual powers he is certainly approached by the brutes,
and, man's whole system duly considered, those powers cannot
be considered other than means to an end, that is, to morality.

In this scene, as it proceeds, is displayed the impression made
by Ferdinand and Miranda on each other; it is love at first
sight; –

> at the first sight
> They have changed eyes: –

and it appears to me, that in all cases of real love, it is at one
moment that it takes place. That moment may have been
prepared by previous esteem, admiration, or even affection, –
yet love seems to require a momentary act of volition, by which a
tacit bond of devotion is imposed, – a bond not to be thereafter
broken without violating what should be sacred in our nature.
How finely is the true Shakspearian scene contrasted with
Dryden's vulgar alteration of it, in which a mere ludicrous
psychological experiment, as it were, is tried – displaying nothing
but indelicacy without passion. Prospero's interruption of the
courtship has often seemed to me to have no sufficient motive;
still his alleged reason –

> lest too light winning
> Make the prize light –

is enough for the ethereal connexions of the romantic imagination, although it would not be so for the historical. The whole
courting scene, indeed, in the beginning of the third act, between
the lovers is a masterpiece; and the first dawn of disobedience
in the mind of Miranda to the command of her father is very
finely drawn, so as to seem the working of the Scriptural com-

mand, *Thou shalt leave father and mother*, &c. O! with what exquisite purity this scene is conceived and executed! Shakspeare may sometimes be gross, but I boldly say that he is always moral and modest. Alas! in this our day decency of manners is preserved at the expense of morality of heart, and delicacies for vice are allowed, whilst grossness against it is hypocritically, or at least morbidly, condemned.

In this play are admirably sketched the vices generally accompanying a low degree of civilization; and in the first scene of the second act Shakspeare has, as in many other places, shown the tendency in bad men to indulge in scorn and contemptuous expressions, as a mode of getting rid of their own uneasy feelings of inferiority to the good, and also, by making the good ridiculous, of rendering the transition of others to wickedness easy. Shakspeare never puts habitual scorn into the mouths of other than bad men, as here in the instances of Antonio and Sebastian. The scene of the intended assassination of Alonzo and Gonzalo is an exact counterpart of the scene between Macbeth and his lady, only pitched in a lower key throughout, as designed to be frustrated and concealed, and exhibiting the same profound management in the manner of familiarizing a mind, not immediately recipient, to the suggestion of guilt, by associating the proposed crime with something ludicrous or out of place, – something not habitually matter of reverence. By this kind of sophistry the imagination and fancy are first bribed to contemplate the suggested act, and at length to become acquainted with it. Observe how the effect of this scene is heightened by contrast with another counterpart of it in low life, – that between the conspirators Stephano, Caliban, and Trinculo in the second scene of the third act, in which there are the same essential characteristics.

In this play and in this scene of it are also shown the springs of the vulgar in politics, – of that kind of politics which is inwoven with human nature. In his treatment of this subject, wherever it occurs, Shakspeare is quite peculiar. In other writers we find the particular opinions of the individual; in Massinger it is rank republicanism; in Beaumont and Fletcher even *jure*

*divino* principles are carried to excess; – but Shakspeare never
promulgates any party tenets. He is always the philosopher and
the moralist, but at the same time with a profound veneration
for all the established institutions of society, and for those
classes which form the permanent elements of the state –
especially never introducing a professional character, as such,
otherwise than as respectable. If he must have any name, he
should be styled a philosophical aristocrat, delighting in those
hereditary institutions which have a tendency to bind one age to
another, and in that distinction of ranks, of which, although few
may be in possession, all enjoy the advantages. Hence, again,
you will observe the good nature with which he seems always to
make sport with the passions and follies of a mob, as with an
irrational animal. He is never angry with it, but hugely content
with holding up its absurdities to its face; and sometimes you
may trace a tone of almost affectionate superiority, something
like that in which a father speaks of the rogueries of a child. See
the good-humoured way in which he describes Stephano passing
from the most licentious freedom to absolute despotism over
Trinculo and Caliban. The truth is, Shakspeare's characters are
all *genera* intensely individualized; the results of meditation, of
which observation supplied the drapery and the colors necessary
to combine them with each other. He had virtually surveyed all
the great component powers and impulses of human nature, –
had seen that their different combinations and subordinations
were in fact the individualizers of men, and showed how their
harmony was produced by reciprocal disproportions of excess
or deficiency. The language in which these truths are expressed
was not drawn from any set fashion, but from the profoundest
depths of his moral being, and is therefore for all ages.

*William Hazlitt*

## UNITY AND VARIETY IN
## SHAKESPEARE'S DESIGN (1817)

*The Tempest* is one of the most original and perfect of Shakespear's productions, and he has shewn in it all the variety of his
powers. It is full of grace and grandeur. The human and
imaginary characters, the dramatic and the grotesque, are
blended together with the greatest art, and without any appearance of it. Though he has here given 'to airy nothing a local
habitation and a name', yet that part which is only the fantastic
creation of his mind, has the same palpable texture, and coheres
'semblably' with the rest. As the preternatural part has the air of
reality, and almost haunts the imagination with a sense of truth,
the real characters and events partake of the wildness of a dream.
The stately magician, Prospero, driven from his dukedom, but
around whom (so potent is his art) airy spirits throng numberless
to do his bidding; his daughter Miranda ('worthy of that name')
to whom all the power of his art points, and who seems the
goddess of the isle; the princely Ferdinand, cast by fate upon
the haven of his happiness in this idol of his love; the delicate
Ariel; the savage Caliban, half brute, half demon; the drunken
ship's crew – are all connected parts of the story, and can hardly
be spared from the place they fill. Even the local scenery is of a
piece and character with the subject. Prospero's enchanted
island seems to have risen up out of the sea; the airy music, the
tempest-tost vessel, the turbulent waves, all have the effect of
the landscape background of some fine picture. Shakespear's
pencil is (to use an allusion of his own) 'like the dyer's hand,
subdued to what it works in'. Every thing in him, though it
partakes of 'the liberty of wit', is also subjected to 'the law' of
the understanding. For instance, even the drunken sailors, who
are made reeling-ripe, share, in the disorder of their minds and

bodies, in the tumult of the elements, and seem on shore to be
as much at the mercy of chance as they were before at the mercy
of the winds and waves. These fellows with their sea-wit are the
least to our taste of any part of the play: but they are as like
drunken sailors as they can be, and are an indirect foil to Caliban,
whose figure acquires a classical dignity in the comparison. The
character of Caliban is generally thought (and justly so) to be
one of the author's masterpieces. It is not indeed pleasant to
see this character on the stage any more than it is to see the god
Pan personated there. But in itself it is one of the wildest and
most abstracted of all Shakespear's characters, whose deformity
whether of body or mind is redeemed by the power and truth
of the imagination displayed in it. It is the essence of grossness,
but there is not a particle of vulgarity in it. Shakespear has
described the brutal mind of Caliban in contact with the pure
and original forms of nature; the character grows out of the soil
where it is rooted, uncontrouled, uncouth and wild, uncramped
by any of the meannesses of custom. It is 'of the earth, earthy'.
It seems almost to have been dug out of the ground, with a soul
instinctively superadded to it answering to its wants and origin.
Vulgarity is not natural coarseness, but conventional coarseness,
learnt from others, contrary to, or without an entire conformity
of natural power and disposition; as fashion is the common-place
affectation of what is elegant and refined without any feeling
of the essence of it. Schlegel, the admirable German critic on
Shakespear, observes that Caliban is a poetical character, and
'always speaks in blank verse'. He first comes in thus:

> Caliban. As wicked dew as e'er my mother brush'd
> With raven's feather from unwholesome fen,
> Drop on you both: a south-west blow on ye,
> And blister you all o'er!
> Prospero. For this, be sure, to-night thou shalt have cramps,
> Side-stitches that shall pen thy breath up; urchins
> Shall, for that vast of night that they may work,
> All exercise on thee: thou shalt be pinched
> As thick as honey-combs, each pinch more stinging
> Than bees that made them.

*Caliban.* I must eat my dinner.
   This island's mine by Sycorax my mother,
   Which thou tak'st from me. When thou camest first,
   Thou stroak'dst me, and mad'st much of me; would'st
      give me
   Water with berries in't; and teach me how
   To name the bigger light and how the less
   That burn by day and night; and then I lov'd thee,
   And shew'd thee all the qualities o' th' isle,
   The fresh springs, brine-pits, barren place and fertile:
   Curs'd be I that I did so! All the charms
   Of Sycorax, toads, beetles, bats, light on you!
   For I am all the subjects that you have,
   Who first was mine own king; and here you sty me
   In this hard rock, whiles you do keep from me
   The rest o' th' island.

And again, he promises Trinculo his services thus, if he will
free him from his drudgery.

   I'll shew thee the best springs; I'll pluck thee berries,
   I'll fish for thee, and get thee wood enough.
   I pr'ythee let me bring thee where crabs grow,
   And I with my long nails will dig thee pig-nuts:
   Shew thee a jay's nest, and instruct thee how
   To snare the nimble marmozet: I'll bring thee
   To clust'ring filberds; and sometimes I'll get thee
   Young sea-mells from the rock.

In conducting Stephano and Trinculo to Prospero's cell,
Caliban shews the superiority of natural capacity over greater
knowledge and greater folly; and in a former scene, when Ariel
frightens them with his music, Caliban to encourage them
accounts for it in the eloquent poetry of the senses.

   – Be not afraid, the isle is full of noises,
   Sounds, and sweet airs, that give delight and hurt not.
   Sometimes a thousand twanging instruments
   Will hum about mine ears, and sometimes voices,
   That if I then had waked after long sleep,
   Would make me sleep again; and then in dreaming,

The clouds methought would open, and shew riches
Ready to drop upon me: when I wak'd,
I cried to dream again.

This is not more beautiful than it is true. The poet here shews us the savage with the simplicity of a child, and makes the strange monster amiable. Shakespear had to paint the human animal rude and without choice in its pleasures, but not without the sense of pleasure or some germ of the affections. Master Barnardine in *Measure for Measure*, the savage of civilized life, is an admirable philosophical counterpart to Caliban.

Shakespear has, as it were by design, drawn off from Caliban the elements of whatever is ethereal and refined, to compound them in the unearthly mould of Ariel. Nothing was ever more finely conceived than this contrast between the material and the spiritual, the gross and delicate. Ariel is imaginary power, the swiftness of thought personified. When told to make good speed by Prospero, he says, 'I drink the air before me'. This is something like Puck's boast on a similar occasion, 'I'll put a girdle round about the earth in forty minutes.' But Ariel differs from Puck in having a fellow feeling in the interests of those he is employed about. How exquisite is the following dialogue between him and Prospero!

*Ariel.* Your charm so strongly works them,
    That if you now beheld them, your affections
    Would become tender.
*Prospero.* Dost thou think so, spirit?
*Ariel.* Mine would, sir, were I human.
*Prospero.* And mine shall.
    Hast thou, which art but air, a touch, a feeling
    Of their afflictions, and shall not myself,
    One of their kind, that relish all as sharply,
    Passion'd as they, be kindlier moved than thou art?

It has been observed that there is a peculiar charm in the songs introduced in Shakespear, which, without conveying any distinct images, seem to recall all the feelings connected with them, like snatches of half-forgotten music heard indistinctly and at intervals. There is this effect produced by Ariel's songs, which (as we are told) seem to sound in the air, and as if the person playing them were invisible.

# Edward Dowden

## THE SERENITY OF *THE TEMPEST*
### (1875)

OVER the beauty of youth and the love of youth, there is shed, in these plays of Shakspere's final period, a clear yet tender luminousness, not elsewhere to be perceived in his writings. In his earlier plays, Shakspere writes concerning young men and maidens, their loves, their mirth, their griefs, as one who is among them, who has a lively, personal interest in their concerns, who can make merry with them, treat them familiarly, and, if need be, can mock them into good sense. There is nothing in these early plays wonderful, strangely beautiful, pathetic about youth and its joys and sorrows. In the histories and tragedies, as was to be expected, more massive, broader, or more profound objects of interest engaged the poet's imagination. But in these latest plays, the beautiful pathetic light is always present. There are the sufferers, aged, experienced, tried – Queen Katharine, Prospero, Hermione. And over against these there are the children absorbed in their happy and exquisite egoism, – Perdita and Miranda, Florizel and Ferdinand, and the boys of old Belarius.

The same means to secure ideality for these figures, so young and beautiful, is in each case (instinctively perhaps rather than deliberately) resorted to. They are lost children, – princes or a princess, removed from the court, and its conventional surroundings, into some scene of rare, natural beauty. There are the lost princes – Arviragus and Guiderius, among the mountains of Wales, drinking the free air, and offering their salutations to the risen sun. There is Perdita, the shepherdess-princess, 'queen of curds and cream', sharing with old and young her flowers, lovelier and more undying than those that Proserpina let fall from Dis's waggon. There is Miranda, (whose very name is significant of wonder), made up of beauty, and love, and womanly pity, neither courtly nor rustic, with the breeding of an island of enchantment, where Prospero is her tutor and protector, and Caliban her servant, and the Prince of Naples her lover. In each of these plays we can see Shakspere, as it were, tenderly bending over the joys and sorrows of youth. We recognise this rather through the total characterization, and through a feeling and a presence, than through definite incident or statement. But some of this feeling escapes in the disinterested joy and admiration of old Belarius when he gazes at the princely youths, and in Camillo's loyalty to Florizel and Perdita; while it obtains more distinct expression in such a word as that which Prospero utters, when from a distance he watches with pleasure Miranda's zeal to relieve Ferdinand from his task of log-bearing: – 'Poor worm, thou art infected'.*

It is not chiefly because Prospero is a great enchanter, now about to break his magic staff, to drown his book deeper than ever plummet sounded, to dismiss his airy spirits, and to return to the practical service of his Dukedom, that we identify Prospero in some measure with Shakspere himself. It is rather because the temper of Prospero, the grave harmony of his character, his self-mastery, his calm validity of will, his sensitiveness to wrong, his unfaltering justice, and with these, a certain abandonment, a remoteness from the common joys and sorrows of the world, are characteristic of Shakspere as discovered to us in all his latest plays. Prospero is a harmonious and fully developed *will*. In the earlier play of fairy enchantments, *A Midsummer Night's Dream*, the 'human mortals' wander to and fro in a maze of error, misled by the mischievous frolic of Puck, the jester and clown of Fairyland. But here the spirits of the elements, and Caliban the gross genius of brute-matter, – needful for the service of life, – are brought under subjection to the human will of Prospero.

* The same feeling appears in the lines which end Act III, scene i.

*Prospero.* So glad of this as they I cannot be,
   Who are surprised with all; but my rejoicing
   At nothing can be more.

What is more, Prospero has entered into complete possession of himself. Shakspere has shown us his quick sense of injury, his intellectual impatience, his occasional moment of keen irritability, in order that we may be more deeply aware of his abiding strength and self-possession, and that we may perceive how these have been grafted upon a temperament, not impassive or unexcitable. And Prospero has reached not only the higher levels of moral attainment; he has also reached an altitude of thought from which he can survey the whole of human life, and see how small and yet how great it is. His heart is sensitive, he is profoundly touched by the joy of the children, with whom in the egoism of their love he passes for a thing of secondary interest; he is deeply moved by the perfidy of his brother. His brain is readily set a-work, and can with difficulty be checked from eager and excessive energizing; he is subject to the access of sudden and agitating thought. But Prospero masters his own sensitiveness, emotional and intellectual: –

> We are such stuff
> As dreams are made on, and our little life
> Is rounded with a sleep. Sir, I am vexed;
> Bear with my weakness; my old brain is troubled:
> Be not disturb'd with my infirmity;
> If you be pleased, retire into my cell
> And there repose; a turn or two I'll walk,
> To still my beating mind.

'Such stuff as dreams are made on.' Nevertheless, in this little life, in this dream, Prospero will maintain his dream rights and fulfil his dream duties. In the dream, he, a Duke, will accomplish Duke's work. Having idealized everything, Shakspere left everything real. Bishop Berkeley's foot was no less able to set a pebble flying than was the lumbering foot of Dr. Johnson. Nevertheless, no material substance intervened between the soul of Berkeley and the immediate presence of the play of Divine power.

A thought which seems to run through the whole of *The Tempest*, appearing here and there like a coloured thread in

some web, is the thought that the true freedom of man consists
in service. Ariel, untouched by human feeling, is panting for his
liberty; in the last words of Prospero are promised his en-
franchisement and dismissal to the elements. Ariel reverences
his great master, and serves him with bright alacrity; but he is
bound by none of our human ties, strong and tender, and he will
rejoice when Prospero is to him as though he never were.*
To Caliban, a land-fish, with the duller elements of earth and
water in his composition, but no portion of the higher elements,
air and fire, though he receives dim intimations of a higher
world, – a musical humming, or a twangling, or a voice heard
in sleep – to Caliban, service is slavery.† He hates to bear his
logs; he fears the incomprehensible power of Prospero, and
obeys, and curses. The great master has usurped the rights of
the brute-power Caliban. And when Stephano and Trinculo
appear, ridiculously impoverished specimens of humanity, with
their shallow understandings and vulgar greeds, this poor earth-
monster is possessed by a sudden *schwärmerei*, a fanaticism for
liberty! –

> 'Ban, 'ban, Ca'-Caliban,
> Has a new master; get a new man.
> Freedom, heyday! heyday, freedom! freedom! freedom,
> heyday, freedom!

His new master also sings his impassioned hymn of liberty,
the *Marseillaise* of the enchanted island:

* Ariel is promised his freedom after two days, Act I, scene ii. Why
two days? The time of the entire action of the Tempest is only three
hours. What was to be the employment of Ariel during two days?
To make the winds and seas favourable during the voyage to Naples.
Prospero's island therefore was imagined by Shakspere as within two
days' quick sail of Naples.

† The conception of Caliban, the 'servant-monster', 'plain fish and
no doubt marketable', the 'tortoise', 'his fins like arms', with 'a very
ancient and fish-like smell', who gabbled until Prospero taught him
language – this conception was in Shakspere's mind when he wrote
*Troilus and Cressida.* Thersites describes Ajax (III, iii): *'He's grown
a very land-fish, languageless, a monster.'*

> Flout 'em and scout 'em,
> And scout 'em and flout 'em;
> Thought is free.

The leaders of the revolution, escaped from the stench and foulness of the horse-pond, King Stephano and his prime minister Trinculo, like too many leaders of the people, bring to an end their great achievement on behalf of liberty by quarrelling over booty, – the trumpery which the providence of Prospero had placed in their way. Caliban, though scarce more truly wise or instructed than before, at least discovers his particular error of the day and hour:

> What a thrice-double ass
> Was I, to take this drunkard for a god,
> And worship this dull fool!

It must be admitted that Shakspere, if not, as Hartley Coleridge asserted, 'a Tory and a gentleman', had within him some of the elements of English conservatism.

But while Ariel and Caliban, each in his own way, is impatient of service, the human actors, in whom we are chiefly interested, are entering into bonds – bonds of affection, bonds of duty, in which they find their truest freedom. Ferdinand and Miranda emulously contend in the task of bearing the burden which Prospero has imposed upon the prince:

> I am in my condition
> A prince, Miranda; I do think, a king:
> I would, not so! and would no more endure
> This wooden slavery than to suffer
> The flesh-fly blow my mouth. Hear my soul speak:
> The very instant that I saw you, did
> My heart fly to your service; there resides,
> To make me slave to it; and for your sake
> Am I this patient log-man.

And Miranda speaks with the sacred candour from which spring the nobler manners of a world more real and glad than the world of convention and proprieties and pruderies:

> Hence, bashful cunning!
> And prompt me, plain and holy innocence!
> I am your wife, if you will marry me;
> If not, I'll die your maid: to be your fellow
> You may deny me; but I'll be your servant
> Whether you will or no.
> *Fer.* My mistress, dearest;
> And I thus humble ever.
> *Mir.* My husband, then?
> *Fer.* Ay, with a heart as willing
> As bondage e'er of freedom.

In an earlier part of the play, this chord which runs through it had been playfully struck in the description of Gonzalo's imaginary commonwealth, in which man is to be enfranchised from all the laborious necessities of life. Here is the ideal of notional liberty, Shakspere would say, and to attempt to realise it at once lands us in absurdities and self-contradictions:

> For no kind of traffic
> Would I admit: no name of magistrate;
> Letters should not be known: riches, poverty,
> And use of service none; contract, succession,
> Bourn, bound of land, tilth, vineyard, none;
> No use of metal, corn, or wine, or oil;
> No occupation; all men idle, all,
> And women too, but innocent and pure;
> No sovereignty.
> *Seb.* Yet he would be king on't.*

Finally, in the Epilogue, which was written perhaps by Shakspere, perhaps by some one acquainted with his thoughts, Prospero in his character of a man, no longer a potent enchanter, petitions the spectators of the theatre for two things, pardon and freedom. It would be straining matters to discover in this

---

* Act II, scene i. – The prolonged and dull joking of Sebastian in this scene cannot be meant by Shakspere to be really bright and witty. It is meant to shew that the intellectual poverty of the conspirators is as great as their moral obliquity. They are monsters more ignoble than Caliban. Their laughter is 'the crackling of thorns under a pot'.

Epilogue profound significances. And yet in its playfulness it curiously falls in with the moral purport of the whole. Prospero, the pardoner, implores pardon. Shakspere was aware – whether such be the significance (aside – for the writer's mind) of this Epilogue or not – that no life is ever lived which does not need to receive as well as to render forgiveness. He knew that every energetic dealer with the world must seek a sincere and liberal pardon for many things. Forgiveness and freedom: these are keynotes of the play. When it was occupying the mind of Shakspere, he was passing from his service as artist to his service as English country gentleman. Had his mind been dwelling on the question of how he should employ his new freedom, and had he been enforcing upon himself the truth that the highest freedom lies in the bonds of duty?*

* Mr Furnivall, observing that in these later plays breaches of the family bond are dramatically studied, and the reconciliations are domestic reconciliations in *Cymbeline* and *The Winter's Tale*, suggests to me that they were a kind of confession on Shakspere's part that he had inadequately felt the beauty and tenderness of the common relations of father and child, wife and husband; and that he was now quietly resolving to be gentle, and wholly just to his wife and his home. I cannot altogether make this view of the later plays my own, and leave it to the reader to accept and develop as he may be able.

# Henry James

## INTRODUCTION TO *THE TEMPEST* (1907)

IF the effect of the Plays and Poems, taken in their mass, be most of all to appear often to mock our persistent ignorance of so many of the conditions of their birth, and thereby to place on the rack again our strained and aching wonder, this character has always struck me as more particularly kept up for them by *The Tempest*; the production, of the long series, in which the Questions, as the critical reader of Shakespeare must ever comprehensively and ruefully call them and more or less resignedly live with them, hover before us in their most tormenting form. It may seem no very philosophic state of mind, the merely baffled and exasperated view of one of the supreme works of all literature; though I feel, for myself, that to confess to it now and then, by way of relief, is no unworthy tribute to the work. It is not, certainly, the tribute most frequently paid, for the large body of comment and criticism of which this play alone has been the theme abounds much rather in affirmed conclusions, complacencies of conviction, full apprehensions of the meaning and triumphant pointings of the moral. The Questions, in the light of all this wisdom, convert themselves with comparatively small difficulty, into smooth and definite answers; the innumerable dim ghosts that flit, like started game at eventide, through the deep dusk of our speculation, with just form enough to quicken it and no other charity for us at all, bench themselves along the vista as solidly as Falstaff and as vividly as Hotspur. Everything has thus been attributed to the piece before us, and every attribution so made has been in turn brushed away; merely to glance at such a monument to the interest inspired is to recognise a battleground of opposed factions, not a little enveloped in sound and smoke. Of these

copious elements, produced for the most part to the best
intention, we remain accordingly conscious; so that to approach
the general bone of contention, as we can but familiarly name it,
for whatever purpose, we have to cross the scene of action at a
mortal risk, making the fewest steps of it and trusting to the
probable calm at the centre of the storm. There in fact, though
there only, we find that serenity; find the subject itself intact
and unconscious, seated as unwinking and inscrutable as a
divinity in a temple, save for that vague flicker of derision, the
only response to our interpretative heat, which adds the last
beauty to its face. The divinity never relents – never, like the
image of life in *The Winter's Tale*, steps down from its pedestal;
it simply leaves us to stare on through the ages, with this fact
indeed of having crossed the circle of fire, and so got into the
real and right relation to it, for our one comfort.

The position of privilege of *The Tempest* as the latest example,
to all appearance, of the author's rarer work, with its distance
from us in time thereby shortened to the extent of the precious
step or two, was certain to expose it, at whatever final cost, we
easily see, to any amount of interpretative zeal. With its first
recorded performance that of February 1613, when it was given
in honour of the marriage of the Princess Elizabeth, its finished
state cannot have preceded his death by more than three years,
and we accordingly take it as the finest flower of his experience.
Here indeed, as on so many of the Questions, judgments sharply
differ, and this use of it as an ornament to the nuptials of the
daughter of James I and the young Elector Palatine may have
been but a repetition of previous performances; though it is not
in such a case supposable that these can have been numerous.
They would antedate the play, at the most, by a year or two, and
so not throw it essentially further back from us. *The Tempest*
speaks to us, somehow, convincingly, as a *pièce de circonstance*,
and the suggestion that it was addressed, in its brevity, its rich
simplicity, and its free elegance, to court-production, and above
all to providing, with a string of other dramas, for the 'intellectual' splendour of a wedding-feast, is, when once entertained,
not easily dislodged. A few things fail to fit, but more fit

strikingly. I like therefore to think of the piece as of 1613. To
refer it, as it is referred by other reckonings, to 1611 is but to
thicken that impenetrability of silence in which Shakespeare's
latest years enfold him. Written as it must have been on the
earlier calculation, before the age of forty-seven, it has
that rare value of the richly mature note of a genius who, by
our present measure of growth and fulness, was still young
enough to have had in him a world of life: we feel behind it the
immense procession of its predecessors, while we yet stare
wistfully at the plenitude and the majesty, the expression as of
something broad-based and ultimate, that were not, in any but a
strained sense, to borrow their warrant from the weight of years.
Nothing so enlarges the wonder of the whole time-question in
Shakespeare's career as the fact of this date, in easy middle life,
of his time-climax; which, if we knew less, otherwise, than we do
about him, might affect us as an attempt, on the part of treacherous History, to pass him off as one of those monsters of precocity
who, fortunately for their probable reputation, the too likely
betrayal of short-windedness, are cut off in their comparative
prime. The transmuted young rustic who, after a look over
London, brief at the best, was ready at the age of thirty to
produce *The Merchant of Venice* and *A Midsummer Night's
Dream* (and this after the half-dozen splendid prelusive things
that had included, at twenty-eight, *Romeo and Juliet*), had been
indeed a monster of precocity – which all geniuses of the first
order are not; but the day of his paying for it had neither arrived
nor, however faintly, announced itself, and the fathomless
strangeness of his story, the abrupt stoppage of his pulse after
*The Tempest,* is not, in charity, lighted for us by a glimmer of
explanation. The explanation by some interposing accident is as
absent as any symptom of 'declining powers'.

His powers declined, that is – but declined merely to obey
the spring we should have supposed inherent in them; and their
possessor's case derives from this, I think, half the secret of its
so inestimably mystifying us. He died, for a nature so organized,
too lamentably soon; but who knows where we should have
been with him if he had not lived long enough so to affirm, with

many other mysteries, the mystery of his abrupt and complete cessation? There is that in *The Tempest,* specifically, though almost all indefinably, which seems to show us the artist consciously tasting of the first and rarest of his gifts, that of imaged creative Expression, the instant sense of some copious equivalent of thought for every grain of the grossness of reality; to show him as unresistingly aware, in the depths of his genius, that nothing like it had ever been known, or probably would ever be again known, on earth, and as so given up, more than on other occasions, to the joy of sovereign *science.* There are so many sides from which any page that shows his stamp may be looked at that a handful of reflections can hope for no coherency, in the chain of association immediately formed, unless they happen to bear upon some single truth. Such a truth then, for me, is this comparative – by which one can really but mean this superlative – artistic value of the play seen in the meagre circle of the items of our knowledge about it. Let me say that our knowledge, in the whole connection, is a quantity that shifts, surprisingly, with the measure of a felt need; appearing to some of us, on some sides, adequate, various, large, and appearing to others, on whatever side, a scant beggar's portion. We are concerned, it must be remembered, here – that is for getting *generally* near our author – not only with the number of the mustered facts, but with the kind of fact that each may strike us as being: never unmindful that such matters, when they are few, may go far for us if they be individually but ample and significant; and when they are numerous, on the other hand, may easily fall short enough to break our hearts if they be at the same time but individually small and poor. Three or four stepping-stones across a stream will serve if they are broad slabs, but it will take more than may be counted if they are only pebbles. Beyond all gainsaying then, by many an estimate, is the penury in which even the most advantageous array of the Shakespearean facts still leaves us: strung together with whatever ingenuity they remain, for our discomfiture, as the pebbles across the stream.

To balance, for our occasion, this light scale, however, *The Tempest* affects us, taking its complexity and its perfection together, as the rarest of all examples of literary art. There may be other things as exquisite, other single exhalations of beauty reaching as high a mark and sustained there for a moment, just as there are other deep wells of poetry from which cupfuls as crystalline may, in repeated dips, be drawn; but nothing, surely, of equal length and variety lives so happily and radiantly as a whole: no poetic birth ever took place under a star appointed to blaze upon it so steadily. The felicity enjoyed is enjoyed longer and more intensely, and the art involved, completely revealed, as I suggest, to the master, holds the securest revel. The man himself, in the Plays, we directly touch, to my consciousness, positively nowhere: we are dealing too perpetually with the artist, the monster and magician of a thousand masks, not one of which we feel him drop long enough to gratify with the breath of the interval that strained attention in us which would be yet, so quickened, ready to become deeper still. Here at last the artist is, comparatively speaking, so generalised, so consummate and typical, so frankly amused with himself, that is with his art, with his power, with his theme, that it is as if he came to meet us more than his usual half-way, and as if, thereby, in meeting *him*, and touching him, we were nearer to meeting and touching the man. The man everywhere, in Shakespeare's work, is so effectually locked up and imprisoned in the artist that we but hover at the base of thick walls for a sense of him; while, in addition, the artist is so steeped in the abysmal objectivity of his characters and situations that the great billows of the medium itself play with him, to our vision, very much as, over a ship's side, in certain waters, we catch, through transparent tides, the flash of strange sea-creatures. What we are present at in this fashion is a series of incalculable plunges – the series of those that have taken effect, I mean, after the great primary plunge, made once for all, of the man into the artist: the successive plunges of the artist himself into Romeo and into Juliet, into Shylock, Hamlet, Macbeth, Coriolanus, Cleopatra, Antony, Lear, Othello, Falstaff, Hotspur; immersions during which, though he always ultimately finds his feet, the very violence of the movements involved troubles and distracts our sight. In

*The Tempest,* by the supreme felicity I speak of, is no violence; he sinks as deep as we like, but what he sinks into, beyond all else, is the lucid stillness of his style.

One can speak, in these matters, but from the impression determined by one's own inevitable standpoint; again and again, at any rate, such a masterpiece puts before me the very act of the momentous conjunction taking place for the poet, at a given hour, between his charged inspiration and his clarified experience: or, as I should perhaps better express it, between his human curiosity and his aesthetic passion. Then, if he happens to have been, all his career, with his equipment for it, more or less the victim and the slave of the former, he yields, by way of a change, to the impulse of allowing the latter, for a magnificent moment, the upper hand. The human curiosity, as I call it, is always there – with no more need of making provision for it than use in taking precautions against it; the surrender to the luxury of expertness may therefore go forward on its own conditions. I can offer no better description of *The Tempest* as fresh re-perusal lights it for me than as such a surrender, sublimely enjoyed; and I may frankly say that, under this impression of it, there is no refinement of the artistic consciousness that I do not see my way – or feel it, better, perhaps, since we but grope, at the best, in our darkness – to attribute to the author. It is a way that one follows to the end, because it is a road, I repeat, on which one least misses some glimpse of him face to face. If it be true that the thing was concocted to meet a particular demand, that of the master of the King's revels, with his prescription of date, form, tone and length, this, so far from interfering with the Poet's perception of a charming opportunity to taste for *himself,* for himself above all, and as he had almost never so tasted, not even in *A Midsummer Night's Dream,* of the quality of his mind and the virtue of his skill, would have exceedingly favoured the happy case. Innumerable one may always suppose these delicate debates and intimate understandings of an artist with himself. 'How much *taste,* in the world, may I conceive that I have? – and what a charming idea to snatch a moment for finding out! What moment could be better than this – a bridal evening before the Court, with extra candles and the handsomest company – if I can but put my hand on the right "scenario"?' We can catch, across the ages, the searching sigh and the look about; we receive the stirred breath of the ripe, amused genius; and, stretching, as I admit I do at least, for a still closer conception of the beautiful crisis, I find it pictured for me in some such presentment as that of a divine musician who, alone in his room, preludes or improvises at close of day. He sits at the harpsichord, by the open window, in the summer dusk; his hands wander over the keys. They stray far, for his motive, but at last he finds and holds it; then he lets himself go, embroidering and refining: it is the thing for the hour and his mood. The neighbours may gather in the garden, the nightingale be hushed on the bough; it is none the less a private occasion, a concert of one, both performer and auditor, who plays for his own ear, his own hand, his own innermost sense, and for the bliss and capacity of his instrument. Such are the only hours at which the artist *may*, by any measure of his own (too many things, at others, make heavily against it); and their challenge to him is irresistible if he has known, all along, too much compromise and too much sacrifice.

The face that beyond any other, however, I seem to see *The Tempest* turn to us is the side on which it so superlatively speaks of that endowment for Expression, expression as a primary force, a consuming, an independent passion, which was the greatest ever laid upon man. It is for Shakespeare's power of constitutive speech quite as if he had swum into our ken with it from another planet, gathering it up there, in its wealth, as something antecedent to the occasion and the need, and if possible quite in excess of them; something that was to make of our poor world a great flat table for receiving the glitter and clink of outpoured treasure. The idea and the motive are more often than not so smothered in it that they scarce know themselves, and the resources of such a style, the provision of images, emblems, energies of every sort, laid up in advance, affects us as the storehouse of a king before a famine or a siege – which not only, by its scale, braves depletion or exhaustion, but bursts,

through mere excess of quantity or presence, out of all doors and
windows. It renders the poverties and obscurities of our world,
as I say, in the dazzling terms of a richer and better. It constitutes,
by a miracle, more than half the author's material; so much
more usually does it happen, for the painter or the poet, that
life itself, in its appealing, overwhelming crudity, offers itself
as the paste to be kneaded. Such a personage works in general
in the very elements of experience; whereas we see Shakespeare
working predominantly in the terms of expression, *all* in the
terms of the artist's specific vision and genius; with a thicker
cloud of images to attest his approach, at any point than the
comparatively meagre given case ever has to attest its own
identity. He points for us as no one else the relation of style to
meaning and of manner to motive; a matter on which, right and
left, we hear such rank ineptitudes uttered. Unless it be true
that these things, on either hand, are inseparable; unless it be
true that the phrase, the cluster and order of terms, *is* the object
and the sense, in as close a compression as that of body and
soul, so that any consideration of them as distinct, from the
moment style is an active, applied force, becomes a gross
stupidity: unless we recognise this reality the author of *The
Tempest* has no lesson for us. It is by his expression of it exactly
as the expression stands that the particular thing is created,
created as interesting, as beautiful, as strange, droll or terrible –
as related, in short, to our understanding or our sensibility; in
consequence of which we reduce it to naught when we begin
to talk of either of its presented parts as matters by themselves.

All of which considerations indeed take us too far; what it is
important to note being simply our Poet's high testimony to
this independent, absolute value of Style, and to its need
thoroughly to project and seat itself. It had been, as so seating
itself, the very home of his mind, for his all too few twenty
years; it had been the supreme source to him of the joy of life.
It had been in fine his material, his plastic clay; since the more
subtly he applied it the more secrets it had to give him, and the
more these secrets might appear to him, at every point, one with
the lights and shades of the human picture, one with the myriad

pulses of the spirit of man. Thus it was that, as he passed from one application of it to another, tone became, for all its suggestions, more and more sovereign to him, and the subtlety of its secrets an exquisite interest. If I see him, at the last, over *The Tempest*, as the composer, at the harpsichord or the violin, extemporising in the summer twilight, it is exactly that he is feeling there for tone and, by the same token, finding it – finding it as *The Tempest*, beyond any register of ours, immortally gives it. This surrender to the highest sincerity of virtuosity, as we nowadays call it, is to my perception *all The Tempest*; with no possible depth or delicacy in it that such an imputed character does not cover and provide for. The subject to be treated was the simple fact (if one may call anything in the matter simple) that refinement, selection, economy, the economy not of poverty, but of wealth a little weary of congestion – the very air of the lone island and the very law of the Court celebration – were here implied and imperative things. Anything was a subject, always, that offered to sight an aperture of size enough for expression and its train to pass in and deploy themselves. If they filled up all the space, none the worse; they occupied it as nothing else could do. The subjects of the Comedies are, without exception, old wives' tales – which we are not too insufferably aware of only because the iridescent veil so perverts their proportions. The subjects of the Histories are no subjects at all; each is but a row of pegs for the hanging of the cloth of gold that is to muffle them. Such a thing as *The Merchant of Venice* declines, for very shame, to be reduced to its elements of witless 'story'; such things as the two Parts of *Henry the Fourth* form no more than a straight convenient channel for the procession of evoked images that is to pour through it like a torrent. Each of these productions is none the less of incomparable splendour; by which splendour we are bewildered till we see how it comes. Then we see that every inch of it is personal tone, or in other words brooding expression raised to the highest energy. Push such energy far enough – far enough if you can! – and, being what it is, it then inevitably provides for Character. Thus we see character, in every form of which the

'story' gives the thinnest hint, marching through the pieces I
have named in its habit as it lives, and so filling out the scene that
nothing is missed. The 'story' in *The Tempest* is a thing of
naught, for any story will provide a remote island, a shipwreck
and a coincidence. Prospero and Miranda, awaiting their relatives,
are, in the present case, *for* the relatives, the coincidence – just
as the relatives are the coincidence for them. Ariel and Caliban,
and the island-airs and island-scents, and all the rest of the
charm and magic and the ineffable delicacy (a delicacy positively
at its highest in the conception and execution of Caliban) are
the style handed over to its last disciplined passion of curiosity;
a curiosity which flowers, at this pitch, into the freshness of
each of the characters.

There are judges for whom the piece is a tissue of symbols;
symbols of the facts of State then apparent, of the lights of
philosophic and political truth, of the 'deeper meanings of life',
above all, of a high crisis in its author's career. At this most
relevant of its mystic values only we may glance; the conse-
crated estimate of Prospero's surrender of his magic robe and
staff as a figure for Shakespeare's own self-despoilment, his
considered purpose, at this date, of future silence. Dr. George
Brandes works out in detail that analogy; the production becomes,
on such a supposition, Shakespeare's 'farewell to the stage';
his retirement to Stratford, to end his days in the care of his
property and in oblivion of the theatre, was a course for which
his arrangements had already been made. The simplest way to
put it, since I have likened him to the musician at the piano, is
to say that he had decided upon the complete closing of this
instrument, and that in fact he was to proceed to lock it with the
sharp click that has reverberated through the ages, and to spend
what remained to him of life in walking about a small, squalid
country-town with his hands in his pockets and an ear for no
music now but the chink of the coin they might turn over there.
This is indeed in general the accepted, the imposed view of the
position he had gained: this freedom to 'elect', as we say, to
cease, intellectually, to exist: this ability, exercised at the zenith
of his splendour, to shut down the lid, from one day to another,

on the most potent aptitude for vivid reflection ever lodged in a human frame and to conduct himself thereafter, in all ease and comfort, not only as if it were not, but as if it had never been. I speak of our 'accepting' the prodigy, but by the established record we have no choice whatever; which is why it is imposed, as I say, on our bewildered credulity. With the impossibility of proving that the author of *The Tempest* did, after the date of that production, ever again press the spring of his fountain, ever again reach for the sacred key or break his heart for an hour over his inconceivable act of sacrifice, we are reduced to behaving as if we understood the strange case; so that any rubbing of our eyes, as under the obsession of a wild dream, has been held a gesture that, for common decency, must mainly take place in private. If I state that my small contribution to any renewed study of the matter can amount, accordingly, but to little more than an irresistible need to rub mine in public, I shall have done the most that the condition of our knowledge admits of. We can 'accept', but we can accept only in stupefaction – a stupefaction that, in presence of *The Tempest*, and of the intimate meaning so imputed to it, must despair of ever subsiding. These things leave us in darkness – in gross darkness about the Man; the case of which they are the warrant is so difficult to embrace. None ever appealed so sharply to some light of knowledge, and nothing could render our actual knowledge more contemptible. What manner of human being was it who *could* so, at a given moment, announce his intention of capping his divine flame with a twopenny extinguisher, and who then, the announcement made, could serenely succeed in carrying it out? Were it a question of a flame spent or burning thin, we might feel a little more possessed of matter for comprehension; the fact being, on the contrary, one can only repeat, that the value of *The Tempest* is, exquisitely, in its refinement of power, its renewed artistic freshness and roundness, its mark as of a distinction unequalled, on the whole (though I admit that we here must take subtle measures), in any predecessor. Prospero has simply waited, to cast his magic ring into the sea, till the jewel set in it shall have begun to burn as never before.

So it is then; and it puts into a nutshell the eternal mystery,
the most insoluble that ever was, the complete rupture, for our
understanding, between the Poet and the Man. There are
moments, I admit, in this age of sound and fury, of connections,
in every sense, too maddeningly multiplied, when we are willing
to let it pass as a mystery, the most soothing, cooling, consoling
too perhaps, that ever was. But there are others when, speaking
for myself, its power to torment us intellectually seems scarcely
to be borne; and we know these moments best when we hear
it proclaimed that a comfortable clearness reigns. I have been
for instance reading over Mr. Halliwell-Phillipps, and I find him
apparently of the opinion that it is all our fault if everything in
our author's story, and above all in this last chapter of it, be not
of a primitive simplicity. The complexity arises from our
suffering our imagination to meddle with the Man at all; who
is quite sufficiently presented to us on the face of the record.
For critics of this writer's complexion the only facts we are
urgently concerned with are the facts of the Poet, which are
abundantly constituted by the Plays and the Sonnets. The Poet
is *there*, and the Man is outside: the Man is for instance in such a
perfectly definite circumstance as that he could never miss, after
*The Tempest*, the key of his piano, as I have called it, since he
could play so freely with the key of his cash-box. The supreme
master of expression had made, before fifty, all the money he
wanted; therefore what was there more to express? This view
is admirable if you can get your mind to consent to it. It must
ignore any impulse, in presence of Play or Sonnet (whatever
vague stir behind either may momentarily act as provocation)
to try for a lunge at the figured arras. In front of the tapestry
sits the immitigably respectable person whom our little slateful
of gathered and numbered items, heaven knows, does amply
account for, since there is nothing in him to explain; while the
undetermined figure, on the other hand – undetermined whether
in the sense of respectability or of anything else – the figure who
supremely interests us, remains as unseen of us as our Ariel,
on the enchanted island, remains of the bewildered visitors.
Mr. Halliwell-Phillipps's theory, as I understand it – and I refer

to it but as an advertisement of a hundred others – is that we
too are but bewildered visitors, and that the state of mind of the
Duke of Naples and his companions is our proper critical
portion.

If our knowledge of the greatest of men consists therefore
but of the neat and 'proved' addition of two or three dozen
common particulars, the rebuke to a morbid and monstrous
curiosity is no more than just. We know enough, by such an
implication, when we admire enough, and as difficulties would
appear to abound on our attempting to push further, this is an
obvious lesson to us to stand as still as possible. Not difficulties –
those of penetration, exploration, interpretation, those, in the
word that says everything, of appreciation – are the approved
field of criticism, but the very forefront of the obvious and the
palpable, where we may go round and round, like holiday-
makers on hobby-horses, at the turning of a crank. Differences
of estimate, in this relation, come back, too clearly, let us
accordingly say, to differences of view of the character of genius
in general – if not, in truth, more exactly stated, to that strangest
of all fallacies, the idea of the separateness of a great man's parts.
His genius places itself, under this fallacy, on one side of the line
and the rest of his identity on the other; the line being that, for
instance, which, to Mr. Halliwell-Phillipps's view, divides the
author of *Hamlet* and *The Tempest* from the man of exemplary
business-method whom alone we may propose to approach at
all intimately. The stumbling-block here is that the boundary
exists only in the vision of those able to content themselves with
arbitrary marks. A mark becomes arbitrary from the moment
we have no authoritative sign of where to place it, no sign of
higher warrant than that it smoothes and simplifies the ground.
But though smoothing and simplifying, on such terms, may, by
restricting our freedom of attention and speculation, make, on
behalf of our treatment of the subject, for a livelier effect of
business – that business as to a zealous care for which we seem
taught that our author must above all serve as our model – it
will see us little further on any longer road. The fullest appreciation possible is the high tribute we must offer to greatness,

and to make it worthy of its office we must surely know where
we are with it. In greatness as much as in mediocrity the man is,
under examination, *one*, and the elements of character melt into
each other. The genius is a part of the mind, and the mind a
part of the behaviour; so that, for the attitude of inquiry,
without which appreciation means nothing, where does one of
these provinces end and the other begin? We may take the
genius first or the behaviour first, but we inevitably proceed
from the one to the other; we inevitably encamp, as it were, on
the high central table-land that they have in common. How are
we to arrive at a relation with the object to be penetrated if we
are thus forever met by a locked door flanked with a sentinel
who merely invites us to take it for edifying? We take it ourselves
for attaching – which is the very essence of mysteries – and
profess ourselves doomed forever to hang yearningly about it.
An obscurity endured, in fine, one inch further, or one hour
longer, than our necessity truly holds us to, strikes us but as an
artificial spectre, a muffled object with waving arms, set up to
keep appreciation down.

For it is never to be forgotten that we are here in presence
of the human character the most magnificently endowed, in all
time, with the sense of the life of man, and with the apparatus
for recording it; so that of *him*, inevitably, it goes hardest of all
with us to be told that we have nothing, or next to nothing, to
do with the effect in him of this gift. If it does not satisfy us that
the effect was to make him write *King Lear* and *Othello*, we are
verily difficult to please: so it is, meanwhile, that the case for the
obscurity is argued. That is sovereign, we reply, so far as it
goes; but it tells us nothing of the effect on him of being *able*
to write Lear and Othello. No scrap of testimony of what this
may have been is offered us; it is the quarter in which our
blankness is most blank, and in which we are yet most officiously
put off. It is true of the poet in general – in nine examples out
of ten – that his life is mainly inward, that its events and revolu-
tions are his great impressions and deep vibrations, and that his
'personality' is all pictured in the publication of his verse.
Shakespeare, we essentially feel, is the tenth, is the millionth

example; not the sleek bachelor of music, the sensitive harp set once for all in the window to catch the air, but the spirit in hungry quest of every possible experience and adventure of the spirit, and which, betimes, with the boldest of all intellectual movements, was to leap from the window into the street. We are in the street, as it were, for admiration and wonder, when the incarnation alights, and it is of no edification to shrug shoulders at the felt impulse (when made manifest) to follow, to pursue, all breathlessly to track it on its quickly-taken way. Such a quest of imaginative experience, we can only feel, has itself constituted one of the greatest observed adventures of mankind; so that no point of the history of it, however far back seized, is premature for our fond attention. Half our connection with it is our desire to 'assist' at it; so how can we fail of curiosity and sympathy? The answer to which is doubtless again that these impulses are very well, but that as the case stands they can move but in one channel. We are free to assist in the Plays themselves – to assist at whatever we like; so long, that is, as, after the fashion I have noted, we rigidly limit our inductions from them. It is put to us once more that we can make no bricks without straw, and that, rage as we may against our barrier, it none the less stubbornly exists. Granted on behalf of the vaulting spirit all that we claim for it, it still, in the street, as we say – and in spite of the effect we see it as acrobatically producing there – absolutely defies pursuit. Beyond recovery, beyond curiosity, it was to lose itself in the crowd. The crowd, for that matter, the witnesses we must take as astonished and dazzled, has, though itself surviving but in a dozen or two dim, scarce articulate ghosts, been interrogated to the last man and the last distinguishable echo. This has practically elicited nothing – nothing, that is, of a nature to gratify the indiscreetly, the morbidly inquisitive; since we find ourselves not rarely reminded that morbidity may easily become a vice. *He* was notoriously not morbid; he stuck to his business – save when he so strangely gave it up; wherefore his own common sense about things in general is a model for the tone he should properly inspire. 'You speak of his career as a transcendent "adventure," as *the* conspicuously transcendent adventure – even to the sight of his contemporaries – of the mind of man; but no glimmer of any such story, of any such figure or "presence," to use your ambiguous word, as you desire to read into the situation, can be discerned in any quarter. So what is it you propose we should do? What evidence do you suggest that, with this absence of material, we should put together? We have what we have; we are not concerned with what we have not.'

In some such terms as that, one makes out, does the best attainable 'appreciation' appear to invite us to let our great personage, the mighty adventurer, slink past. He slunk past in life: that was good enough for him, the contention appears to be. Why therefore should he not slink past in immortality? One's reply can indeed only be that he evidently must; yet I profess that, even while saying so, our poor point, for which *The Tempest* once more gives occasion, strikes me as still, as always, in its desperate way, worth the making. The question, I hold, will eternally interest the student of letters and of the human understanding, and the envied privilege of our play in particular will be always to keep it before him. *How* did the faculty so radiant there contrive, in such perfection, the arrest of its divine flight? By what inscrutable process was the extinguisher applied and, when once applied, kept in its place to the end? What became of the checked torrent, as a latent, bewildered presence and energy, in the life across which the dam was constructed? What other mills did it set itself turning, or what contiguous country did it – rather indeed did it *not*, in default of these – inevitably ravage? We are referred, for an account of the matter, to recorded circumstances which are only not supremely vulgar because they are supremely dim and few; in which character they but mock, and as if all consciously, as I have said, at our unrest. The one at all large indication they give is that our hero may have died – since he died so soon – of his unnatural effort. Their quality, however, redeems them a little by having for its effect that they throw us back on the work itself with a rebellious renewal of appetite and yearning. The secret that baffles us being the secret of the Man, we know, as I have granted, that we shall never touch the Man *directly* in the Artist. We stake our hopes thus on indirectness, which may contain possibilities; we take that very truth for our counsel of despair, try to look at it as helpful for the Criticism of the future. That of the past has been too often infantile; one has asked one's self how it *could*, on such lines, get at him. The figured tapestry, the long arras that hides him, is always there, with its immensity of surface and its proportionate underside. May it not then be but a question, for the fulness of time, of the finer weapon, the sharper point, the stronger arm, the more extended lunge?

# W. H. Auden

## CALIBAN TO THE AUDIENCE

### (1945)

IF now, having dismissed your hired impersonators with verdicts ranging from the laudatory orchid to the disgusted and disgusting egg, you ask and, of course, notwithstanding the conscious fact of his irrevocable absence, you instinctively *do* ask for our so good, so great, so dead author to stand before the finally lowered curtain and take his shyly responsible bow for this, his latest, ripest production, it is I – my reluctance is, I can assure you, co-equal with your dismay – who will always loom thus wretchedly into your confused picture, for, in default of the all-wise, all-explaining master you would speak *to*, who else at least can, who else indeed must respond to your bewildered cry, but its very echo, the begged question you would speak to him *about*.

\*     \*     \*

We must own [*for the present I speak your echo*] to a nervous perplexity not unmixed, frankly, with downright resentment. How *can* we grant the indulgence for which in his epilogue your personified type of the creative so lamely, tamely pleaded? Imprisoned, by you, in the mood doubtful, loaded, by you, with distressing embarrassments, we are, we submit, in no position to set *anyone* free.

Our native Muse, heaven knows and heaven be praised, is not exclusive. Whether out of the innocence of a child-like heart to whom all things are pure, or with the serenity of a status so majestic that the mere keeping up of tones and appearances, the suburban wonder as to what the strait-laced Unities might possibly think, or sad sour Probability possibly say, are questions for which she doesn't because she needn't, she hasn't in her lofty maturity any longer to care a rap, she invited, dear generous-hearted creature that see is, just *tout le monde* to drop in at any time so that her famous, memorable, sought-after evenings present to the speculative eye an ever-shining, never-tarnished proof of her amazing unheard-of power to combine and happily contrast, to make *every* shade of the social and moral palette contribute to the general richness, of the skill, un-approached and unattempted by Grecian aunt or Gaelic sister, with which she can skate full tilt toward the forbidden inco-herence and then, in the last split second, on the shuddering edge of the bohemian standardless abyss effect her breathtaking triumphant turn.

No timid segregation by rank or taste for her, no prudent listing into those who will, who might, who certainly would not get on, no nicely graded scale of invitations to heroic formal Tuesdays, young comic Thursdays, al fresco farcical Saturdays. No, the real, the only test of the theatrical as of the gastronomic, her practice confidently wagers, is the mixed perfected brew.

As he looks in on her, so marvellously at home with all her cosy swarm about her, what accents will not assault the new arrival's ear, the magnificent tropes of tragic defiance and despair, the repartee of the high humour, the pun of the very low, cultured drawl and manly illiterate bellow, yet all of them gratefully doing their huge or tiny best to make the party go?

And if, assured by her smiling wave that of course he may, he should presently set out to explore her vast and rambling mansion, to do honour to its dear odd geniuses of local con-venience and proportion, its multiplied deities of mysterious stair and interesting alcove, not one of the laughing groups and engrossed warmed couples that he keeps 'surprising' – the never-ending surprise for him is that he doesn't seem to – but affords some sharper instance of relations he would have been the last to guess at, choleric prince at his ease with lymphatic butler, moist hand-taking so to dry, youth getting on quite famously with stingy cold old age, some stranger vision of the large loud liberty violently rocking yet never, he is persuaded, finally upsetting the jolly crowded boat.

What, he may well ask, has the gracious goddess done to all these people that, at her most casual hint, they should so trustingly, so immediately take off those heavy habits one thinks of them as having for their health and happiness day and night to wear, without in this unfamiliar unbuttoned state – the notable absence of the slightest shiver or not-quite-inhibited sneeze is indication positive – for a second feeling the draught? Is there, could there be, *any* miraculous suspension of the wearily historic, the dingily geographic, the dully drearily sensible beyond her faith, her charm, her love, to command? Yes, there could be, yes, alas, indeed yes, O there is, right here, right now before us, the situation present.

How *could* you, you who are one of the oldest habitués at these delightful functions, one, possibly the closest, of her trusted inner circle, how could you be guilty of the incredible unpardonable treachery of bringing along the one creature, as you above all men must have known, whom she cannot and will not under any circumstances stand, the solitary exception she is not at any hour of the day or night at home to, the unique case that her attendant spirits have absolute instructions never, neither at the front door nor at the back, to admit?

At Him and at Him only does she draw the line, not because there are any limits to her sympathy but precisely because there are none. Just because of all she is and all she means to be, she cannot conceivably tolerate in her presence the represented principle of *not* sympathizing, *not* associating, *not* amusing, the only child of her Awful Enemy, the rival whose real name she will never sully her lips with – 'that envious witch' is sign sufficient – who does not rule but defiantly is the unrectored chaos.

All along and only too well she has known what would happen if, by any careless mischance – of conscious malice she never dreamed till now – He should ever manage to get in. She foresaw what He would do to the conversation, lying in wait for its vision of private love or public justice to warm to an Egyptian brilliance and then with some fish-like odour or *bruit insolite* snatching the visionaries back tongue-tied and blushing to the here and now; she foresaw what He would do to the arrangements, breaking, by a refusal to keep in step, the excellent order of the dancing ring, and ruining supper by knocking over the loaded appetizing tray; worst of all, she foresaw, she dreaded what He would end up by doing to her, that, not content with upsetting her guests, with spoiling their fun, His progress from outrage to outrage would not relent before the gross climax of His making, horror unspeakable, a pass at her virgin self.

Let us suppose, even, that in your eyes she is by no means as we have always fondly imagined, your dear friend, that what we have just witnessed was not what it seemed to us, the inexplicable betrayal of a life-long sacred loyalty, but your long-premeditated just revenge, the final evening up of some ancient never-forgotten score, then even so, why make us suffer who have never, in all conscience, done you harm? Surely the theatrical relation, no less than the marital, is governed by the sanely decent general law that, before visitors, in front of the children or the servants, there shall be no indiscreet revelation of animosity, no 'scenes', that, no matter to what intolerable degrees of internal temperature and pressure restraint may raise both the injured and the guilty, nevertheless such restraint is applied to tones and topics, the exhibited picture must be still as always the calm and smiling one the most malicious observer can see nothing wrong with, and not until the last of those whom manifested anger or mistrust would embarrass or amuse or not be good for have gone away or out or up, is the voice raised, the table thumped, the suspicious letter snatched at or the outrageous bill furiously waved.

For we, after all – you cannot have forgotten this – are strangers to her. We have never claimed her acquaintance, knowing as well as she that we do not and never could belong on her side of the curtain. All we have ever asked for is that for a few hours the curtain should be left undrawn, so as to allow our humble ragged selves the privilege of craning and gaping at the splendid goings-on inside. We most emphatically do *not* ask that she should speak to us, or try to understand us; on the contrary our one desire has always been that she should preserve for ever her old high strangeness, for what delights us about her world is just that it neither is nor possibly could become one in which we could breathe or behave, that in her house the right of innocent passage should remain so universal that the same neutral space accommodates the conspirator and his victim; the generals of both armies, the chorus of patriots and the choir of nuns, palace and farmyard, cathedral and smugglers' cave, that time should never revert to that intransigent element we are so ineluctably and only too familiarly in, but remain the passive good-natured creature she and her friends can by common consent do anything they like with − (it is not surprising that they should take advantage of their strange power and so frequently skip hours and days and even years: the dramatic mystery is that they should always so unanimously agree upon exactly how many hours and days and years to skip) − that upon their special constitutions the moral law should continue to operate so exactly that the timid not only deserve but actually win the fair, and it is the socially and physically unemphatic David who lays low the gorilla-chested Goliath with one well-aimed custard pie, that in their blessed climate, the manifestation of the inner life should always remain so easy and habitual that a sudden eruption of musical and metaphorical power is instantly recognized as standing for grief and disgust, an elegant *contrapposto* for violent death, and that consequently the picture which they in there present to us out here is always that of the perfectly tidiable case of disorder, the beautiful and serious problem exquisitely set without a single superfluous datum and insoluble with less, the expert landing of all the passengers with all their luggage safe and sound in the best of health and spirits and without so much as a scratch or a bruise.

Into that world of freedom without anxiety, sincerity without loss of vigour, feeling that loosens rather than ties the tongue, we are not, we reiterate, so blinded by presumption to our proper status and interest as to expect or even wish at any time to enter, far less to dwell there.

Must we − it seems oddly that we must − remind you that our existence does not, like hers, enjoy an infinitely indicative mood, an eternally present tense, a limitlessly active voice, for in our shambling, slovenly makeshift world any two persons, whether domestic first or neighbourly second, require and necessarily presuppose in both their numbers and in all their cases, the whole inflected gamut of an alien third since, without a despised or dreaded Them to turn the back *on*, there could be no intimate or affectionate Us to turn the eye *to*; that, *chez nous*, space to never the whole uninhabited circle but always some segment, its eminent domain upheld by two co-ordinates. There always has been and always will be not only the vertical boundary, the river on this side of which initiative and honesty stroll arm in arm wearing sensible clothes, and beyond which is a savage elsewhere swarming with contagious diseases, but also its horizontal counterpart, the railroad above which houses stand in their own grounds, each equipped with a garage and a beautiful woman, sometimes with several, and below which huddled shacks provide a squeezing shelter to collarless herds who eat blancmange and have never said anything witty. Make the case as special as you please; take the tamest congregation or the wildest faction; take, say, a college. What river and railroad did for the grosser instance, lawn and corridor do for the more refined, dividing the tender who value from the tough who measure, the superstitious who still sacrifice to causation from the heretics who have already reduced the worship of truth to bare description, and so creating the academic fields to be guarded with umbrella and learned periodical against the trespass of any unqualified stranger, not a whit less jealously than the game-preserve is protected from the poacher by the unamiable shot-gun. For without these prohibitive frontiers we should never know who we were or what we wanted. It is they who donate to neighbourhood all its accuracy and vehemence. It is thanks to them that we do know with whom to associate, make love, exchange recipes and jokes, go mountain climbing or sit side by side fishing from piers. It is thanks to them, too, that we know against whom to rebel. We *can* shock our parents by visiting the dives below the railroad tracks, we *can* amuse ourselves on what would otherwise have been a very dull

evening indeed, in plotting to seize the post office across the
river.

Of course these several private regions must together com-
prise one public whole – we would never deny that logic and
instinct require that – of course. We and They are united in the
candid glare of the same commercial hope by day, and the soft
refulgence of the same erotic nostalgia by night – and this is
our point – without our privacies of situation, our local idioms
of triumph and mishap, our different doctrines concerning the
transubstantiation of the larger pinker bun on the terrestrial
dish for which the mature sense may reasonably water and the
adult fingers furtively or unabashedly go for, our specific
choices of which hill it would be romantic to fly away over or
what sea it would be exciting to run away to, our peculiar visions
of the absolute stranger with a spontaneous longing for the lost
who will adopt our misery not out of desire but pure compassion,
without, in short, our devoted pungent expression of the partial
and contrasted, the Whole would have no importance and its
Day and Night no interest.

So, too, with Time who, in our auditorium, is not her dear
old buffer so anxious to please everybody, but a prim magistrate
whose court never adjourns, and from whose decisions, as he
laconically sentences one to loss of hair and talent, another to
seven days' chastity, and a third to boredom for life, there is
no appeal. We should not be sitting here now, washed, warm,
well-fed, in seats we have paid for, unless there were others
who are not here; our liveliness and good-humour, such as
they are, are those of survivors, conscious that there are others
who have not been so fortunate, others who did not succeed in
navigating the narrow passage or to whom the natives were not
friendly, others whose streets were chosen by the explosion or
through whose country the famine turned aside from ours to
go, others who failed to repel the invasion of bacteria or to
crush the insurrection of their bowels, others who lost their
suit against their parents or were ruined by wishes they could
not adjust or murdered by resentments they could not control;
aware of some who were better and bigger but from whom,

only the other day, Fortune withdrew her hand in sudden
disgust, now nervously playing chess with drunken sea-captains
in sordid cafés on the equator or the Arctic Circle, or lying, only
a few blocks away, strapped and screaming on iron beds or
dropping to naked pieces in damp graves. And shouldn't you
too, dear master, reflect – forgive us for mentioning it – that we
might very well not have been attending a production of yours
this evening, had not some other and maybe – who can tell? –
brighter talent married a barmaid or turned religious and shy
or gone down in a liner with all his manuscripts, the loss
recorded only in the corner of some country newspaper below
A Poultry Lover's Jottings?

You yourself, we seem to remember, have spoken of the
conjured spectacle as 'a mirror held up to nature', a phrase
misleading in its aphoristic sweep but indicative at least of one
aspect of the relations between the real and the imagined, their
mutual reversal of value, for isn't the essential artistic strangeness
to which your citation of the sinisterly biased image would
point just this: that on the far side of the mirror the general
will to compose, to form at all costs a felicitous pattern, becomes
the *necessary cause* of any particular effort to live or act or love
or triumph or vary, instead of being as, in so far as it emerges
at all, it is on this side, their *accidental effect?*

Does Ariel – to nominate the spirit of reflection in your
terms – call for manifestation? Then neither modesty nor fear of
reprisals excuses the one so called on from publicly confessing
that she cheated at croquet or that he committed incest in a dream.
Does He demand concealment? Then their nearest and dearest
must be deceived by disguises of sex and age which anywhere
else would at once attract the attentions of the police or the
derisive whistle of the awful schoolboy. That is the price asked,
and how promptly and gladly paid, for universal reconciliation
and peace, for the privilege of all galloping together past the
finishing post neck and neck.

How then, we continue to wonder, knowing all this, could
you act as if you did not, as if you did not realize that the
embarrassing compresence of the absolutely natural, incorrigibly

right-handed, and, to any request for co-operation, utterly negative, with the enthusiastically self-effacing would be a simultaneous violation of both worlds, as if you were not perfectly well aware that the magical musical condition, the orphic spell that turns the fierce dumb greedy beasts into grateful guides and oracles who will gladly take one anywhere and tell one everything free of charge, is precisely and simply that of his finite immediate note *not*, under any circumstances, being struck, of its not being tentatively whispered, far less positively banged.

Are we not bound to conclude, then, that, whatever snub to the poetic you may have intended incidentally to administer, your profounder motive in so introducing Him to them among whom, because He doesn't belong, He couldn't appear as anything but His distorted parody, a deformed and savage slave, was to deal a mortal face-slapping insult to us among whom He does and is, moreover, all grossness turned to glory, no less a person than the nude august elated archer of our heaven, the darling single son of Her who, in her right milieu, is certainly no witch but the most sensible of all the gods, whose influence is as sound as it is pandemic, on the race-track no less than in the sleeping cars of the Orient Express, our great white Queen of Love herself?

But even that is not the worst we suspect you of. If your words have not buttered any parsnips, neither have they broken any bones.

He, after all, can come back to us now to be comforted and respected, perhaps, after the experience of finding himself for a few hours and for the first time in His life not wanted, more fully and freshly appreciative of our affection than He has always been in the past; as for His dear mother, She is far too grand and far too busy to hear or care what you say or think. If only we were certain that your malice was confined to the verbal affront, we should long ago have demanded our money back and gone whistling home to bed. Alas, in addition to resenting what you have openly said, we fear even more what you may secretly have done. Is it possible that, not content with inveigling Caliban into Ariel's kingdom, you have also let loose Ariel in

Caliban's? We note with alarm that when the other members of the final tableau were dismissed, He was not returned to His arboreal confinement as He should have been. Where is He now? For if the intrusion of the real has disconcerted and incommoded the poetic, that is a mere bagatelle compared to the damage which the poetic would inflict if it ever succeeded in intruding upon the real. We want no Ariel here, breaking down our picket fences in the name of fraternity, seducing our wives in the name of romance, and robbing us of our sacred pecuniary deposits in the name of justice. Where is Ariel? What have you done with Him? For we won't, we daren't leave until you give us a satisfactory answer.

# PART TWO

# Recent Studies

# J. Middleton Murry

## SHAKESPEARE'S DREAM (1936)

IN *The Tempest* this 'sensation' of the final Shakespeare achieves
its perfect dramatic form. The relation between it and its
predecessors is made sensible by Alonso's question to Prospero:

> When did you lose your daughter?
> *Pros.* In this last tempest.          (v i 152–3)

Marina was lost in an actual tempest; Perdita, first, in the
tempest of her father's jealousy, and then exposed in an actual
tempest: but Miranda is not involved in a tempest at all. Her
tempest is one in which others are overwhelmed, wherein she is
engulfed by her imagination alone:

> O, I have suffered
> With those that I saw suffer: a brave vessel
> Who had, no doubt, some noble creature in her,
> Dash'd all to pieces. O, the cry did knock
> Against my very heart.          (1 ii 5–9)

And, when the noble creature emerges, it is in love of him that
she is lost. Miranda sees Ferdinand first, by Prospero's art. It
was needed to safeguard her; for when at last she sees the others
of the company before her, she cries:

> O wonder!
> How many goodly creatures are there here!
> How beauteous mankind is! O brave new world
> That has such people in it!          (v i 181–4)

And Prospero's wise-sad answer to her ecstasy is simply: "Tis
new to thee'. Of the four chief actors who are before her eyes,
three are evil; or, more truly, were evil. The one untainted is

Gonzalo, whose loving-kindness had saved Prospero from death, and steaded him with the means of life, and more:

> Knowing I loved my books, he furnish'd me
> From mine own library with volumes that
> I prize above my dukedom.          (1 ii 166–8)

From Prospero's study of these volumes comes his power. He is the votary of wisdom. Because he had been so 'transported and rapt in secret studies', he had fallen a victim to the machinations of his brother and lost his dukedom.

Because I am by temperament averse to reading Shakespeare as allegory I am struck by my own impression that *The Tempest* is more nearly symbolical than any of his plays. I find it impossible to deny that Prospero is, to some extent, an imaginative paradigm of Shakespeare himself in his function as poet; and that he does in part embody Shakespeare's self-awareness at the conclusion of his poetic career.

To this conclusion I am forced by many considerations. The simplest and weightiest of them all is this. That there is a final period in Shakespeare's work, which exists in reality and is as subtly homogeneous as a living thing, is to me indubitable. It is equally certain that *The Tempest* is, artistically, imaginatively and 'sensationally', the culmination of that period. And, finally, it is certain that Prospero's function in the drama of *The Tempest* is altogether peculiar. He is its prime mover; he governs and directs it from the beginning to the end; he stands clean apart from all Shakespeare's characters in this, or any other period of his work. He is the quintessence of a quintessence of a quintessence.

To what extent Prospero is Shakespeare, I do not seek to determine. I have no faith in allegorical interpretation, because I am certain that allegory was alien to Shakespeare's mind. I can conceive innumerable interpretations of Prospero beginning thus: 'It is through his dedication to the pursuit of secret wisdom that he loses his dukedom; so Shakespeare, through his dedication to the mystery of Poetry, forwent the worldly eminence which his genius could have achieved.' That kind of thing means nothing to me, and I find no trace of it in the length and breadth of Shakespeare's work. When I reach the conclusion that Prospero is, in some sense, Shakespeare, I mean no more than that, being what he is, fulfilling his unique function in a Shakespeare play, and that in all probability Shakespeare's last, it was inevitable that Prospero should be, as it were, uniquely 'shot with' Shakespeare. I mean no more than that it is remarkable and impressive that Shakespeare should have given his last play this particular form, which carried with it this particular necessity: which is no other than that of coming as near to projecting the last phase of his own creative imagination into the figure of a single character as Shakespeare could do without shattering his own dramatic method. But, in saying this, I do not mean that Shakespeare deliberately contrived *The Tempest* to this end. He wanted, simply, to write a play that would satisfy himself, by expressing something, or many things, that still were unexpressed. For this purpose, a Prospero was necessary.

He was necessary to make accident into design. *The Winter's Tale* is a lovely story, but it is in substance (though not in essence) a simple tale, a sequence of chances. There is no chance in *The Tempest*; everything is foreordained. Of course, this is appearance only. The events of *The Winter's Tale* are no less foreordained than those of *The Tempest*; both are foreordained by Shakespeare. But in *The Tempest*, Shakespeare employs a visible agent to do the work. That is the point. For it follows, first, that the visible agent of Shakespeare's poetic mind must be one endowed with supernatural powers, a 'magician'; and, second, that what he foreordains must be, in some quintessential way, human and humane. Once grant a character such powers, their use must satisfy us wholly. Chance may be responsible for the loss and saving of Perdita, and the long severance of Hermione and Leontes, but not humane omnipotence.

It may be said that this is to put the cart before the horse, and that Shakespeare was concerned primarily with the solution of a 'technical' problem. It may be that his central 'idea' was the

obliteration of the evil done and suffered by one generation
through the love of the next, and that his problem was to represent that 'idea' with the same perfection as he had in the past
represented the tragedy of the evil done and suffered. (Though
to call this a merely technical problem is fantastic: a whole
religion is implicit in it.) In *The Winter's Tale* he had pretty
completely humanized the crude story of *Pericles*: but Leontes'
jealousy was extravagant, Antigonus' dispatch a joke, the oracle
clumsy, and Hermione's disguise as statue a theatrical trick.
The machinery was unworthy of the theme. It stood in the way
of the theme's significance.

We are driven back to the same conclusion. In order to
precipitate the significance of the theme out of a condition of
solution, a palpable directing intelligence was required. What
seemed to be accident must now be felt as design. There is but
one accident in *The Tempest*, the accident which brings the ship
to the Island. And Shakespeare is emphatic that this is accident:

> *Mir.* And now, I pray you, sir,
>   For still 'tis beating in my mind, your reason
>   For raising this sea-storm?
> *Pros.* Know thus far forth,
>   By accident most strange, bountiful Fortune,
>   Now my dear lady, hath mine enemies
>   Brought to this shore; and by my prescience
>   I find my zenith doth depend upon
>   A most auspicious star, whose influence
>   If now I court not but omit, my fortunes
>   Will ever after droop.                    (I ii 175–83)

Initial accident there must be. If Prospero's power extended to
the world beyond the Island, so that he could compel the
voyage thither, the drama would be gone. Prospero would be
omnipotent indeed; and the presence of evil and wrong in the
world he controlled would be evidence of devilishness in his
nature. *The Tempest* implies a tremendous criticism of vulgar
religion. I do not think that Shakespeare intended this deliberately; it was the spontaneous outcome of the working of his

imagination. But I think there was a moment in the writing of his drama when he was deeply disturbed by the implications of the method to which he had been brought by the natural effort towards complete utterance of his 'sensation'.

The Island is a realm where God is Good, where true Reason rules; it is what would be if Humanity – the best in man – controlled the life of man. And Prospero is a man in whom the best in man has won the victory: not without a struggle, of which we witness the reverberation:

> *Ari.* Your charm so strongly works them
> That if you now beheld them, your affections
> Would become tender.
> *Pros.* Dost thou think so, spirit?
> *Ari.* Mine would, sir, were I human.
> *Pros.* And mine shall.
> Hast thou, which art but air, a touch, a feeling
> Of their afflictions, and shall not myself,
> One of their kind, that relish all as sharply,
> Passion as they, be kindlier moved than thou art?
> Though with their high wrongs I am struck to the quick,
> Yet with my nobler reason 'gainst my fury
> Do I take part: the rarer action is
> In virtue than in vengeance; they being penitent,
> The sole drift of my purpose doth extend
> Not a frown further. Go, release them, Ariel:
> My charms I'll break, their senses I'll restore,
> And they shall be themselves.          (v i 17–32)

'Themselves' – not what they were, but what they should be. This is no stretch of interpretation. Gonzalo drives it home afterwards. 'All of us found ourselves, when no man was his own.'

The Island is a realm, then; controlled by a man who has become himself, and has the desire, the will and the power to make other men themselves. Miranda is what she is because she has been his pupil:

> Here
> Have I, thy schoolmaster, made thee more profit

> Than other princess' can that have more time
> For vainer hours; and tutors not so careful.
>
> (I ii 171–4)

Here is a difference between Miranda and Perdita; and an important one, for it belongs, as we shall see, to the essence of Shakespeare's thinking. It is not a difference in the imaginative substance of those lovely creatures. We must not say that Perdita is the child of nature, and Miranda the child of art. They are creatures of the same kind. The difference is only that in *The Tempest* Shakespeare wants to make clear what he means: that men and women do not become their true selves by Nature merely, but by Nurture. So it is that, for all his power, Prospero cannot transmute Caliban, for he is one

> on whose nature
> Nurture can never stick; on whom my pains
> Humanely taken, all, all lost, quite lost.  (IV i 188–91)

The thought is vital to *The Tempest*. The Island is a realm where by Art or Nurture Prospero transforms man's Nature to true Human Nature. The process, in the case of the evil-doers, must by dramatic necessity be sudden, and as it were magical; but we must understand its import. For this process is the meaning of Prospero.

We can approach Prospero by way of Gonzalo, who was, to the limit of his power, Prospero's loyal and understanding friend in the evil past. Gonzalo has his own dream. After the shipwreck, he looks upon the beauty and richness of the enchanted island. 'Had I plantation of this isle, my lord' – if it were his to colonize and rule – 'what would I do?' And he answers; or rather Shakespeare answers for him. It is significant that Shakespeare takes his words from Montaigne. We have a choice: either the passage from Montaigne's essay 'Of the Caniballes' was so familiar to Shakespeare that he knew it by heart, or he wrote Gonzalo's words with the passage from Florio's Montaigne before his eyes. Other solution there is none. This is not reminiscence, but direct copying. I am sorry, says

Montaigne, that the 'cannibals' were not discovered long ago, when there were living men who could have appreciated their significance:

I am sorie, *Lycurgus* and *Plato* had it not: for me seemeth that what in those nations we see by experience, doth not only exceed all the pictures wherewith licentious Poesie hath proudly imbellished the golden age, and all her quaint inventions to faine a happy condition of man, but also the conception and desire of Philosophy. They could not imagine a genuitie so pure and simple, as we see it by experience; nor ever beleeve our societie might be maintained with so little art and humane combination.

The words are worth the scrutiny. We know that Shakespeare read and studied them while he was writing *The Tempest*. There are very few passages, outside North's Plutarch, of which we can certainly say so much: and assuredly no passage of the few we know that Shakespeare studied bears so nearly upon the heart of his final theme as this one.

Montaigne says that he regrets that Plato and Lycurgus did not know of the 'cannibals'. Those great lawmakers – one the legislator of an actual, the other of an ideal society – would have seen in the society of the South American savages something that exceeded 'the conception and desire of philosophy'. They could never have believed that a society of men might be maintained with so little art and humane combination – that is to say, with so little artifice and contrivance. Montaigne is saying that the life of the South American Indians proves that mankind is capable of living peacefully, happily and humanely without the constraint of law, or the institution of private property:

It is a nation, would I answer Plato, that hath no kinde of traffike, no knowledge of Letters, no intelligence of numbers, no name of magistrate, nor of politike superioritie; no use of service, of riches or of povertie; no contracts, no successions, no partitions, no occupation but idle; no respect of kindred, but common, no apparel but naturall, no manuring of lands, no use of wine, corne, or mettle. The very words that import lying, falsehood, treason, dissimulations, covetousnes, envie, detrac-

tion, and pardon, were never heard of amongst them. How
dissonant would hee finde his imaginarie commonwealth from
this perfection!

Gonzalo imagines that he has the empty island to colonize.
What would I do? he says:

> I' the commonwealth I would by contraries
> Execute all things: for no kind of traffic
> Would I admit; no name of magistrate;
> Letters should not be known; riches, poverty
> And use of service, none; contract, succession,
> Bourne, bound of land, tilth, vineyard, none;
> No use of metal, corn, or wine, or oil;
> No occupation; all men idle, all;
> And women, too, but innocent and pure;
> No sovereignty . . .
> All things in common nature should produce
> Without sweat or endeavour: treason, felony,
> Sword, pike, knife, gun, or need of any engine
> Would I not have; but nature should bring forth,
> Of its own kind, all foison, all abundance,
> To feed my innocent people.                    (II i 143–60)

What Shakespeare has done is singular, and revealing.
Montaigne, true sceptic that he was, had pitted the savage
against the civilized. Shakespeare omits from Montaigne's
picture the incessant fighting, the plurality of wives, the cannibalism itself, and puts his words in Gonzalo's mouth as a description of the ideal; and at the same time he sets before us, in
Caliban, his own imagination of the savage, in which brutality
and beauty are astonishingly one nature. So Shakespeare makes
clear his conviction that it is not by a return to the primitive
that mankind must advance. Yet he is as critical as Montaigne
himself of the world of men. The wise Gonzalo when he looks
upon the 'strange shapes' who bring in the unsubstantial banquet
and 'dance about it with gentle actions of salutation, inviting
the king to eat', says:

> If in Naples
> I should report this now, would they believe me?

> If I should say, I saw such islanders –
> For, certes, these are people of the island –
> Who, though they are of monstrous shape, yet, note
> Their manners are more gentle-kind than of
> Our human generation you shall find
> Many, nay almost any.                    (III iii 27–34)

But these are not savages; they are Prospero's spirits.

This reaction to Montaigne, this subtle change of Montaigne, might be put down to a purely instinctive motion in Shakespeare, were it not for the fact that Shakespeare had used this essay of Montaigne before. He had been reading it at the time he was writing *The Winter's Tale*, for Polixenes' memorable defence of the Art which mends Nature, and is therefore itself Nature, is a reply to the passage in Montaigne's essay which immediately precedes those we have quoted. Montaigne begins by declaring that there is nothing in the Indians – head-hunting, cannibalism, incessant warfare, and community of wives, included – that is either barbarous or savage 'unless men call that barbarisme which is not common to them'. He is, of course, turning it all to the account of his ethical scepticism: Truth this side of the Alps, falsehood the other. He goes on:

> They are even savage, as we call those fruits wilde, which nature of her selfe, and of her ordinarie progresse hath produced: whereas indeed they are those which our selves have altered by our artificiall devices, and diverted from their common order, we should rather terme savage. In those are the true and most profitable vertues, and naturall properties most lively and vigorous, which in these we have bastardized, applying them to the pleasure of our corrupted taste. And if notwithstanding, in divers fruits of those countries that were never tilled, we shall finde, that in respect of ours they are most excellent, and as delicate unto our taste; there is no reason, art should gaine the point of honour of our great and puissant mother Nature . . . Those nations seem therefore so barbarous to me because they have received very little fashion from humane wit, and are yet neere their originall naturalitie. The lawes of nature do yet commande them, which are but little bastardized by ours . . .

Precisely so, did Perdita exclude 'carnations and streaked gillyvors' from her garden, because they are called 'nature's bastards', because

There is an art which in their piedness shares
With great creating nature.

Shakespeare will have nothing to do with that false antithesis between Art and Nature. Says Polixenes: 'Nature is made better by no mean but Nature makes that mean'. The Art that makes Nature better is Nature's Art. That is the true distinction, between Nature's art and man's, and it has perhaps never been more simply or subtly formulated. Where man's art improves nature, it is nature's art in man; where it makes nature worse, it is man's art alone. In *The Winter's Tale*, we have first, Shakespeare's casual, in *The Tempest* his deliberate reply to the scepticism of Montaigne.

And thus it is that Shakespeare, in Gonzalo's words, with splendid irony changes Montaigne's report of the Indians, from mere nature, to a picture of nature's art in man, working on man. He discards the savagery, and retains only what belongs to the ideal and human. It is the innocence not of the primitive, but of the ultimate, which he seeks to embody. And that is manifest from the very structure of *The Tempest*. Caliban is the primitive; but Miranda and Ferdinand are the ultimate. There is no confusion possible between them, and the sophistry of Montaigne is exorcised by a wave of the wand. Nature and Nurture alone can make human Nature. But the nurture that is Nature's own is hard to find.

In *The Tempest* there is Prospero to govern the process, and to work the miracle of a new creation. Poised between Caliban, the creature of the baser elements – earth and water – and Ariel, the creature of the finer – fire and air – is the work of Prospero's alchemy: the loving humanity of Ferdinand and Miranda. Miranda is a new creature; but Ferdinand must be made new. He is made new by the spell of Ariel's music.

> Sitting on a bank,
> Weeping again the king my father's wreck,
> This music crept by me upon the waters,
> Allaying both their fury and my passion
> With its sweet air: thence I have follow'd it,
> Or it hath drawn me rather. But 'tis gone.
> No, it begins again.

> ARIEL *sings*
> Full fathom five thy father lies;
>    Of his bones are coral made;
> Those are pearls that were his eyes:
>    Nothing of him that doth fade
> But doth suffer a sea-change
> Into something rich and strange.
> Sea-nymphs hourly ring his knell:
>        *Burthen.* Ding-dong!
> Hark, now I hear them – Ding-dong, bell.
>                    (I ii 392–407)

From the ecstasy of that transforming music, Ferdinand awakes to behold Miranda, and Miranda beholds him. *Jam nova progenies* . . .

Beneath a like transforming spell, eventually all the company pass – Alonzo, the false brother, Sebastian and Antonio, the traitors. In the men of sin it works madness, or what seems like madness, but is a desperation wrought by the dreadful echoing of the voice of conscience by the elements:

> *Gon.* I' the name of something holy, sir, why stand you
>    In this strange stare?
> *Alon.* O, it is monstrous, monstrous!
>    Methought the billows spoke, and told me of it;
>    The winds did sing it to me; and the thunder,
>    That deep and dreadful organ-pipe, pronounced
>    The name of Prosper; it did bass my trespass.
>    Therefore my son i' the ooze is bedded, and
>    I'll seek him deeper than e'er plummet sounded,
>    And with him there lie mudded.                    [*Exit*
> *Seb.* But one fiend at a time!
>    I'll fight their legions o'er.
> *Ant.* I'll be thy second.                    [*Exeunt* SEB. *and* ANT.

> *Gon.* All three of them are desperate: their great guilt,
> Like poison given to work a great time after,
> Now 'gins to bite the spirits.                    (III iii 94–106)

That which Christian theology imposes on evil men at the Judgment-Day – 'The tortures of the damned' – by Prospero's art they experience in life. They are rapt out of time by his spells. To Gonzalo, whose life is clear, it brings only such change as that which Ariel's music works upon Ferdinand. But by these different paths, they reach the condition which Gonzalo describes: 'All of us found ourselves, when no man was his own.'

So that when Miranda looks upon them, and cries for joy at 'the brave new world that has such creatures in it', they really are new creatures that she sees. They have suffered a sea-change. And Prospero's wise-sad word: ''Tis new to thee', if we were to take it precisely, applies only to the world beyond the island, not to those of its creatures he has transformed. But it is not the word of Prospero; it is of Prospero 'shot by' Shakespeare, who knows it is not so easy to transform men, still less a world.

And it is a sudden pang of this awareness which works in the strange conclusion of the lovely masque which Prospero sets before Ferdinand and Miranda, to celebrate their betrothal. He has promised to bestow on them 'some vanity of mine art'. It is the kind of lovely thing that Shakespeare found it natural to write: a vision of Nature's beauty, ministering to the natural beauty of Ferdinand's and Miranda's love. Ferdinand, enchanted, cries:

> Let me live here ever:
> So rare a wonder'd father and a wife
> Make this place Paradise.                    (IV i 122–4)

Suddenly, towards the end of the concluding dance, Prospero remembers the clumsy plot of Caliban and Stephano against his life. He is in no danger, nor could he be conceived to be in danger. Yet he is profoundly disturbed, strangely disturbed, and the strangeness of the disturbance is strangely insisted on.

> *Fer.* This is strange: your father's in some passion
> That works him strongly.

*Mir.* Never till this day
  Saw I him touch'd with anger so distemper'd.
*Pros.* You do look, my son, in a moved sort,
  As if you were dismay'd; be cheerful, sir.
  Our revels now are ended. These our actors,
  As I foretold you, were all spirits and
  Are melted into air, into thin air:
  And, like the baseless fabric of this vision,
  The cloud-capp'd towers, the gorgeous palaces,
  The solemn temples, the great globe itself,
  Yea, all which it inherit, shall dissolve
  And, like this unsubstantial pageant faded,
  Leave not a rack behind. We are such stuff
  As dreams are made on, and our little life
  Is rounded with a sleep. Sir, I am vex'd;
  Bear with my weakness; my old brain is troubled:
  Be not disturb'd with my infirmity:
  If you be pleased, retire into my cell
  And there repose: a turn or two, I'll walk
  To still my beating mind.
*Fer. Mir.* We wish your peace.          (IV i 143–63)

It is not the plot against his life which has produced this
disturbance. It is the thought of what the plot means: the
Nature on which Nurture will never stick. The disturbance and
the thought come from beyond the visible action of the drama
itself.

What Prospero seems to be thinking concerning the vanity
of his art, has been disturbed and magnified by what Shakespeare is thinking concerning the vanity of his. He has imagined
a mankind redeemed, transformed, re-born; the jewel of the
wood become the jewel of the world. As the recollection of
Caliban's evil purpose seems to wake Prospero, so does the
recollection of the world of reality wake Shakespeare: and these
two awakings are mingled with one another. In *The Tempest*
Shakespeare had embodied his final dream – of a world created
anew, a new race of men and women. Was it also *only* a dream?

# E. M. W. Tillyard

## THE TRAGIC PATTERN (1938)

IT is a common notion that *Cymbeline* and *The Winter's Tale* are experiments leading to the final success of *The Tempest*. I think it quite untrue of *The Winter's Tale*, which, in some ways though not in others, deals with the tragic pattern more adequately than the later play. Certainly it deals with the destructive portion more directly and fully. On the other hand, *The Tempest*, by keeping this destructive portion largely in the background and dealing mainly with regeneration, avoids the juxtaposition of the two themes, which some people (of whom I am not one) find awkward in *The Winter's Tale*. The simple truth is, that if you cram a trilogy into a single play something has to be sacrificed. Shakespeare chose to make a different sacrifice in each of his two successful renderings of the complete tragic pattern: unity in *The Winter's Tale*, present rendering of the destructive part of the tragic pattern in *The Tempest*.

Many readers, drugged by the heavy enchantments of Prospero's island, may demur at my admitting the tragic element to the play at all. I can cite in support one of the latest studies of the play, Dover Wilson's[1] (although I differ somewhat in the way I think the tragic element is worked out). Of the storm scene he writes:

> It is as if Shakespeare had packed his whole tragic vision of life into one brief scene before bestowing his new vision upon us.

But one has only to look at the total plot to see that in its main lines it closely follows those of *Cymbeline* and *The Winter's Tale*, and that tragedy is an organic part of it. Prospero, when one first hears of him, was the ruler of an independent state and beloved of his subjects. But all is not well, because the King of Naples is his enemy. Like Basilius in Sidney's *Arcadia*, he commits the error of not attending carefully enough to affairs of state. The reason for this error, his Aristotelian ἁμαρτία, is his love of study. He hands over the government to his brother Antonio, who proceeds to call in the King of Naples to turn Prospero out of his kingdom. Fearing the people, Antonio refrains from murdering Prospero and his infant daughter, but sets them adrift in a boat. Now, except for this last item, the plot is entirely typical of Elizabethan revenge tragedy. Allow Prospero to be put to death, give him a son instead of a daughter to live and to avenge him, and your tragic plot is complete. Such are the affinities of the actual plot of *The Tempest*. And in the abstract it is more typically tragic in the fashion of its age than *The Winter's Tale*, with its debt to the Greek romances.

In handling the theme of regeneration, Shakespeare in one way alters his method. Although a royal person had previously been the protagonist, it had been only in name. Cymbeline had indeed resembled Prospero in having his enemies at his mercy and in forgiving them, but he owed his power not to himself, but to fortune and the efforts of others. As for Leontes, he has little to do with his own regeneration; for it would be perverse to make too much of his generosity in sheltering Florizel and Perdita from the anger of Polixenes. But Prospero is the agent of his own regeneration, the parent and tutor of Miranda; and through her and through his own works he changes the minds of his enemies. It was by this centring of motives in Prospero as well as by subordinating the theme of destruction that Shakespeare gave *The Tempest* its unified structure.

In executing his work, Shakespeare chose a method new to himself but repeated by Milton in *Samson Agonistes*. He began his action at a point in the story so late that the story was virtually over; and he included the total story either by narrating the past or by re-enacting samples of it: a complete reaction from the method of frontal attack used in *The Winter's Tale*.

For the re-enactment of tragedy it is possible to think with Dover Wilson that the storm scene does this. But it does nothing to re-enact the specific tragic plot in the play, the fall of Prospero;

and one of its aims is to sketch (as it does with incomparable
swiftness) the characters of the ship's company. The true re-
enactment is in the long first scene of the second act where
Antonio, in persuading Sebastian to murder Alonso, personates
his own earlier action in plotting against Prospero, thus drawing
it out of the past and placing it before us in the present. This
long scene, showing the shipwrecked King and courtiers and
the conspiracy, has not had sufficient praise nor sufficient
attention. Antonio's transformation from the cynical and lazy
badgerer of Gonzalo's loquacity to the brilliantly swift and
unscrupulous man of action is a thrilling affair. Just so Iago
awakes from his churlish 'honesty' to his brilliant machinations.
Antonio is indeed one of Shakespeare's major villains:

> *Ant.* Will you grant with me
>    That Ferdinand is drown'd?
> *Seb.* He's gone.
> *Ant.* Then, tell me,
>    Who's the next heir to Naples?
> *Seb.* Claribel.
> *Ant.* She that is queen of Tunis; she that dwells
>    Ten leagues beyond man's life; she that from Naples
>    Can have no note, unless the sun were post —
>    The man i' the moon's too slow — till new-born chins
>    Be rough and razorable; she that from whom
>    We all were sea-swallow'd, though some cast again,
>    And by that destiny, to perform an act
>    Whereof what's past is prologue, what to come,
>    In yours and my discharge.
> *Seb.* What stuff is this! how say you?
>    'Tis true my brother's daughter's queen of Tunis;
>    So is she heir of Naples; 'twixt which regions
>    There is some space.
> *Ant.* A space whose every cubit
>    Seems to cry out, 'How shall that Claribel
>    Measure us back to Naples? Keep in Tunis,
>    And let Sebastian wake.' Say this were death
>    That now hath seized them; why, they were no worse
>    Than now they are. There be that can rule Naples

>As well as he that sleeps; lords that can prate
>As amply and unnecessarily
>As this Gonzalo; I myself could make
>A chough of as deep chat. O, that you bore
>The mind that I do! What a sleep were this
>For your advancement! Do you understand me?

We should do wrong to take the conspiracy very seriously in itself. We know Prospero's power, and when Ariel enters and wakes the intended victims we have no fears for their future safety. But all the more weight should the scene assume as recalling the past.

Dover Wilson[2] greatly contributes to a right understanding of the play by stressing the first lines of the fifth act, when Prospero declares to Ariel that he will pardon his enemies, now quite at his mercy:

>*Ari.* Your charm so strongly works 'em
>    That if you now beheld them, your affections
>    Would become tender.
>*Pros.* Dost thou think so, spirit?
>*Ari.* Mine would, sir, were I human.
>*Pros.* And mine shall.
>    Hast thou, which art but air, a touch, a feeling
>    Of their afflictions, and shall not myself,
>    One of their kind, that relish all as sharply,
>    Passion as they, be kindlier moved than thou art?
>    Though with their high wrongs I am struck to the quick,
>    Yet with my nobler reason 'gainst my fury
>    Do I take part: the rarer action is
>    In virtue than in vengeance: they being penitent,
>    The sole drift of my purpose doth extend
>    Not a frown further.

But when Dover Wilson would have this to represent Prospero's sudden conversion from a previously intended vengeance, I cannot follow him. It is true that Prospero shows a certain haste of temper up to that point of the play, and that he punishes Caliban and the two other conspirators against his life with some asperity; but his comments on them, after his supposed conversion, have for me the old ring:

> Mark but the badges of these men, my lords,
> Then say if they be true. This mis-shapen knave,
> His mother was a witch, and one so strong
> That could control the moon, make flows and ebbs,
> And deal in her command without her power.
> These three have robb'd me; and this demi-devil –
> For he's a bastard one – had plotted with them
> To take my life. Two of these fellows you
> Must know and own; this thing of darkness I
> Acknowledge mine.

The last words express all Prospero's old bitterness that Caliban has resisted him and refused to respond to his nurture.[3] Indeed, Prospero does not change fundamentally during the play, though, like Samson's, his own accomplished regeneration is put to the test. If he had seriously intended vengeance, why should he have stopped Sebastian and Antonio murdering Alonso? That he did stop them is proof of his already achieved regeneration from vengeance to mercy. This act, and his talk to Ariel of taking part with his reason against his fury, are once again a re-enactment of a process now past, perhaps extending over a period of many years. I do not wish to imply that the re-enactment is weak or that the temptation to vengeance was not there all the time. Prospero's fury at the thought of Caliban's conspiracy, which interrupts the masque, must be allowed full weight. It is not for nothing that Miranda says that –

> never till this day
> Saw I him touch'd with anger so distemper'd.

We must believe that Prospero felt thus, partly because Caliban's conspiracy typifies all the evil of the world which has so perplexed him, and partly because he is still tempted to be revenged on Alonso and Antonio. He means to pardon them, and he will pardon them. But beneath his reason's sway is this anger against them, which, like Satan's before the sun in *Paradise Lost*, disfigures his face. When Dover Wilson calls Prospero 'a terrible old man, almost as tyrannical and irascible as Lear at the opening of his play', he makes a valuable comparison, but it should concern Prospero as he once was, not the character who meets us in the play, in whom these traits are mere survivals.

The advantage of this technique of re-enactment was economy, its drawback an inevitable blurring of the sharp outline. The theme of destruction, though exquisitely blended in the whole, is less vivid than it is in *The Winter's Tale*. Having made it so vivid in that play, Shakespeare was probably well content to put the stress on the theme of re-creation. And here he did not work solely by re-enactment. He strengthened Prospero's re-enacted regeneration by the figures of Ferdinand and Miranda. I argued above that, in view of his background of Elizabethan chivalrous convention, Ferdinand need not have been as insignificant as he is usually supposed. Similarly, Miranda's character has been unduly diminished in recent years. To-day, under the stress of the new psychology, men have become nervous lest they should be caught illicitly attaching their day-dreams of the perfect woman to a character in fiction. They laugh at the Victorians for falling unawares into this error, and Miranda may have been one of the most popular victims. Hence the anxiety not to admire her too much. E. K. Chambers has written:

Unless you are sentimentalist inveterate, your emotions will not be more than faintly stirred by the blameless loves at first sight of Ferdinand and Miranda.

Schücking goes further and considers Miranda a poor imitation of Beaumont and Fletcher's idea of the chaste female, an idea that could be dwelt on so lovingly and emphatically only in a lascivious age. In depicting her with her talk of 'modesty, the jewel in my dower' and her protests that if Ferdinand will not marry her, 'I'll die your maid', and in making Prospero so insistent that she should not lose her maidenhead before marriage, Shakespeare, according to Schücking, is yielding to the demands of his age against his own better judgment. But Miranda is sufficiently successful a symbolic figure for it to matter little if she makes conventional and, in her, unnatural remarks. And even this defence may be superfluous. Since Miranda had never seen a young man, it might reasonably be doubted whether she would behave herself with entire propriety when she did. Prospero, too, had made enough mistakes in his life to be very careful to make no more. Further, Miranda was the heiress to the Duchy of Milan and her father hoped she would be Queen of Naples. What most strikingly emerged from the abdication of our late King was the strong 'anthropological' feeling of the masses of the people concerning the importance of virginity in a King's consort. The Elizabethans were not less superstitious than ourselves and would have sympathised with Prospero's anxiety that the future Queen of Naples should keep her maidenhead till marriage: otherwise ill luck would be sure to follow.

To revert to Miranda's character, like Perdita she is both symbol and human being, yet in both capacities somewhat weaker. She is the symbol of 'original virtue,' like Perdita, and should be set against the devilish figure of Antonio. She is the complete embodiment of sympathy with the men she thinks have been drowned: and her instincts are to create, to mend the work of destruction she has witnessed. She is – again like Perdita, though less clearly – a symbol of fertility. Stephano asks of Caliban, 'Is it so brave a lass?' and Caliban answers,

> Ay, lord; she will become thy bed, I warrant,
> And bring thee forth brave brood.

Even if *The Tempest* was written for some great wedding, it need not be assumed that the masque was inserted merely to fit the occasion. Like the goddesses in Perdita's speeches about the flowers, Juno and Ceres and the song they sing may be taken to reinforce the fertility symbolism embodied in Miranda:

> *Juno.* Honour, riches, marriage-blessing,
>         Long continuance, and increasing,
>         Hourly joys be still upon you!
>         Juno sings her blessings on you.
> *Cer.* Earthës increase, foison plenty,
>         Barns and garners never empty,
>         Vines with clustering bunches growing,
>         Plants with goodly burthen bowing;

> Spring come to you at the farthest
> In the very end of harvest!
> Scarcity and want shall shun you;
> Ceres' blessing so is on you.

The touches of ordinary humanity in Miranda – her siding with Ferdinand against a supposedly hostile father, for instance – are too well known to need recalling. They do not amount to a very great deal and leave her vaguer as a human being than as a symbol. Middleton Murry is not at his happiest when he says that 'they are so terribly, so agonizingly real, these women of Shakespeare's last imagination.' As far as Miranda is concerned, any agonizing sense of her reality derives from the critic and not from the play. But this does not mean that, judged by the play's requirements (which are not those of brilliant realism), Miranda is not perfection. Had she been more weakly drawn, she would have been insignificant, had she been more strongly, she would have interfered with the unifying dominance of Prospero.

Not only do Ferdinand and Miranda sustain Prospero in representing a new order of things that has evolved out of destruction; they also vouch for its continuation. At the end of the play Alonso and Prospero are old and worn men. A younger and happier generation is needed to secure the new state to which Prospero has so painfully brought himself, his friends, and all his enemies save Caliban.

## NOTES

1. *The Meaning of the Tempest,* the Robert Spence Watson Memorial Lecture for 1936, delivered before the Literary and Philosophical Society of Newcastle upon Tyne, on 5 Oct. 1936.

2. Op. cit., pp. 14–18.

3. See the admirable discussion of 'nature' and 'nurture' in *The Tempest* in Middleton Murry's *Shakespeare* (1936) pp. 396 ff. (reproduced on pp. 114-18 above).

# G. Wilson Knight

## THE SHAKESPEARIAN SUPERMAN
## (1947)

As Zarathustra thus discoursed he stood nigh unto the entrance of his cave; but with the final words he slipped away from his guests and fled for a brief while into the open air.

O clean odours around me! he cried. O blessed stillness around me! But where are my beasts? Draw nigh, mine Eagle and my Serpent!

Tell me, my beasts – all these Higher men, smell they, perchance, not sweet? O clean odours around me! Now only do I know and feel how I love you, my beasts!

*Thus Spake Zarathustra*, The Song of Melancholy

WE have seen how these final plays tend to refashion old imagery into some surprising dramatic incident; of which the most striking examples are the jewel-thrown-into-the-sea, Thaisa in her casket-coffin; Pericles on board his storm-tossed ship; the co-presence of actual storm and bear, an old poetic association, in *The Winter's Tale*; the appearance of Jupiter the Thunderer in *Cymbeline*. In these we find a variation of a normal Shakespearian process; for Shakespeare is continually at work splitting up and recombining already used plots, persons, and themes, weaving something 'new and strange' from old material. Much of his later tragedy and history is contained in *Titus Andronicus* and *Henry VI*; much of later comedy in *Love's Labour's Lost* and *The Two Gentlemen of Verona*. The opposition of cynic and romantic in *Romeo and Juliet* gives us Mercutio and Romeo; the same opposition – with what a difference! – becomes Iago and Othello; and again, Enobarbus and Antony. Prince Hal and Hotspur together make Henry V; and as for Falstaff, his massive bulk contains in embryo much of the later tragedies in their nihilistic, king-shattering, impact; though, as comedian, he stands between Sir Toby and Autolycus. One could go on, and on.

The last plays are peculiar in their seizing on poetry itself, as it were, for their dominating effects; and in doing this also find themselves often reversing the logic of life as we know it, redeveloping the discoveries and recognitions of old comedy into more purposeful conclusions, impregnated with a far higher order of dramatic belief. The finding of Aemilia as an abbess in *The Comedy of Errors* forecasts the finding of Thaisa as priestess of Diana in *Pericles*; the recovery of Hero, supposed dead, in *Much Ado about Nothing* that of Hermione; Juliet and Imogen endure each a living death after use of similar potions. What is first subsidiary, or hinted by the poetry itself, as when Romeo or Cleopatra dream of reunion beyond, or within, death (*Romeo and Juliet* V i 1–9; *Antony and Cleopatra* V ii 75–100), is rendered convincing later.

This tendency *The Tempest* drives to the limit. For once, Shakespeare has no objective story before him from which to create. He spins his plot from his own poetic world entirely, simplifying the main issues of his total work – plot, poetry, persons; whittling off the non-essential and leaving the naked truth exposed. *The Tempest*, patterned of storm and music, is thus an interpretation of Shakespeare's world.

Its originating action is constructed, roughly, on the pattern of *The Comedy of Errors* and *Twelfth Night*, wherein wreck in tempest leads to separation of certain persons and their reunion on a strange shore; the plots being entwined with magic and amazement, as in Antipholus of Syracuse's comment on Ephesus as a land of 'Lapland sorcerers' (*The Comedy of Errors* IV iii 11), and Sebastian's amazement at Olivia's welcome (*Twelfth Night* IV iii 1–21; see also Viola's pun on Illyria and Elysium at I ii 2–3). There is an obvious further relation of *The Tempest* to *A Midsummer Night's Dream*, both plays showing a fairy texture, with Puck and Ariel, on first acquaintance, appearing as blood-brethren, though the differences are great. The balance of tempests and music, not only in imagery but in plot too, throughout the Comedies (including *A Mid-*

*summer Night's Dream* and *The Merchant of Venice*) here reaches its consummation; but the Tragedies, wherein tempests and music are yet more profoundly important, are also at work within our new pattern of shipwreck and survival.

Prospero is a composite of many Shakespearian heroes; not in 'character', since there is no one quite like him elsewhere, but rather in his fortunes and the part he plays. As a sovereign wrongfully dethroned he carries the overtones of tragic royalty enjoyed by Richard II. Ejected from his dukedom by a wicked brother – 'That a brother should be so perfidious' (I ii 67) – he is placed, too, like the unfortunate Duke in *As You Like It* and as Don Pedro might have been placed had Don John's rebellion succeeded in *Much Ado about Nothing*. Clarence, Orlando and Edgar suffer from similar betrayals.

Now Prospero's reaction is one of horror at such betrayal of a 'trust' and a 'confidence sans bound' (I ii 96) by 'one whom', as he tells Miranda, 'next thyself of all the world I lov'd' (I ii 69). So Valentine suffers from Proteus' betrayal in *The Two Gentlemen of Verona* and Antonio, as he thinks, from Sebastian's in *Twelfth Night*. King Henry treats the faithless lords in *Henry V* to a long tirade of withering blank-verse on ingratitude and betrayal comparable with Richard II's scathing denunciation of his betrayers. Ingratitude generally is basic to the emotions, speeches, and songs of *As You Like It*; and in *King Lear* we have a 'filial ingratitude' (III iv 14), corresponding to Prospero's viewing of himself as 'a good parent', too kindly begetting in his child (meaning his brother) a corresponding 'falsehood' (I ii 94; cp. *King Lear*, 'Your old kind father whose frank heart gave all' at III iv 20). Loyalty to king, master, friend, wife, husband, is a continual theme. It is basic in *Julius Caesar*, in Brutus' relation to Caesar, in Portia's to Brutus, in the friendship of Brutus and Cassius: it vitalizes the whole of *Antony and Cleopatra*, with the subtly defined, personal, tragedy of Enobarbus – 'a master-leaver and a fugitive' (IV ix 22). There are the loyal friends: Antonio to Sebastian; Horatio to Hamlet; or servants – the Bastard in *King John*, Adam, Kent; Gonzalo here winning a corresponding honour. The extensions into sexual jealousy are equally, or more, important; as in *The Merry Wives of Windsor, Much Ado about Nothing, Troilus and Cressida, Hamlet* (felt on the father's behalf by the son), *Othello, Antony and Cleopatra, The Winter's Tale, Cymbeline.*

There is a recurring sense of desertion, of betrayal, very strong in *Troilus and Cressida*; and also in *King Lear,* the old man's age underlining his helplessness. In *King Lear,* and often elsewhere, the result is a general nausea at human falsity; the poet continually driving home a distinction of falsehood, and especially flattery, and true, unspectacular, devotion (as in Theseus' words to Hippolyta, *A Midsummer Night's Dream* v i 89–105). This disgust tends to project the action into wild nature, conceived, as in *The Two Gentlemen of Verona, As You Like It,* and *King Lear,* as an improvement on the falsities of civilization. In *King Lear* the return to nature is acted by Edgar and endured, for his purgation, by Lear on the tempest-torn heath; while many variations are played throughout on the comparison and contrast of human evil with the beasts and elemental forces. The pattern of *The Winter's Tale* shows a similar movement from falsehood through rugged nature to an idealized rusticity. Of all this the great prototype, or archetype, is *Timon of Athens,* where the princely hero, conceived as a sublime patron and lover of humanity, is so thunder-struck by discovery of falsehood and ingratitude that he rejects man and all his works and in uncompromising bitterness retires in naked-ness to a cave by the sea-shore, where he denounces to all who visit him the vices of civilization and communes, in savage solitude, with all of nature that is vast and eternal; his story finally fading into the ocean surge. *The Tempest* shows a similar movement. Prospero, like Timon and Belarius – for Belarius is another, driven to the mountains by the ingratitude of Cymbeline – lives (presumably) in a cave; like Timon, by the sea.

He is akin, too, to all princes whose depth of understanding accompanies or succeeds political failure: to Hamlet, Brutus, Richard II, Henry VI. Hamlet, like Timon, is an archetypal figure, being a complex of many heroes. He is out of joint with a society of which he clearly sees the decadence and evil.

Through his ghostly converse and consequent profundity of
spiritual disturbance, he is unfitted for direct action, while
nevertheless doing much to control the other persons, indeed
dominating them, half magically, from within. Hamlet is a
student and scholar; and in this too, as in his surface (though
not actual) ineffectuality and his revulsion from an evil society,
he forecasts the learned Prospero, whose dukedom was

> reputed
> In dignity, and for the liberal arts,
> Without a parallel.                                      (I ii 72)

Such enlightenment was bought at a cost:

> these being all my study,
> The government I cast upon my brother,
> And to my state grew stranger, being transported
> And rapt in secret studies.                             (I ii 74)

Prospero is in straight descent from those other impractical
governors, Agamemnon in *Troilus and Cressida,* whose philosophic attitude to his army's disaster (I iii 1–30) calls forth
Ulysses' famous speech on order; and Vincentio, Duke of
Vienna, in *Measure for Measure,* whose depth of study and
psychological insight make execution of justice impossible. All
these are in Prospero; while the surrounding action, both
serious and comic, condenses the whole of Shakespeare's
political wisdom.

He is also a recreation of Cerimon in *Pericles.* Listen to
Cerimon:

> I hold it ever
> Virtue and cunning were endowments greater
> Than nobleness or riches; careless heirs
> May the two latter darken and expend;
> But immortality attends the former,
> Making a man a god.                      (*Pericles,* III ii 26)

And to Prospero:

> I, thus neglecting worldly ends, all dedicated
> To closeness and the bettering of my mind

With that which, but by being so retir'd,
O'erpriz'd all popular rate . . .                    (I ii 89)

The lines set the disadvantage of the monastic life against the
supreme end it pursues. Duke Prospero was, like Lord Cerimon
(also a nobleman), a religious recluse on the brink of magical
power; and may be compared with those earlier religious
persons, Friar Laurence in *Romeo and Juliet*, whose magic arts
control the action (and who speaks, like Prospero, of his 'cell'),
and Friar Francis in *Much Ado about Nothing*, who negotiates
Hero's death and reappearance. These are people of spiritual
rather than practical efficiency; like Duke Vincentio and Hamlet
(who so mysteriously dominates his society, by play-production
and otherwise), they are plot-controllers; Duke Vincentio,
disguised as a Friar, organizing the whole action, and being
directly suggestive of 'power divine' (*Measure for Measure*
v i 370). So, too, Prospero manipulates his own plot like a god.
He is a blend of Theseus and Oberon.

Prospero is a matured and fully self-conscious embodiment
of those moments of fifth-act transcendental speculation to which
earlier tragic heroes, including Macbeth, were unwillingly
forced. He cannot be expected to do more than typify; there
is not time; and, as a person, he is, no doubt, less warm, less
richly human, than most of his poetic ancestors. But only
if we recognize his inclusiveness, his summing of nearly all
Shakespeare's more eminent persons, shall we understand
clearly what he is about. He, like others, Vincentio and Oberon
pre-eminently, is controlling our plot, composing it before our
eyes; but, since the plot is, as we shall see, so inclusive an
interpretation of Shakespeare's life-work, Prospero is controlling,
not merely a Shakespearian play, but the Shakespearian world.
He is thus automatically in the position of Shakespeare himself,
and it is accordingly inevitable that he should often speak as
with Shakespeare's voice.

Ariel incorporates all those strong picturizations of angels
aerially riding observed in our recent analysis of the Vision in
*Cymbeline*.[1] To these we may add the Dauphin's humorous

but poetically revealing comparison of his horse to a Pegasus
in *Henry V*:

When I bestride him, I soar, I am a hawk: he trots the air; the
earth sings when he touches it; the basest horn of his hoof is more
musical than the pipe of Hermes. . . . It is a beast for Perseus; he
is pure air and fire; and the dull elements of earth and water never
appear in him but only in patient stillness while his rider mounts
him; he is indeed a horse. . . . It is a theme as fluent as the sea.
(III vii 11–44)

Precisely from this complex of air, fire, music and lightly
apprehended sea in contrast to the duller Caliban-elements of
earth and water Ariel is compounded. He personifies all
Shakespeare's more volatile and aerial impressionism (he is
called a 'bird' at IV i 184, 'chick' at V i 316, and 'an airy
spirit' in the *dramatis personae*), especially those images or
phrases involving 'swift' (i.e. either intuitional or emotional)
thought (a vein of poetry discussed in *The Shakespearian
Tempest*, Appendix A, particularly pp. 308–11). A good
example occurs in the association of thought's swiftness and
'feathered Mercury' at *King John* IV ii 174. Ariel is mercurial
and implicit in both the agile wit and Queen Mab fantasies of
the aptly-named Mercutio; compare his definition of dreams, 'as
thin of substance as the air' (*Romeo and Juliet* I iv 100), with
Prospero's 'thou, which art but air' (V i 21), addressed to
Ariel. Ariel is implicit often in Shakespeare's love-poetry:
though he is not an Eros-personification, yet, wherever we find
emphasis on love's lightning passage, as at *Romeo and Juliet*
II ii 118–20 or *A Midsummer Night's Dream* I i 141–9; on
its uncapturable perfection, as throughout *Troilus and Cressida*
(with strong emphasis on volatility and speed at III ii 8–15
and IV ii 14); on its spiritual powers, as in the aerial imagery
and energy of *Antony and Cleopatra*, with Cleopatra at death as
'fire and air' (V ii 291); or on its delicate and tender sweetness,
as in the 'piece of tender air', Imogen (*Cymbeline* V v 436–53);
wherever such elusive and intangible excellences are our matter,
there Ariel is forecast. He is the spirit of love's aspiration 'all

compact of fire' in *Venus and Adonis* 149. He is made of Biron's speech of elaborate love-psychology with its contrast of 'slow arts' and the quicksilver swiftnesses of love's heightened consciousness, its new delicacy of perception and increased power, all entwined with fire, thoughts of mythology, poetry and music, and the ability (shown by Ariel's music in *The Tempest* at III ii 123–50 and IV i 175–8) to

> ravish savage ears
> And plant in tyrants mild humility;

while at the limit touching, as does Ariel (at v i 19), 'charity' (*Love's Labour's Lost* IV iii 320–65). Closely similar is Falstaff's speech on sherris-sack, which makes the brain 'apprehensive, quick, forgetive, full of nimble, fiery and delectable shapes which, deliverer'd o'er to the voice, the tongue, which is the birth, becomes excellent wit' (*2 Henry IV* IV iii 107). Ariel is also forecast by other passages on wit (in the modern sense), so often, as is Mercutio's, levelled *against* love; as when the shafts of feminine mockery are compared to the swiftness of 'arrows, bullets, wind, thought' at *Love's Labour's Lost* v ii 262. Ariel exists in a dimension overlooking normal categories of both reason and emotion: he is the 'mutual flame' in which the winged partners of *The Phoenix and the Turtle* transcend their own duality.

Since, moreover, he personifies these subtle and overruling powers of the imagination, he becomes automatically a personification of poetry itself. His sudden appearance depends, precisely, on Prospero's 'thought' (IV i 164–5; cp. 'the quick forge and working-house of thought', *Henry V* v chor. 23). He is the poetic medium, whatever the subject handled, his powers ranging over the earthy and the ethereal, tragic and lyric, with equal ease. As a dramatic person, he certainly descends from Puck and also, in view of his songs and trickery – he is a 'tricksy spirit' (v i 226; a word associated with Launcelot Gobbo in *The Merchant of Venice* III v 75) – from the jesters Feste, Touchstone, even Lear's Fool; all of whom enjoy a share of the poet's own, critical, awareness, as in certain of

Puck's generalized speeches and his final epilogue, the philosophic detachment of Feste's and Touchstone's wit, and the Fool's
perceptual clarity. Ariel likewise is apart: he is emotionally
detached, though actively engaged, everyone and everything,
except Prospero and Miranda, being the rough material of
creation on which the Ariel-spirit of poetry works; an opposition
seen most starkly in his piping to Caliban.

Ariel is accordingly shown as the agent of Prospero's purpose.
He is Prospero's instrument in controlling and developing the
action. Through him Prospero raises the tempest, Ariel (like
mad Tom in *Lear*) being part of it, acting it (I ii 195–215).
He puts people to sleep, so tempting the murderers, but wakes
them just in time (II i), thunderously interrupts the feast,
pronouncing judgement and drawing the moral (III iii). He
plays tricks on the drunkards (III ii), hears their plot and leads
them to disaster (III ii; IV i 171–84). His music leads Ferdinand
to Miranda (I ii). He puts the ship safely in harbour (I ii 226)
and later releases and conducts the mariners (V i). He is Prospero's stage-manager; more, he is the enactor of Prospero's
conception: Prospero is the artist, Ariel the art. He is a spirit of
'air' (V i 21) corresponding to the definition of poetry as 'airy
nothing' in *A Midsummer Night's Dream* (V i 16). His powers
range freely over and between the thunderous and the musical,
tragic and lyric, extremes of Shakespearian drama.

Caliban condenses Shakespeare's concern, comical or satiric,
with the animal aspect of man; as seen in Christopher Sly and
the aptly-named Bottom (whose union with Titania drives
fantasy to an extreme), Dogberry, writ down 'an ass' (*Much Ado
about Nothing* IV ii 75–93), Sir Toby Belch; and Falstaff,
especially in *The Merry Wives of Windsor*, where his animality
is punished by fairies (that Falstaff should show contacts with
both Ariel and Caliban exactly defines the universal nature of his
complexity). Caliban also symbolizes all brainless revolution,
such as Jack Cade's in *2 Henry VI*, and the absurdities of mob-
mentality in *Julius Caesar* and *Coriolanus*. So much is fairly
obvious; but there is more.

Caliban derives from other ill-graced cursers, a 'misshapen

knave' and 'bastard' (v i 268–73) like the deformed Thersites ('bastard begot, bastard instructed, bastard in mind, bastard in valour, in everything illegitimate', *Troilus and Cressida* v vii 17) and bitter as Apemantus; from the 'indigest deformed lump', 'abortive rooting hog', 'poisonous bunch-back'd toad' and 'cacodemon', Richard III (*3 Henry VI* v vi 51; *Richard III* I iii 228, 246, 144; cp. Caliban as 'demi-devil' at v i 272); and from all Shakespeare's imagery of nausea and evil expressed through reptiles or, since we must not forget Sycorax (who may be allowed to sum all Shakespeare's evil women), creatures of black magic, as in *Macbeth*. He derives from all bad passion, as when Lear and Coriolanus are called dragons (*King Lear* I i 124; *Coriolanus* v iv 14). He combines the infra-natural evil of *Macbeth* with the bestial evil of *King Lear,* where man's suicidal voracity is compared to 'monsters of the deep' (*King Lear* IV ii 50). He is himself a water-beast, growing from the ooze and slime of those stagnant pools elsewhere associated with vice, being exactly defined by Thersites' description of Ajax as 'a very land-fish, languageless, a monster' (*Troilus and Cressida* III iii 266). But he has a beast's innocence and pathos too, and is moved by music as are the 'race of youthful and unhandled colts' of *The Merchant of Venice* (v i 71–9; cp. the comparison of the music-charmed Caliban to 'unback'd colts' at IV i 176–8). He sums up the ravenous animals that accompany tempest-passages, the boar, bull, bear; especially the much-loathed boar of *Venus and Adonis*. In him is the ugliness of sexual appetite from *Lucrece* onwards, and also the ugliness vice raises in those who too much detest it, the ugliness of hatred itself and loathing, the ugliness of Leontes. Man, savage, ape, water-beast, dragon, semi-devil – Caliban is all of them; and because he so condenses masses of great poetry, is himself beautiful. He is the physical as opposed to the spiritual; earth and water as opposed to air and fire. That he may, like Ariel, be considered in closest relation to Prospero himself is witnessed by Prospero's admission: 'This thing of darkness I acknowledge mine' (v i 275).

These three main persons present aspects of Timon. Besides

Prospero's resemblance already observed, Ariel's thunderous
denunciation (at III iii 53) recalls Timon's prophetic fury,
both addressed to a society that has rejected true nobility for a
sham, while Caliban reproduces his naked savagery and the
more ugly, Apemantus-like, affinities of his general hatred. This
especial inclusiveness marks Timon's archetypal importance.

To turn to the subsidiary persons. Alonso and his party
present a varied assortment of more or less guilty people. We
have, first, a striking recapitulation of *Macbeth*, Antonio
persuading Sebastian to murder the sleeping king in phrases
redolent of Duncan's murder:

> What might,
> Worthy Sebastian? O! what might? – No more:
> And yet methinks I see it in *thy face*,
> What thou should'st be. *The occasion speaks thee*; and
> My strong imagination sees a *crown*
> Dropping upon thy head.                    (II i 199)

We remember 'Your face, great thane, is as a book . . .'; 'Nor
time, nor place, did then adhere and yet you would make
both; they have made themselves . . .'; and 'all that impedes
thee from the golden round . . .' (*Macbeth* I v 63; I vii 51;
I v 29). Antonio's

> O!
> If you but knew how you the purpose cherish
> Whiles thus you mock it . . .                    (II i 218)

is a crisp capitulation of Lady Macbeth's soliloquy on her
husband's divided will (I v 17–30). *Macbeth* is resurrected in
both phrase and verse-texture:

> And by that destiny to perform an *act*
> Whereof what's past is *prologue*, what to come
> Is yours and my discharge.                    (II i 247)

Compare Macbeth's 'happy *prologues* to the swelling *act* of the
imperial theme' and Lady Macbeth's 'Leave all the rest to me'
(*Macbeth* I iii 128; I v 74). Death and sleep are all but identified
in both (II i 255–7; *Macbeth* II ii 54). Antonio's attitude to

conscience ('Ay, sir, where lies that?' at II i 271) parallels Lady
Macbeth's, while her 'Who dares receive it other?' (*Macbeth*
I vii 77) is expanded into Antonio's scornful certainty that 'all
the rest' will

> take suggestion as a cat laps milk;
> They'll tell the clock to any business that
> We say befits the hour . . . (II i 283)

– where even the cat, a comparatively rare Shakespearian
animal, harks back to 'the poor cat i' the adage' (*Macbeth* I vii
45). In both plays the victim's weariness is brutally advanced
as an assurance of sleep: compare Duncan's 'day's hard labour',
which shall 'invite' him to sound sleep (*Macbeth* I vii 62)
with 'now they are oppressed with travel' (III iii 15). That
*Macbeth* should be singled out for so elaborate a re-enactment
is not strange, since, standing alone in point of absolute and
abysmal evil, it shares only slightly (via Sycorax) in the general
recapitulation covered by Caliban, whom Prospero specifically
acknowledges. Thus poetic honesty leaves Antonio's final
reformation doubtful.

Alonso is less guilty, nor is there here any so vivid correspondence to be observed. Sebastian blames him for insisting
on marrying his daughter Claribel against her and his subjects'
will to an African (II i 119–31); and, since Gonzalo partly
sanctions the criticism, we must, it would seem, perhaps with
some faint reference to Desdemona's ill-starred marriage, regard
Alonso's action as a fault. He was also a silent accomplice to
Antonio's original treachery, and Ariel later asserts that he is
being punished for it by his son's loss (III iii 75). As one of
Shakespeare's many autocratic fathers and also as a king rather
pathetically searching for his child, he is a distant relative of
Lear. Both are purgatorial figures: he realizes his 'trespass'
(III iii 99).

The faithful and garrulous old lord Gonzalo is a blend of
Polonius, Adam and Kent. The courtiers Adrian and Francisco
are not particularized. The wit of Antonio and Sebastian on their
first entry needs, however, a remark.

It is cynical and cruel. The points made are of slight importance except for the extraordinary reiteration of 'widow Dido' (II i 73–97). There is presumably a sneer at an unmarried woman who has been deserted by her lover being given the status of 'widow'; and this we may tentatively relate to *Antony and Cleopatra*, wherein 'Dido and her Aeneas' are once compared to the protagonists (IV xii 53) and which in Cleopatra's phrase 'Husband, I come!' (v ii 289) reaches a compact self-interpretation in direct answer to such cynicism as Antonio's. The whole dialogue, starting with criticism of Gonzalo's and Adrian's insistence on the isle's fertility (the island varies mysteriously according to the nature of the spectator) and leading through ridicule of Gonzalo's phrase 'widow Dido' and his identification of Tunis and Carthage, to a final flowering in his Utopian dream, serves very precisely to define an opposition of cynic and romantic.[2] The points at issue are less important than the points of view:

> *Antonio*. He misses not much.
> *Sebastian*. No. He doth but mistake the truth totally.
>
> (II i 54)

That is cynical keenness in good form; and our dialogue takes us accordingly to the threshold at least of *Antony and Cleopatra*, the supreme answer of romanticism, wherein human love, though criticized as filth, wins through to glory. There is further corroboration: not only do the phrases 'such a paragon to their queen', 'miraculous harp' and 'impossible matter' (II i 71, 83, 85) raise, ironically or otherwise, suggestion of the marvellous harking back to *Antony and Cleopatra*, but we have one direct reminder:

> *Sebastian*. I think he will carry this island home in his *pocket*, and give it his son for an apple.
> *Antonio*. And, sowing the kernels of it in the sea, bring forth more *islands*.                    (II i 86)

Compare Cleopatra's dream, with its 'realms and *islands* were as plates dropt from his *pocket*' (*Antony and Cleopatra* v ii 91). We find the romantic extreme, whether in jocular cynicism or in visionary earnest, reaching definition in similar terms. Certainly one expects some trace of the earlier play, some honest facing in this austere work of its golden sexuality; and perhaps the easiest way to honour it was through the self-negating cynicism of an Antonio.[3]

To return to the marriage of Claribel to the King of Tunis. Any further correspondences (outside *Othello*) may again be sought in *Antony and Cleopatra*, where a west-east conflict in relation to marriage is strongly developed; and again in the Prince of Morocco, in *The Merchant of Venice* (see also *The Winter's Tale* v i 156–67). Criticism of the marriage originates from Sebastian, the cynic being naturally hostile, as in *Othello*, to the eastern glamour; while Gonzalo changes his view later, regarding it as part of the general happiness (v i 209). To Shakespeare Africa and the Orient are at once glamorous and dangerous (Sycorax came from Argier), with something of the disturbing magic wielded by the Indian fairies in *A Midsummer Night's Dream*: perhaps that is why Antonio seems to regard Tunis as an *infinite* distance from Milan.

The central experience of this group is the offering and sudden withdrawal of the mysterious banquet, with Ariel's appearance as a harpy and speech of denunciation.

Feasts are regularly important throughout Shakespeare, but are so obvious that one accepts them without thought. It is the mark of greatest literature to play on such fundamentals of human existence and we must remember their importance in Homer and the New Testament; in the one direct, in the other, in event, miracle and parable, carrying symbolic overtones. Shakespeare ends his two morality farces, *The Taming of the Shrew* and *The Merry Wives of Windsor*, with feasts, acted or announced, to convey a sense of general good-will succeeding horse-play. In *Romeo and Juliet* a feast and dance relate neatly to the family feud, raising questions of daring, adventure and hospitality. There is the rough feasting in Arden and Belarius' cave, both characterized by hospitality. Eating and drinking are continually given dramatic emphasis, with various ethical implications: they are important throughout *Antony and*

*Cleopatra*, with one gorgeous feast-scene celebrating union after hostility, though nearly ruined by treachery. An elaborate banquet occurs in *Pericles*, with Thaisa as 'queen of the feast' (II iii 17) pointing on, as we have seen, to Perdita as 'mistress of the feast' (IV iii 68) in *The Winter's Tale*. Important examples occur in *Timon of Athens* and *Macbeth*. In *Timon* there are two: the first (I ii) conceived as a sacrament of love and friendship (with New Testament reminiscence at line 51), crowned by Timon's speech and negatively underlined by Apemantus' cynicism; the second (III vi), planned as a deadly serious practical joke, in which Timon, after raising his false friends' hopes, speaks an ironic grace, overturns (probably) their tables, and douses them with luke-warm water. In *Macbeth*, we have first the irony of the feasting of Duncan (I vii), and later on (IV i) the *inverted* good of the 'hell-broth' brewed by the Weird Women; and, in between (III iv), the feast to which Banquo has been carefully invited and which he attends as a ghost, smashing up the conviviality and social health so vividly emphasized in the text, and thus denying to Macbeth's tyrannous and blood-stained rule all such sacraments of brotherhood. These two *broken* feasts in *Timon of Athens* and *Macbeth*, related to the two main Shakespearian evils of unfaithfulness and crime, are key-scenes; and their shattering stage-power derives precisely from the simplicity of the effects used, planted squarely as they are on fundamentals.

The meaning of the feast offered but denied to Alonso, Sebastian and Antonio will now be clear; and also its relevance to the Shakespearian world.

The 'solemn and strange music' (III iii 18) of the feast is followed by Ariel's appearance as a Harpy to 'thunder and lightning' (III iii 53). The sequence recalls the Vision in *Cymbeline*, and Ariel's harpy-appearance drives home the similarity. Like Jupiter, he enters as a figure of overruling judgement, speaking scornfully of the lesser beings who think to dispute the ordinances of 'fate' (III iii; cp. 'How dare you ghosts . . .' *Cymbeline* v iv 94). Both epitomize the Shakespearian emphasis on thunder as the voice of the gods, or God. So

Ariel acts the more awe-inspiring attributes of Shakespeare's tempest-poetry before our eyes, and in a long speech drives home its purgatorial purpose.

Besides Alonso and his party, we have the comic group of Stephano and Trinculo, in association with Caliban. The comedy is delightful, but scarcely subtle. Stephano the butler is an unqualified, almost professional, drunkard, with nothing of the philosophic quality of Falstaff or the open if unprincipled *bonhomie* of Sir Toby. Both those are, in their way, gentlemen, and yet their new representative (as drunkard) is of a low type socially; as are Dogberry, Bottom and the Gravediggers, though Stephano is a poor equivalent, lacking natural dignity. Trinculo is an equally poor successor to Touchstone, Feste, Yorick and Lear's Fool. Note that their representative quality is nevertheless emphasized by their joint embodiment of the two main sorts of clown: the natural and the artificial.

*The Tempest* is an austere work. The poet, while giving his clowns full rein in comic appeal, allows them no dignity. In writing of Autolycus we have observed Shakespeare's tendency there, as with Falstaff, earlier, to show his humorist as disintegrating; both as losing dignity and revealing ugly tendencies. So, too, with Sir Toby: in spite of his admirable 'cakes and ale' (*Twelfth Night* II iii 125) he is carefully made to lose dignity towards the play's conclusion, the balance of conviviality and reproof being carefully held.

Both Falstaff and Autolycus, as their glow of humour pales, show themselves as rather cheaply ambitious: whilst bearers of the comic spirit, they are, for a while, the superiors of kings; but when they, in their turn, ape the courtier, join in the vulgar scramble for show, they fall lower than their meanest dupes. Falstaff in *2 Henry IV* is enjoying his advance, ordering new clothes, being the grand man. Here the distinction is subtle; but the way is open for his final disintegration in *The Merry Wives of Windsor*. So, too, with Autolycus: he dresses as a courtier, apes a courtier's grandiosity and trades sadistically on the Shepherd's and Clown's anguish. He is finally shown as cringing to his former dupe. Now, remembering, too, Hamlet's

disgust at the heavy drinking of Claudius' court, observe
what happens to our comic trio, especially Stephano.

First, he drinks and sings maudlin songs. Next, he becomes
a petty tyrant and engages in a bloody plot, aiming to make
himself lord of the island. He is a burlesque of the power-quest,
with all the absurdity of a barbaric despotism, having his foot
licked by Caliban and posing as king, resembling Marlowe's
Tamburlaine and the Macbeth of

> Now does he feel his title
> Hang loose about him, like a giant's robe
> Upon a dwarfish thief.                 (*Macbeth* v ii 20)

Stephano parodies the essential absurdity of tyrannic ambition.
Now he and his companions are lured by Ariel to a filthy pool:

> at last I left them
> I' the filthy-mantled pool beyond your cell,
> There dancing up to the chins, that the foul lake
> O'erstunk their feet.                      (IV i 181)

Stagnant water occurs regularly to suggest filth and indignity.
Poor Tom in *King Lear* has been led by the foul fiend 'through
fire and through flame, through ford and whirlpool, o'er bog
and quagmire'; and an utmost degradation is suggested by his
eating 'the swimming frog, the toad, the tadpole, the wall-
newt and the water' and drinking 'the green mantle of the
standing pool' (*King Lear* III iv 50; 132, 137). The lascivious
Falstaff is ducked in *The Merry Wives of Windsor*; in flowing
water, certainly, but the dirty-linen basket supplies the rest.
There is also the final entry of the absurd braggart, Parolles,
in *All's Well that Ends Well*, bedraggled, with filthy clothes,
and admitting that he is 'muddied in Fortune's mood' and
smelling 'somewhat strong of her strong displeasure'; with a
developed dialogue on bad smells, an 'unclean fish-pond',
'carp', etc. (v ii 1–27). Notice that (i) lust – there is direct
association of pools to sexual vice at *The Winter's Tale* I ii 195
and *Cymbeline* I iv 103 – and (ii) braggadocio are involved.
Stephano, the would-be tyrant, meant to possess Miranda after

murdering Prospero; Caliban has already tried to rape her; and all three are accordingly left in the 'filthy-mantled pool'.

Our buffoons are next tempted, like Autolycus, by an array of 'trumpery' (IV i 186), of 'glistering apparel' (IV i 193). Rich clothes were a more pressing masculine temptation in Shakespeare's day than in ours. One of Faustus' ambitions was to clothe Wittenberg's students in silk, and *Macbeth*'s power-quest is characterized in terms of a 'a giant's robe' (*Macbeth* v ii 21; cp. *The Tempest* II i 267). Shakespeare reiterates his scorn for the latest (usually foreign) fashions, for all tinsel of clothes, speech, or manners, in play after play; as with Claudio, Sir Andrew and his 'flame-colour'd stock' (*Twelfth Night* I iii 146), Kent's 'a tailor made thee' (*King Lear* II ii 59), Osric, and many others. The prim Malvolio is fooled in his yellow stockings; Christopher Sly dressed absurdly in a nobleman's robes; Katharina the Shrew tormented with finery. This vein of satire beats in our present symbolic incident: the two fools are ensnared by a tinsel glitter, though Caliban, being closer to nature, has more sense (the temptation is perhaps slightly out of character for the others too, whose job here is, however, to parody their social superiors). All three are next chased off by Prospero's hounds. The pool and the show of garments will be now understood, but what of the hounds? Hounds are impregnated with a sense of healthy, non-brutal, and (like Shakespeare's horses) man-serving virility, occurring favourably at *Venus and Adonis* 913–24; *Henry V* III i 31; and *Timon of Athens* I ii 198. Hunting is a noble sport, though sympathy can be accorded the hunted hare (at *Venus and Adonis* 679–708, and *3 Henry VI* II v 130). Courteous gentlemen, such as Theseus and Timon, necessarily hunt, especially important being the long description of Theseus' *musical* hounds, with reference also to those of Hercules, baying the bear in Crete (*A Midsummer Night's Dream* IV i 112–32). Hounds are adversaries to the bear and (in *Venus and Adonis*) the boar, both 'tempest-beasts', and, though the fawning of dogs is used satirically, hounds, as such, may be musically, almost spiritually, conceived: hence their picturesque names in *The Tempest*:

'Mountain', 'Silver', 'Fury' and 'Tyrant'.⁴ They are spirit-
essences directed against the bestial Caliban and his companions.

So, too, the fleshly and 'corrupt' Falstaff was punished by
fairies or supposed fairies in *The Merry Wives of Windsor* by
pinching, conceived as a punishment of 'sinful fantasy', 'lust'
and 'unchaste desire' by spirits (v v 96–108). Here Caliban
regularly (I ii 327–32, 371–3; II ii 4), and now Stephano and
Trinculo, too, are thoroughly *pinched* and given cramps and
aches (IV i 258–61).⁵

Such is Shakespeare's judgement on drunkenness, sexual
lust and braggart ambition. Such evils have, variously, held
dignity, as in Falstaff's speech on sherris-sack (*2 Henry IV*
IV iii 92), the riotous love of Antony and Cleopatra and, for
the power-quest, *Macbeth*; but it is a tight-rope course; one
slip and the several vices appear in their nakedness. That
naked essence, in all its lewd and ludicrous vulgarity, is here
emphasized.

There remain Ferdinand and Miranda. These are representative of beautiful and virtuous youth as drawn in former plays
(Marina, Florizel and Perdita, Guiderius and Arviragus), though
lacking something of their human impact. Our new pair illustrate
humility (as in Ferdinand's log-piling), innocence, faith and
purity; their words being characterized by utter simplicity and
sincerity. They are whittled down to these virtues with slight
further realization, and in comparison with earlier equivalents
must be accounted pale. As elsewhere, essences are abstracted
and reclothed. Except for Prospero, Ariel and Caliban, the
people scarcely exist in their own right. The real drama consists
of the actions and interplay of our three major persons with the
natural, human and spiritual powers in which their destiny is
entangled.

Prospero, who controls this comprehensive Shakespearian
world, automatically reflects Shakespeare himself. Like Hamlet,
he arranges dramatic shows to rouse his sinning victims'
conscience: the mock-feast (whose vanishing, as we have seen,
recalls Macbeth's ghost-shattered banquet), brought in by
a 'living drollery' of 'shapes' (III iii 21); and the masque of

goddesses and dancers (IV i), which, like the Final Plays themselves (of whose divinities these goddesses are pale reflections), is addressed to the purer consciousness (Ferdinand's). This tendency, as in *Hamlet*, reflects some degree of identification of the protagonist with the playwright, whose every work is a parable. Prospero himself delivers what is practically a long prologue in Act I, and in his own person speaks the epilogue. He is, even more than the Duke in *Measure for Measure*, a designer of the drama in which he functions as protagonist. We have seen how many of Shakespeare's tragic themes are covered by him; and that his farewell might have been spoken by Shakespeare is a correspondence demanded by the whole conception.

He addresses (v i 33–57) the various powers (drawn from folk-lore and called, with a grand humility, 'weak') by whose aid he has 'bedimm'd the noontide sun' (as 'the travelling lamp' is strangled in *Macbeth* II iv 7) and loosed the 'mutinous winds' to 'set roaring war' between sea and sky, thereby recalling such tempests throughout the great tragedies, in *Julius Caesar*, *Othello*, *Macbeth*, *King Lear*, with their many symbolic undertones of passionate conflict here crisply recapitulated in thought of war betwixt 'sea' and 'sky'. He has used 'Jove's own bolt' to blast (as at *Measure for Measure* II ii 116 and *Coriolanus* v iii 152) Jove's tree, the oak, recalling Jupiter the Thunderer in *Cymbeline*. From such images the speech moves inevitably to:

> Graves at my command
> Have wak'd their sleepers, op'd, and let them forth
> By my so potent art.                    (v i 48)

The statement, with its parallel in the resurrections of *Pericles* and *The Winter's Tale* and the less vivid restoration of Imogen in *Cymbeline*, may seem to apply more directly to Shakespeare than to Prospero; though the miraculous preservation of the ship and its crew must be regarded as an extension of earlier miracles. Prospero's speech, ending in 'heavenly' or 'solemn' (v i 52, 57) music, forms a recapitulation of Shakespeare's artistic progress from tempest-torn tragedy to resurrection and music (cp. the 'music of the spheres' at *Pericles* v i 231, and the resurrection music of *Pericles* III ii 88, 91; and *The Winter's Tale* v iii 98) corresponding to its forecast in *Richard II*.

Prospero uses his tempest-magic to draw his enemies to the island, and there renders them harmless. He wrecks and saves, teaches through disaster, entices and leads by music, getting them utterly under his power, redeeming and finally forgiving. What are the Shakespearian analogies? The poet himself labours to master and assimilate that unassuaged bitterness and sense of rejection so normal a lot to humanity (hence the popularity of *Hamlet*) by drawing the hostile elements within his own world of artistic creation; and this he does mainly through tragedy and its thunderous music; and by seeing that, in spite of logic, his creation is good. By destroying his protagonists, he renders them deathless; by expressing evil, in others and in himself, he renders it innocent. And throughout this tumult of creative activity, turning every grief to a star, making of his very loathing something 'rich and strange', there is a danger: a certain centre of faith or love must be preserved, this centre at least kept free from the taint of that rich, wild, earthy, lustful, violent, cursing, slimy yet glittering thing that is creation itself, or Caliban; that uses cynicism (born of the knowledge of lust) to ruin Desdemona, though not Othello's love for her; that tries in vain, but only just in vain, to make of Timon an Apemantus. Therefore Prospero keeps Miranda intact, though threatened by Caliban, just as Marina was threatened in the brothel of Mitylene. Alone with her he had voyaged far to his magic land, cast off in a wretched boat,

> To cry to the sea that roar'd to us; to sigh
> To the winds whose pity, sighing back again,
> Did us but loving wrong.                    (I ii 149)

What an image of lonely, spiritual voyage, like that of Wordsworth's Newton 'voyaging through strange seas of thought, alone'; while echoing back, through the long story of Shakespearian 'sea-sorrow' (I ii 170), to the Nordic origins of our literature in *The Wanderer* and *The Seafarer*. Prospero, unlike

Lear, Pericles and Leontes, guards his Miranda, and with her survives on his island of poetry, with Ariel and Caliban. Who are these? The one, clearly, his art, his poetry in action; the other, the world of creation, smelling of earth and water, with the salt tang of the physical, of sexual energy, and with, too, all those revulsions and curses to which it gives birth. Prospero finds both Ariel and Caliban on the island, releasing the one (as genius is regularly characterized less by inventiveness than by the ability to release some dormant power) and aiming to train the other; and both must be strictly controlled. Prospero, Ariel, Caliban, Miranda: all are aspects of Shakespeare himself. Prospero, corresponding to the poet's controlling judgement, returns to Milan, uniting his daughter, his human faith, to his enemy's son; and Shakespeare's life-work, in *Henry VIII*, draws to its conclusion.

It is, indeed, remarkable how well the meanings correspond. Prospero has been on the island for twelve years (I ii 53); and it is roughly twelve years since the sequence of greater plays started with *Hamlet*. Before that, Ariel had been prisoned in a tree for another twelve years (I ii 279); again, roughly, the time spent by Shakespeare in his earlier work, before the powers of bitterness and abysmal sight projected him into the twilit, lightning-riven and finally transcendent regions; rather as Herman Melville passed from *Typee* and *White Jacket* to *Moby Dick*, *Pierre* and his later poetry. And now, as the end draws near, Ariel cries (as does Caliban too) for freedom from ceaseless 'toil':

*Prospero.* How now! moody?
　What is't thou canst demand?
*Ariel.* My liberty.
*Prospero.* Before the time be out? No more! 　　(I ii 244)

Prospero dominates Ariel and Caliban with an equal severity: as Shakespeare may be supposed to have willed, sternly, the safe conclusion of his labour in *Henry VIII*.

That labour is not all easy. Prospero, though still, is not static. Like Hamlet's, his very centrality is dynamic, drawing

others to him, like Timon in his retirement, radiating power;
or rather those earlier spiritual radiations are here given appropriate, symbolic, action, just as, according to Shelley's definition,
poetry itself holds, in its very reserve, its stillness, a myriad
radiations.

## NOTES

1. See G. Wilson Knight, *The Crown of Life*, (1947), p. 187.

2. According to Vergil Dido was widowed before Aeneas' arrival
at Carthage and Gonzalo here, as in his identification of Tunis and
Carthage, is correct. The cynic's sneer is based on lack of information.

3. My suggestion must remain tentative; but it has at least some
confirmation from my brother's reading of Vergil's poetic methods.
(See W. F. Jackson Knight, *Roman Vergil* (1944).)

4. The use of such names as 'Tyrant' and 'Fury' does not lower the
animals' status, since the implied humanizing serves as an idealization;
as with battleships, where the names H.M.S. *Furious* or H.M.S.
*Venomous*, by attributing living status to a machine, witness a respect
not usually offered to ill-temper and snakes.

5. Compare the fairies' song 'Pinch him black and blue' in Lyly's
*Endimion*.

# Reuben A. Brower

# THE MIRROR OF ANALOGY

> *The Mind, that Ocean where each kind*
> *Does streight its own resemblance find;*
> *Yet it creates, transcending these,*
> *Far other Worlds, and other Seas . . .*
>
> ANDREW MARVELL

OF *The Tempest*, we may say what Ferdinand said of the masque,

> This is a most majestic vision, and
> Harmonious charmingly.

The harmony of the play lies in its metaphorical design, in the closeness and completeness with which its rich and varied elements are linked through almost inexhaustible analogies. It is hard to pick a speech at random without coming on an expression that brings us by analogy into direct contact with elements that seem remote because of their place in the action or because of the type of experience they symbolize. Opening the play at the second act we read,

> Four legs and two voices; a most delicate monster!

The last phrase is comic enough as used of Caliban and as issuing from the lips of Stephano, a 'most foul' speaker. But 'delicate' evokes a more subtle incongruity by recalling characters and a world we might suppose were forgotten. Stephano is parodying Prospero when he rebukes Ariel as 'a spirit too delicate / To act her [Sycorax's] earthy and abhorr'd commands' and when he says,

> delicate Ariel,
> I'll set thee free for this!

We have in Stephano's words not only the familiar Shakespearean balancing of comic and serious, but a counterpointing of

analogies that run throughout the play. 'Delicate' as the antithesis of 'earth' points to the opposition of Ariel and Caliban
and to the often recurring earth-air symbolism of *The Tempest*.
'Delicate' used of this remarkable island creature echoes also the
'delicate temperance' of which the courtiers spoke and 'the air'
that 'breathes . . . here most sweetly'. 'Monster' – almost another
name for Caliban – balances these airy suggestions with an
allusion to 'the people of the island . . . of monstrous shape' and
thereby to the strain of fantastic sea lore in *The Tempest*, which
is being parodied in this scene.

So viewed, Shakespeare's analogies may perhaps seem too
much like exploding nebulae in an expanding though hardly
ordered universe. But Shakespeare does not 'multiply variety
in a wilderness of mirrors'; he makes use of a few fairly constant
analogies that can be traced through expressions sometimes the
same and sometimes extraordinarily varied. And the recurrent
analogies (or continuities) are linked through a key metaphor
into a single metaphorical design. Shakespeare is continually
prodding us – often in ways of which we are barely conscious –
to relate the passing dialogue with other dialogues into and
through a super-design of metaphor.

In concentrating on how the design is built up, I am not
forgetting that it is a metaphorical design in a *drama*, that we are
interested in how Shakespeare has linked stages in a presentation
of changing human relationships. Toward the end of the
chapter I hope to show how wonderfully the metaphorical
design is related to the main dramatic sequence of *The Tempest*,
especially in the climactic speeches of Acts IV and V.

The play moves forward, we should remember, from a scene
of tempest to a final promise of 'calm seas, auspicious gales',
and through a series of punishments or trials to a series of
reconciliations and restorations. Although, as Dr. Johnson
might say, there is a 'concatenation of events' running through
Prospero's 'project' and though the play has a curiously exact
time schedule, there is often little chronological or logical connection between successive dialogues or bits of action. To be
sure, Shakespeare has the Elizabethan conventions on his side,

but the freedom of his dramatic composition in *The Tempest* never seems merely conventional or capricious because the linkage of analogy is so varied and so pervasive.

The surest proof of the pervasiveness of Shakespeare's design lies in the mere number of continuities that can be discovered in the play. But some are more important than others because they can be traced through more expressions or in more scenes and because they express analogies more closely related to the key metaphor. The six main continuities, roughly labeled to indicate their character, are: 'strange-wondrous', 'sleep-and-dream', 'sea-tempest', 'music-and-noise', 'earth-air', 'slavery-freedom', and 'sovereignty-conspiracy'.

All of these continuities appear during the second scene of Act I, which is an exposition of Shakespeare's metaphorical and dramatic designs for the entire play. Near the close of the scene, Ariel's two songs offer wonderfully concentrated expressions of both designs. 'Come unto these yellow sands' calms the 'fury' of the waves and Ferdinand's 'passion', thus charting in brief the course of the action. 'Full fathom five' is anticipatory in a very different fashion. It presents in miniature the main lines of the metaphorical design and sounds the key note of 'sea change', Shakespeare's most direct expression of the key metaphor of *The Tempest*. (See I ii 1–186.)

As we trace the first two continuities ('strange-wondrous', 'sleep-and-dream'), the reader can appreciate how unobtrusively they emerge from the developing dramatic pattern. Prospero's narrative, with which the scene opens, tells us of the past and describes the present situation while symbolizing the quality of *The Tempest* world. Prospero explains that his enemies have come to this shore 'by accident most strange', and Miranda, who falls to sleep at the end of his tale, accounts for her lapse by saying,

> The strangeness of your story put
> Heaviness in me.

Prospero's tale was strange indeed: it included a ruler 'rapt in secret studies', a 'false uncle' who 'new created / The creatures' of the state, the miraculous voyage of Prospero and Miranda

(who was 'a cherubin') and their safe arrival 'by Providence
divine'. This 'strangeness' is best defined by Alonso's remarks
near the end of the play:

> These are not natural events; they strengthen
> From strange to stranger . . .
>
> This is as strange a maze as e'er men trod;
> And there is in this business more than nature
> Was ever conduct of . . .

They are 'unnatural' in a broad seventeenth-century sense of
the term; that is, outside the order which includes all created
things. The theme is almost constantly being played on:
'strange', 'strangely', or 'strangeness' occur altogether some
seventeen times, and similar meanings are echoed in 'wondrous',
'monstrous', 'divine'.

Of all the analogies of the play this is probably the vaguest,
the nearest in effect to the atmospheric unity of nineteenth-
century Romantic poetry. But a more precise metaphor of
strangeness appears, the 'strangeness' of 'new created creatures'.
From the 'accident most strange' of the shipwreck we come to
Alonso's ponderous woe:

> O thou, mine heir
> Of Naples and of Milan! what strange fish
> Hath made his meal on thee?

and then to Trinculo's discovery of Caliban – 'A strange fish!'
With a similar comic antiphony, Miranda finds Ferdinand 'a
thing divine', and Ferdinand replies, 'O you wonder'; while a
little later hails Trinculo as his god and cries, 'Thou wondrous
man'. The full significance of these strange births will appear
later.

The vague 'strangeness' of the island world is closely allied
to a state of sleep, both continuities appearing in Miranda's
remark about the 'heaviness' that came over her while listening
to Prospero's story. The feeling that we are entering on an
experience of sleep-and-dream arises beautifully out of the
dramatic and rhythmic texture of the opening dialogue between

father and daughter. The movement of these speeches with their oddly rocking repetitions is in key with the sleepy incredibility of the events about to be described: 'Canst thou remember . . . thou canst . . . I can . . . thy remembrance . . . my remembrance . . . thou remember'st . . . Twelve year since, Miranda, twelve year since . . .' Throughout the story Prospero is continually reminding Miranda to 'attend' to the telling, and it seems perfectly natural that at the end she should be 'inclin'd to sleep'. (Note in passing how neatly Shakespeare has broken a long narrative into dialogue and also given a distinct impression of Prospero's firmness and of Miranda's innocent dependence.) Miranda's images of the past come back to her 'rather like a dream', and Prospero seems to be drawing their story from a world of sleep, 'the dark backward and abysm of time'.

With the next scene (the mourning King and his courtiers) we meet one of Shakespeare's typical analogical progressions. The sleep which affects the courtiers is, like Miranda's, a strange 'heaviness'. Their dialogue runs down, psychologically and rhythmically, through three echoes of Miranda's words:

*Gonzalo.* Will you laugh me asleep, for I am very heavy? . . .
*Sebastian.* Do not omit the heavy offer of it . . .
*Alonso.* Thank you. Wondrous heavy.
*Sebastian.* What a strange drowsiness possesses them!

The conversation that follows between the conspirators shows how Shakespeare uses an analogy to move to a new level of action and experience and to make them harmonious with what precedes and follows. Sebastian and Antonio begin by talking about actual sleep and waking: why are they not drowsy like the others? Then Antonio shifts to talking of sleepiness and alertness of mind, and from that to imagining that he sees 'a crown dropping' upon Sebastian's head. The wit becomes more complex as Sebastian describes Antonio's talk as 'sleepy language' – without meaning – though indicating that it does have meaning. 'There's meaning in thy snores.' This dialogue, which readers are liable to dismiss as so much Elizabethan wit, has its place within the play's metaphorical pattern. The plotting takes on a preposterous dreamy-sleepy character like that of

Prospero's narrative and Miranda's recollections. Through such verbal trifling Shakespeare maintains the continuous quality of his imagined world.

References to similar wakings and sleepings, to dreams and dreamlike states, abound from here to the end of the play, where the sailors are 'brought moping . . . even in a dream', and the grand awakening of all the characters is completed. But up to that point confusion between waking and sleep is the rule, being awake is never far from sleep or dream. In *The Tempest* sleep is always imminent, and more than once action ends in sleep or trance.

The witty talk of the conspirators glides from conceits of 'sleep' to conceits of 'the sea', to talk of 'standing water' and 'flowing' and 'ebbing'. The 'good Gonzalo', in consoling the King, speaks in similar figures:

> It is foul weather in us all, good sir,
> When you are cloudy.

Recurrent expressions of 'sea and tempest', like those of 'sleep and dream', are numerous and have a similar atmospheric value of not letting us forget the special quality of life on Prospero's island. But they also have far more important effects, for many of them become metaphors which are more precisely and more variously symbolic and which link more kinds of experience together.

By tracing two groups of 'tempest' expressions, metaphors of 'sea-swallowing' and images of 'clouds', we may understand how these more complex analogies are built up. We may also see how Shakespeare moves from narrative fact to metaphor, from image or metaphor referring only to narrative fact to metaphor rich in moral and psychological implications. As in creating the analogies of 'strangeness' and 'sleep', Shakespeare starts from a dramatic necessity: the audience must be told what the situation was in the storm scene with which the play opens, and they must learn through an actor (Miranda) how they are to take it. (See I ii 1–186.) Although there is a hint of magic in Miranda's vision of the tempest, she pictures it as a violent actuality:

> Had I been any god of power, I would
> Have sunk the sea within the earth, or e'er
> It should the good ship so have swallow'd and
> The fraughting souls within her.

As if there were an inner rhythm in these responses, this metaphor, like others we have been tracing, recurs in the plotting episode. Antonio is speaking of Ferdinand's sister Claribel, left behind in Tunis:

> she that from whom
> We all were sea-swallow'd, though some cast again,
> And by that destiny to perform an act
> Whereof what's past is prologue, what to come
> In yours and my discharge.

In this new context 'sea-swallow'd' does several things at once. It brings back Miranda's horrified impression; but the magical nature of the storm now being known, the phrase reminds us that there was no 'sea-swallowing', no actual sinking of 'fraughting souls'. Next, with a curiously Shakespearean 'glide and a jump' via the pun on 'cast', 'sea-swallow'd' merges into another metaphor (they are now 'cast' as actors in destiny's drama). 'Sea-swallowing' has become a metaphor that expresses destiny's extraordinary way of bringing Sebastian to the throne.

The irony of Antonio's words, which is clear to the audience is made explicit later in the solemn speech in which Ariel explains the purpose of the tempest:

> You are three men of sin, whom Destiny –
> That hath no instrument this lower world
> And what is in 't – the never-surfeited sea
> Hath caused to belch up you . . .

Few passages could show better how Shakespeare carries his analogies along and at the same time completely renews them. The 'belching up' recalls the wreck and the casting ashore and the earlier connection with destiny. But the sea's action is now described in much grosser terms and with grim sarcasm, while the oddly compact grammar makes 'the never-surfeited sea' very nearly a synonym for 'Destiny'. The violence though

increased is now religious and moral; the imagery has become
expressive of the strenuous punishment and purification of
'three men of sin'. So by the continuity of his varying metaphor
Shakespeare has expressed an unbroken transition from actual
storm to the storm of the soul. This sequence, which expresses
both physical and metaphysical transformations, points very
clearly to the key metaphor of *The Tempest*.

The recurrent cloud images present a similar sequence as
they take on various symbolic meanings in the course of the
play. 'Cloud' does not actually occur in the opening storm
scene, but when Trinculo sees 'another storm brewing' and
speaks of a 'black cloud', we are reminded of the original
tempest. The cloud undergoes an appropriate change in
Trinculo's speech; it 'looks like a foul bombard that would shed
his liquor'. This comic cloud is very different from 'the curl'd
clouds' on which Ariel rides, though they too are associated
with storms. The clouds of Caliban's exquisite speech are those
of Ariel and the deities of the masque:

>                         and then, in dreaming,
> The clouds methought would open and show riches
> Ready to drop upon me . . .

Clouds – here linked with magical riches – become in Prospero's
'cloud-capp'd towers' speech a symbol for the unsubstantial
splendor of the world. One of the subordinate metaphors there,
the 'melting into air' and the 'dissolving' of the clouds, is picked
up in Prospero's later words about the courtiers:

>                   The charm dissolves apace;
> And as the morning steals upon the night,
> Melting the darkness, so their rising senses
> Begin to chase the ignorant fumes that mantle
> Their clearer reason.

This dissolution of night clouds (suggested also by 'fumes')
is a figure for the change from madness to sanity, from evil
ignorance to the clear perceptions of reason. Although the
cloud images of the play are so varied, they have a common
symbolic value, for whether they are clouds of tempest or of

visionary riches or of the soul, they are always magically unsubstantial. The reader is led to feel some touch of likeness among experiences as different as a storm at sea, a bit of drunken whimsy, a vision of heavenly and earthly beauty, and a spiritual regeneration. The cloud sequence, as an arc of metaphor, is in perfect relation to the gradual dramatic movement from tempest and punishment to fair weather and reconciliation, the images having meanings more and more remote from any actual storm.

The 'cloudlike' change in the distracted souls of the guilty nobles was induced (as if in reminiscence of Plato) by *Solemn music* –

> A solemn air and the best comforter
> To an unsettled fancy.

Many of the expressions referring to music, like the stage direction above, are not explicitly metaphorical, but along with the continuities of 'sleep' and 'strangeness' they help maintain the magical character of the action. The music is always the music of spirits and always a sign of more than natural events.

The one fairly constant musical metaphor[1] in *The Tempest* is the symbolic opposition of confused noises, especially storm sounds, and harmonious music. The key word and the central impression of the opening scene is certainly 'noise'[2] in the modern sense. The impression is carried over in the first words of the next scene:

> If by your art, my dearest father, you have
> Put the wild waters in this roar, allay them.

Miranda's request is soon answered by Ariel's first song, 'the wild waves' are 'whist'. The *solemn and strange music* heard when the *strange Shapes* bring a banquet to the courtiers makes Alonso say, 'What harmony is this? my good friends, hark!' Gonzalo replies: 'Marvelous sweet music!' By contrast, when Ariel enters shortly after, in order to inform the 'three men of sin' of their punishment by the storm, there is an offstage sound of *Thunder and lightning*. The masque vision which Ferdinand finds 'harmonious charmingly' is rudely interrupted by *a strange, hollow, and confused noise* which symbolizes the stormy anger expressed by Prospero in the speeches that follow. When in the next scene he prepares to forgive his enemies, he abjures the 'rough magic' by which he

> call'd forth the mutinous winds,
> And 'twixt the green sea and the azur'd vault
> Set roaring war . . .

As the *solemn music* is played the clouds of ignorance 'dissolve', and so the musical metaphor, like the sea metaphor, has moved from outer to inner weather.

The music analogy has some close links with the earth-air continuity which we glanced at in the introductory chapter of the book. Ferdinand, following Ariel's 'yellow sands' song, asks, 'Where should this music be? i' th' air, or th' earth?' And a little later:

> This is no mortal business, nor no sound
> That the earth owes: I hear it now above me.

The connection of air and music can never be long forgotten: Ariel and his spirits of 'thin air' are the musicians of the island.

The earth-air, Caliban-Ariel antithesis coincides at points with what we might call a slavery-freedom continuity, for Caliban is in Prospero's words both 'slave' and 'earth'. Ariel too is called a 'slave' by Prospero, and for the time of the play he is as much a slave as Caliban. (Both are called 'slaves' in I ii, the scene of metaphorical exposition.) He is always asking for his freedom, which is at last granted, his release being symbolically expressed in the airy rovings of his final song. He flies into perpetual summer and, like air, becomes merged with the elements. By contrast, the 'high-day, freedom!' of which Caliban sings is ironically enough simply a change of masters.

The 'slaves' and 'servants' of the play suffer various kinds of imprisonment, from Ariel in his 'cloven pine' to Ferdinand's mild confinement, and before the end of Act IV everyone except Prospero and Miranda has been imprisoned in one way or another. During the course of Act V all the prisoners except

Ferdinand (who has already been released) are set free, each of them by Prospero's special command.

A sovereignty-conspiracy analogy parallels very closely the slavery-freedom analogy, some of the same persons, e.g. Ferdinand and Caliban, appearing as both slaves and conspirators. 'That foul conspiracy / Of the beast Caliban, and his confederates' is of course a parody version of the 'Open-ey'd Conspiracy' of Sebastian and Antonio. Ferdinand, too, is charged fantastically by Prospero with plotting against his island rule. Talk of kings and royalty turns up in many scenes, being connected usually with the denial of kingship, as in 'good Gonzalo's' speech on his golden-age commonwealth where 'he would be king' and yet have 'no sovereignty'. Though no single explicit metaphor for conspiracy or usurpation is often repeated, Shakespeare rings many changes on the theme as he moves from plot to plot. Prospero's brother, we recall, is said to have 'new created the creatures' of state. Antonio's seizure of power is called a 'substitution': 'crediting his own lies', he began to believe 'he was indeed the duke', and from merely playing a part he went on to become 'absolute Milan'. The figure is picked up in the somnolent dialogue of Sebastian and Antonio:

> I remember
> You did supplant your brother Prospero.

In the second of the scenes in which Caliban and his fellows plot to overthrow the island 'tyrant', Sebastian's 'supplant' is recalled with a difference:

> *Caliban.* I would my valiant master would destroy thee; I do not lie.
> *Stephano.* Trinculo, if you trouble him any more in his tale, by this hand, I will supplant some of your teeth.

The figure recurs a little later in a more serious context:

> . . . you three
> From Milan did supplant good Prospero.

In Act v after various supplantings, serious and comic, accomplished or merely projected, all true kings are restored and all false ones dethroned.

The two continuities, sovereignty-conspiracy and slavery-freedom, are also alike in the fact that their metaphorical force is expressed through scenes that are just one step removed from allegory. The more serious of the restorations and releases convey similar kinds of moral meaning. Ferdinand's release from 'wooden slavery' signifies that he is a true lover and a true prince. In being freed from madness Alonso has escaped from 'heart-sorrow' and regained his rightful rank and a 'clear life ensuing'. Both continuities convey an impression of topsy-turvydom in the order of things, an unnatural interchange of status among creatures of every kind. Both express a return to stability after a disturbance of degree.

What then is the key metaphor through which the various continuities are linked, and how are they connected through it? Shakespeare's most direct expression of his key metaphor is 'sea change', the key phrase of Ariel's song. But what does Shakespeare mean by 'sea change'? Ariel sings of 'bones' being made into 'coral' and of 'eyes' becoming 'pearls'. 'A change into something rich and strange', we now understand, is a change 'out of nature'. 'Sea change' is a metaphor for 'magical transformation', for metamorphosis. The key metaphor of the play is 'change' in this special sense, and 'change' is the analogy common to all of the continuities we have been tracing. (I am not forgetting that they are also expressive of many other relationships, or that Shakespeare is often playing with two or three metaphors at once, as in the various figures of 'sea-swallowing'. But all are at least expressive of change, or changeableness.)

Through the first rather vague analogies we traced, of 'strangeness' and 'sleep-and-dream', numerous events and persons in the play are qualified as belonging to a realm where anything may happen. Expressions of 'strangeness' and 'sleep', like many of the references to sea and music, suggest 'far other Worlds and other Seas', where magical change is to be expected. A more particular metaphor of change is expressed through the stress on the 'strangeness' of 'new creations' and on the confusion between sleep and dream and waking. The island is a world of fluid, merging states of being and forms of life. This lack of dependable boundaries between states is also expressed by the many instances of confusion between natural and divine. Miranda says that she might call Ferdinand

> A thing divine; for nothing natural
> I ever saw so noble.

Ferdinand cannot be sure whether she is a goddess or a maid, and Caliban takes Trinculo for a 'brave god'. There is a further comic variation on this theme in Trinculo's difficulty in deciding whether to classify Caliban as fish or man, monster or devil.

But 'change' is most clearly and richly expressed through the sequence of tempest images (especially 'cloud' and 'sea-swallowed') and through the noise-music antithesis. All kinds of sounds, harmonious and ugly, like the manifestations of sea and storm, are expressive of magical transformation. 'The fire and cracks / Of sulfurous roaring' (imagery in which both storm and sound analogies are blended) 'infects' the courtiers' 'reason', and *solemn music* induces the 'clearing' of their understanding. The 'music' and the 'tempest' continuities, taken together as metaphors of 'sea change', are perhaps the most extensive of all the analogies in their organizing power. They recur often, they connect a wide diversity of experiences, and they express in symbolic form some of the main steps in the drama, in particular, the climactic moments of inner change: Ariel's revelation to the courtiers of their guilt, Alonso's first show of remorse, and the final purification.

The earth-air or Caliban-Ariel antithesis may seem to have very little to do with metamorphosis. But the relation of this theme to the key metaphor is clear and important. Air, Ariel, and his music are a blended symbol of change as against the unchanging Caliban, 'the thing of darkness'. He can be punished, but hardly humanized; he is, says Prospero,

> A devil, a born devil, on whose nature
> Nurture can never stick; on whom my pains,
> Humanely taken, are all lost, quite lost.

The other continuities parallel to earth-air, of slavery-freedom
and conspiracy-sovereignty, are frequently expressive of major
and minor changes of status among the inhabitants and temporary
visitors on Prospero's island.

But the interconnection of Shakespeare's analogies through
the key metaphor cannot be adequately described, since we are
able to speak of only one point of relationship at a time. We
can get a better sense of the felt union of various lines of analogy
in *The Tempest* by looking at the two passages where Shakespeare expresses his key metaphor most completely, the 'Full
fathom five' song and Prospero's 'cloud-capp'd towers' speech.

Rereading Ariel's song at this point, we can see how many
of the main continuities are alluded to and related in the description of 'sea change' and how the song anticipates the metaphorical design that emerges through the dialogue of the whole
play. The total metaphorical pattern is to an amazing degree
an efflorescence from this single crystal:

> Full fathom five thy father lies;
> Of his bones are coral made:
> Those are pearls that were his eyes:
> Nothing of him that doth fade,
> But doth suffer a sea change
> Into something rich and strange.
> Sea nymphs hourly ring his knell:
> > *Burthen:* 'Ding-dong!'
> Hark! now I hear them – Ding-dong, bell.

In addition to the more obvious references to the deep sea and
its powers and to the 'strangeness' of this drowning, there are
indirect anticipations of other analogies. 'Fade' prefigures the
'dissolving cloud' metaphor and the theme of tempest changes,
outer and inner. 'Rich', along with 'coral' and 'pearls', anticipates
the opulent imagery of the dream-world passages and scenes,
the 'riches ready to drop' on Caliban and the expressions of
wealth and plenty in the masque. ('Rich' and 'riches' occur no
less than five times in the masque.) The song closes with the
nymphs tolling the bell, the transformation and the 'sea sorrow'
are expressed through sea music. Ferdinand's comment reminds

us that the song has connections with two other lines of analogy:

> The ditty does remember my drown'd father.
> This is no mortal business, nor no sound
> That the earth owes: – I hear it now above me.

The song convinces Ferdinand that he is now King of Naples (the first of the interchanges of sovereignty), and it is a 'ditty' belonging not to the 'earth', but to the 'air'.

The sense of relationship between the many continuities is still more vividly felt in the lines of Prospero's most memorable speech:

> You do look, my son, in a mov'd sort,
> As if you were dismay'd: be cheerful, sir:
> Our revels now are ended. These our actors,
> As I foretold you, were all spirits and
> Are melted into air, into thin air:
> And, like the baseless fabric of this vision,
> The cloud-capp'd towers, the gorgeous palaces,
> The solemn temples, the great globe itself,
> Yea, all which it inherit, shall dissolve
> And, like this insubstantial pageant faded,
> Leave not a rack behind. We are such stuff
> As dreams are made on, and our little life
> Is rounded with a sleep.

In Prospero's words Shakespeare has gathered all the lights of analogy into a single metaphor which sums up the metaphorical design and the essential meaning of *The Tempest*. The language evokes nearly every continuity that we have traced. 'Melted into air', 'dissolve', 'cloud', and 'rack' bring us immediately to Ariel and tempest changes, while 'vision', 'dream', and 'sleep' recall other familiar continuities. 'Revels', 'gorgeous palaces', and 'pageant' (for Elizabethans closely associated with royalty) are echoes of the kingly theme; and 'solemn' is associated particularly with the soft music of change. The 'stuff' of dreams is at once cloud-stuff (air) and cloth, both images being finely compressed in 'baseless fabric'. Taken with 'faded' these images refer obliquely to the garments so miraculously 'new-dyed ... with salt water', one of the first signs of 'sea change' noted by Gonzalo. Within the metaphor of tempest-clearing and of cloudlike transformation, Shakespeare has included allusions to every important analogy of change in the play.

But it is through the twofold progress of the whole figure that the change metaphor is experienced and its most general meaning fully understood. We read first: that like the actors and scenery of the vision, earth's glories and man shall vanish into nothingness. Through a happy mistake we also read otherwise. By the time we have passed through 'dissolve', 'insubstantial', and 'faded', and reached 'leave not a rack behind', we are reading 'cloudcapped towers' in reverse as a metaphor of tower-like clouds. 'Towers', 'palaces', 'temples', 'the great globe', 'all which it inherit' are now taken for cloud forms. Through a sort of Proustian merging of icon and subject, we experience the blending of states of being, of substantial and unsubstantial, or real and unreal, which is the essence of *The Tempest* metamorphosis.

Similar meanings are expressed through the closing dream figure, which grows equally out of the metaphorical context of the speech and the play. 'Rounded', we should take with Kittredge as 'surrounded', but without losing the force of round, as in Donne's 'surrounded with tears'. 'Our little life' is more than sentimental, it is our little life (microcosm) in contrast with 'the great globe' (macrocosm). There may also be an over-image in 'surrounded' of the world in classical myth and geography with its encircling ocean, sleep being the stream that 'rounds' the lesser world. In relation to the metaphorical design of the play, 'rounded with a sleep' and the notion of life ending in dreams express again the sense of confusion between sleep and dream and waking. This metaphor which completes the figure of cloud-change is Shakespeare's most perfect symbol for the closeness of states that to our daylight sense are easily separable. Although the vision here expressed goes far beyond the play, it is still a natural extension of the dramatic moment and a fulfillment of the metaphor that has been implicit since the noisy opening lines of *The Tempest*.

But if Shakespeare's total metaphor is in a sense present everywhere, it is also a design that develops in close relation to the main dramatic movement of the play. As we have noted more than once, a particular metaphor will be varied to fit a new dramatic situation and so serve to express the situation more fully and to anticipate the next step in the development of the drama. The best example of this adaptation of metaphor comes in a speech in which Shakespeare seems to be playing capriciously with his noise-music theme. At first sight the passage seems inconsistent with the symbolic contrast between storm noise and music:

> *Alonso.* O, it is monstrous! monstrous!
> Methought the billows spoke and told me of it;
> The winds did sing it to me; and the thunder,
> That deep and dreadful organ pipe, pronounc'd
> The name of Prosper: it did bass my trespass.

It is admittedly odd that the confused noise of the tempest should, in Alonso's soul, compose a harmony – however gloomy – but the paradox fits in perfectly with the developing structure of the play. Alonso has just been told by Ariel that the storm had a purpose as an instrument of Destiny. Since at this moment remorse first appears in the play and the inner clearing begins, it is exactly right that the storm sounds should seem harmonious and so point forward to the events of the fourth and fifth acts. No use of metaphor in *The Tempest* reveals more clearly Shakespeare's exact sense of the movement of his drama, of the changing human relations and feelings he is presenting.

In building up his metaphorical design, Shakespeare prepares us for the moment in *The Tempest* when the major shift in dramatic relationships takes place. The moment comes in the speech in which Prospero describes the behavior of the King and the courtiers as they slowly return from madness to sanity. The first important step toward this climax, Alonso's acknowledgment of his guilt, was expressed through a metaphor combining both sea and musical changes. The next step, Ferdinand's release from his tempest-trials and from dreamlike

enchantment, is expressed through the masque, which is an
elaborate dramatization of metamorphosis, Ariel's 'meaner
fellows', 'the rabble', being now transformed into majestic
Olympian goddesses. Once again, familiar continuities appear,
and again they are transformed to fit a new occasion. 'Earth',
for example, is no longer 'barren place and fertile', but the earth
enriched by human cultivation and symbolized now by Ceres –
not by Caliban, who is 'nature resisting nurture'. Iris summons
this new Earth in the gorgeous speech beginning 'Ceres, most
bounteous lady, thy rich leas . . .', lines in which we hear a quite
new majesty of tone and movement. The couplet form sets the
dialogue apart from human speech, while the longer periods,
the added stresses, the phrasal balancings are especially appropriate to 'that large utterance of the early gods'. (Here is one of
many instances of how Shakespeare adapts his sound patterns to
his metaphorical and dramatic designs.) Prospero's visionary
speech that ends 'the revels' is not simply a concentration of
metaphor without reference to the dramatic development. It
announces the changes to come, it gives a rich expression of
their meaning, and it anticipates the dreamlike flux of the
psychological events of the last act.

If we now read Prospero's words in Act v, in which he
describes the great changes as they take place, we see many
references back to Shakespeare's metaphorical preparation for
this moment. We also realize that various lines of action and
various lines of analogy are converging almost simultaneously.
The speech opens with Prospero's farewell to his art, after
which he turns his thoughts to 'restoring the senses' of the
courtiers, whom Ariel has just gone to release:

A solemn air and the best comforter
To an unsettled fancy, cure thy brains,
Now useless, boil'd within thy skull! There stand,
For you are spell-stopp'd.
Holy Gonzalo, honorable man,
Mine eyes, even sociable to the show of thine,
Fall fellowly drops. The charm dissolves apace;
And as the morning steals upon the night,

Melting the darkness, so their rising senses
Begin to chase the ignorant fumes that mantle
Their clearer reason. O good Gonzalo!
My true preserver, and a loyal sir
To him thou follow'st, I will pay thy graces
Home, both in word and deed. Most cruelly
Didst thou, Alonso, use me and my daughter:
Thy brother was a furtherer in the act;
Thou'rt pinch'd for 't now, Sebastian. Flesh and blood,
You, brother mine, that entertain'd ambition,
Expell'd remorse and nature; who, with Sebastian –
Whose inward pinches therefore are most strong –
Would here have kill'd your king; I do forgive thee,
Unnatural though thou art! Their understanding
Begins to swell, and the approaching tide
Will shortly fill the reasonable shores
That now lie foul and muddy. Not one of them
That yet looks on me, or would know me. Ariel,
Fetch me the hat and rapier in my cell:    [*Exit* ARIEL.
I will discase me, and myself present,
As I was sometime Milan. Quickly, spirit;
Thou shalt ere long be free.

If this is a climactic moment, what changes in dramatic
relationships are taking place, what is happening dramatically?
The 'men of sin', like Ferdinand, have come to the end of the
trials which began with the storm and continued through
various 'distractions'. Now, as Prospero explains, they are
undergoing a moral as well as a mental regeneration, they are
'pinch'd' with remorse and are being forgiven. The twofold
regeneration is further dramatized in the speeches that follow:
'th' affliction of Alonso's mind amends', he resigns Prospero's
dukedom and 'entreats' him to pardon his 'wrongs'.

But these are the prose facts, the bare bones of the changes
in dramatic relationships. We cannot feel the peculiar quality
of what is taking place or grasp its meaning apart from the
metaphorical language through which it is being expressed.
And the expressions acquire their force and precision from the
whole metaphorical preparation we have been tracing. The

courtiers' senses are restored by 'an airy charm', by magic
similar to that which was worked by Ariel and his spirits. The
allusions to 'heavenly music' and 'a solemn air', in contrast to
the 'rough magic' that Prospero has abjured, remind us that these
changes will be musically harmonious, like the songs of Ariel,
and not noisy and confused like the storm sent to punish
these men and reveal their 'monstrous' guilt. Towards the end
of the speech, the imagery recalls the tempest metaphor, but it is
altered so as to express the mental and moral change that is
taking place. The return of understanding is like an approaching
tide that covers the evidence of a storm (both 'foul' and 'muddy'
have storm associations from earlier occurrences).

But the metaphor that best expresses this clearing is the one
for which the preparation has been most complete:

> The charm dissolves apace;
> And as the morning steals upon the night,
> Melting the darkness, so their rising senses
> Begin to chase the ignorant fumes that mantle
> Their clearer reason.

'Dissolving' and 'melting' and 'fumes' take us back at once to
the grand transformations of the masque speech, to the earlier
cloud transformations both serious and comic; and they take
us back further to the association of clouds with magical tempests, inner storms, and clearing weather. We read of the moral
and psychological transformations with a present sense of these
analogies. They are qualified for us as a dreamlike dissolution
of tempest clouds, as events in the 'insubstantial' region where
reality and unreality merge.

It is through such links that Shakespeare concentrates at this
climactic moment the fullest meaning of his key metaphor.
There is of course no separation in the reader's experience
between the dramatic fact and the metaphorical qualification.
The images that recur in Prospero's speech take us back to felt
qualities, but to felt qualities embedded in particular dramatic
contexts. 'Melting', for example, carries us to the spiritlike
dissolution of 'spirits . . . melted into air, into thin air'; but it

also reminds us of the masque pageantry and of Prospero's calming of Ferdinand's fears. We hear Prospero's soothing and mysterious tone in both the earlier and later uses of the word. The dramatic links and the analogical links are experienced at once, which is to say that metaphorical design and dramatic design are perfectly integrated.

We can now realize that metamorphosis is truly the key metaphor to the *drama,* and not the key metaphor to a detachable design of decorative analogies. Through the echoes in Prospero's speech of various lines of analogy, Shakespeare makes us feel each shift in dramatic relationships as a magical transformation, whether it is the courtiers' return to sanity, or Prospero's restoration to his dukedom, or Ariel's flight into perpetual summer. While all of the 'slaves' and 'prisoners' are being freed, and while all of the 'sovereigns' are being restored, the sense of magical change is never wholly lost. The union of drama and metaphor in *The Tempest* is nowhere more complete than in the last act of the play.

The larger meaning of Shakespeare's total design, which was anticipated in the cloud and dream metaphor of Prospero's visionary speech, is most clearly and fully expressed in these final transformations. In a world where everywhere may become something else, doubts naturally arise, and in the swift flow of change the confusion about what is and what is not becomes fairly acute. When Prospero 'discases' himself and appears as Duke of Milan, Gonzalo says with understandable caution:

> Whether this be,
> Or be not, I'll not swear

And Prospero answers:

> You do yet taste
> Some subtilties o' the isle, that will not let you
> Believe things certain.

Whereas in the earlier acts the characters had often accepted the unreal as real (spirits, shipwrecks, drownings, visions), they now find it difficult to accept the real as truly real. The play concludes with their acceptance of the unexpected change to reality. But for the spectator there remains the heightened sense of the 'thin partitions' that 'do divide' these states. The world that common sense regards as real, of order in nature and society and of sanity in the individual, is a shimmering transformation of disorder. 'We shall all be changed, in a moment, in the twinkling of an eye.' (This or something like it is as near as we can come to describing the total attitude conveyed by *The Tempest*.)

Thus *The Tempest* is, like Marvell's 'Garden', a Metaphysical poem of metamorphosis, though the meaning of change is quite different for the two writers. It is worth noting too that Shakespeare 'had Ovid in his eye', a fact that is obvious from the echoes of Golding's famous translation. There could be no better proof of Shakespeare's maturity than the contrast between the 'sweet witty' Ovidianism of 'Venus and Adonis' and the metaphorical design of *The Tempest*, which gives philosophic meaning to a drama of Ovidian metamorphosis. We remember 'a lily prison'd in a jail of snow' as an isolated 'beauty', but hardly as an apt symbol of the amorous relations of Venus and Adonis, or as symbolic of some larger meaning in their story. (Indeed a 'jail of snow' is rather inept for the fervid goddess of the poem.) 'Those were pearls that were his eyes' revives Ariel's sea music, Ferdinand's melancholy, and a world of fantasy and transshifting states of being. The increased concentration in meaning of the image from *The Tempest* is a sign of a growth in the command of language which is command of life for a poet. As Arnold said of Wordsworth, Shakespeare now 'deals with more of *life*' and 'he deals with *life*, as a whole, more powerfully'. His maturity and power appear in the variety of experience so perfectly harmonized through the imaginative design of *The Tempest*.

## NOTES

1. The music and tempest metaphors have been traced in a very different fashion and with quite different aims by G. Wilson Knight in *The Shakespearian Tempest* (1932). My analysis (which I had worked

out before reading Professor Knight's essay) has a more limited purpose: to show a continuity of analogy and a development of metaphor parallel to that of the other continuities I have traced.

2. The scene is full of expressions such as: *A tempestuous noise of thunder and lightning heard*, 'roarers', 'command these elements to silence', *A cry within*, 'A plague upon this howling! they are louder than the weather, or our office', 'insolent noisemaker', *A confused noise within*, etc.

*Frank Kermode*

# INTRODUCTION TO *THE TEMPEST* (1954)

## NATURE

1. *Natural Men.* The only undisputed source for any part of *The Tempest* is Montaigne's essay 'Of Cannibals'; there are unmistakeable traces of Florio's translation in the text. It has been argued, most recently by A. Lovejoy,[1] that Shakespeare intends a satirical comment upon Montaigne's apparent acceptance of the primitivistic view that a natural society, without the civilized accretions of law, custom, and other artificial restraints, would be a happy one.

Montaigne's essay as a whole is relevant to the play, and it would appear that critical comment has been hampered by a failure to understand this. The essay, like the play, is concerned with the general contrast between natural and artificial societies and men, though Montaigne assumes, in his 'naturalist' way, that the New World offers an example of naturally virtuous life uncorrupted by civilization, whereas Shakespeare obviously does not. Montaigne's general position is stated thus:

They [the Indians] are even savage, as we call those fruits wilde, which nature of her selfe ... hath produced: whereas indeed ... those which our selves have altered by our artificiall devices, and diverted from their common order, we should rather terme savage. In those are the true and most profitable vertues, and naturall properties most lively and vigorous, which in these we have bastardized, applying them to the pleasure of our corrupted taste. And if notwithstanding, in divers fruits of those countries that were never tilled, we shall finde, that in respect of ours they are most excellent, and as delicate unto our taste; there is no reason, art should gaine the point of honour of our great and puissant mother Nature ...[2]

This is a simple 'primitivism', and it uses the traditional horticultural analogy, equally available to those who held that the gardener's art corrupted and those who believed it improved the stock.[3] The dispute is central to *The Winter's Tale*, and is debated by Polixenes, who takes the view that Art acts to the improvement of Nature;* Perdita, who disagrees, is herself the product of careful breeding, of virtuous stock, which can no more be concealed by her rustic milieu than can the nobility of the salvage man and Pastorella in *The Faerie Queene*, book VI, or of the King's sons in *Cymbeline*.

These apparently antithetical views on the natural life to some extent controlled the reports of the voyagers upon whom Montaigne and Shakespeare both depend. They tended to describe the natives as purely virtuous or purely vicious. From Eden to Harcourt they repeat the theme of Montaigne's commonwealth; and yet they also speak of the brutality of the natives, of their treachery, ugliness, and infidelity. The *True Declaration* called them 'human beasts' and the experienced Captain John Smith 'perfidious, inhuman, all Savage'.[4] Literary men saw in the favourable reports a rich affirmation of a traditional theme of poetry; hence the enthusiasm of Drayton, the talk of 'sun-burnt Indians, That know no other wealth but Peace and Pleasure';[5] but a more central humanism expressed the other view, as did Sandys in his comparison of the Indians with the Cyclops, with its emphasis on the social achievement of Art:

... The *Cyclops* were a salvage people ... unsociable amongst themselves, & inhumane to strangers: And no marvaile, when lawlesse, and subject to no government, the bond of society; which gives to every man his owne, suppressing vice, and advancing vertue, the two maine columnes of a Commonwealth ... Man is a politicall and sociable creature: they therefore are to be numbred among beasts who renounce society, whereby they are destitute of lawes, the ordination of civility. Hence it ensues, that man, in creation the best, when averse to justice, is the worst of all creatures. Such *Polyphemus*; ... more salvage ... are the *West-Indians* at this day.[6]

* IV iv. Nature transcends Art when the statue of Hermione moves.

Both these attitudes to primitive man are deeply rooted in the
past; and both found some support in the behaviour of the
natives, which was, as a rule, very amiable at first – as Caliban's
was with Prospero and Stephano – but under provocation, and
sometimes spontaneously, treacherous later. Behind all these
observations are the two opposing versions of the natural; on
the one hand, that which man corrupts, and on the other that
which is defective, and must be mended by cultivation – the
less than human, which calls forth man's authoritative power to
correct and rule. This latter is the view which suits best the
conscience of the colonist. In practice everybody except a few
missionaries treated the savages literally as lesser breeds without
the law; sun- and devil-worshippers, often cannibals, they were
also in occupation of fertile territory, and it was at once virtuous
and expedient to convert and exploit them. In 1493, for example,
the Spanish Ambassador at the Papal Court announced the
discoveries of Columbus on behalf of his sovereigns; 'Christ',
he said, 'has placed under their rule the Fortunate Isles.'[7]
Prospero's assumption of his right to rule the island, 'to be the
lord on't', is the natural assumption of a European prince, as
Purchas on 'The Lawfulness of Discoveries' demonstrates.[8]
The natives were worth some trouble; although they had no
rational language, they did not lack certain mechanic arts, like
the building of dams for fish, upon which the European settler
long remained dependent. Many stratagems were devised to
expedite the subjection of the natives. Stephano's claim to be
descended from the moon was commonly made by unscrupulous
voyagers who seized the chance of turning to account the
polytheism of the Indians.[9] There is ample testimony to the
corrupting effect upon natives of contact with dissolute
Europeans – Christian savages sent to convert heathen savages,
as Fuller put it.[10] Ronsard seems to have been the first to voice
this complaint,[11] and of course it is another element in the
situation which interested both Montaigne and Shakespeare.
Reports of such barbarism would tend to reinforce the nostalgic
primitivism of the literary men, and lead them once more to
reflect upon an ancient theme:

> not all
> That beare the name of men . . .
> . . . Are for to be accounted men: but such as under awe
> Of reasons rule continually doo live in vertues law;
> And that the rest doo differ nought from beasts, but
>                 rather bee
> Much woorse than beasts, bicause they do abace theyr
>                 owne degree.[13]

Gonzalo's half-serious talk about his commonwealth serves
to introduce into the play the theme of the natural life in a
guise more appropriate to pastoral poetry which takes a 'soft'
view of Nature. It is over-simple to assume that this perennial
theme is destroyed by the cheap jeers of Antonio and Sebastian.
There are points in the play at which Shakespeare uses Caliban
to indicate how much baser the corruption of the civilized can
be than the bestiality of the natural, and in these places he is
using his natural man as a criterion of civilized corruption, as
Montaigne had done. At the end of the play we learn Gonzalo's
stature; he is not only the good-natured calm old man of the
wreck, the cheerful courtier of the second act, and the pure
soul of the third; he pronounces the benediction, and we see
that he was all the time as right as it was human to be, even
when to the common sense of the corrupt he was transparently
wrong – wrong about the location of Tunis, wrong about the
commonwealth, wrong about the survival of Ferdinand. And
we see that Nature is not, in *The Tempest,* defined with the
single-minded clarity of a philosophic proposition.[13] Shakespeare's treatment of the theme has what all his mature poetry
has, a richly analytical approach to ideas, which never reaches
after a naked opinion of true or false.

The poetic definition of Nature in the play is achieved largely
by a series of antitheses with Caliban constantly recurring as
one term. He represents the natural man. This figure is not, as
in pastoral generally, a virtuous shepherd, but a salvage and
deformed slave.

II. *A Salvage and Deformed Slave.* Caliban's name is usually
regarded as a development of some form of the word 'Carib',

meaning a savage inhabitant of the New World; 'cannibal' derives from this, and 'Caliban' is possibly a simple anagram of that word.[14] But though he is thus connected with the Indian savage, he is also associated, as were the uncivilized inhabitants of the Indies, with the wild or salvage man of Europe, formerly the most familiar image of mankind without the ordination of civility.

The origins of this type are obscure,[15] but the wild man was a familiar figure in painting, heraldry, pageant, and drama.[16] Several varieties are distinguished; the kind which survived in the drama was a satyr-type, like Bremo in the old play *Mucedorus*, which was revived by Shakespeare's company in 1610. Bremo abducts a virgin; unchastity was a conventional attribute of salvage men, which Shakespeare skilfully exploits. These creatures were believed to occupy an 'intermediate position in the moral scale, below man, just as the angels were above him . . . they are the link between . . . the settled and the wild, the moral and the unmoral'.[17] The term 'salvage', used of Caliban in the Folio 'Names of the Actors', has thus a restricted meaning, as it has in Spenser. Caliban is a salvage man, and the West Indians were salvage men of a topical kind; hence the Indian element in this natural man.

The next thing the 'Names of the Actors' says about Caliban is that he is deformed. He is what Thersites called Ajax, 'a very land-fish, languageless, a monster'.[18] There were reports from the Indies of curious specimens, and these reports may have influenced some of the things that are said about Caliban in the play;[19] but his deformity is visualized in terms of Old World monsters. Caliban's birth, as Prospero insists, was inhuman; he was 'a born devil', 'got by the devil himself upon thy wicked dam'. He was the product of sexual union between a witch and an incubus, and this would account for his deformity, whether the devil-lover was Setebos (all pagan gods were classified as devils) or, as W. C. Curry infers, some aquatic demon.[20]

Caliban's mother, though associated with reports of devil-worship and witchcraft in the New World, belongs to the Old. She is a powerful witch, deliberately endowed with many of

the qualities of classical witches,[21] but also possessing a clearly
defined place in the contemporary demonological scheme. She
is a practitioner of 'natural' magic, a goetist who exploited the
universal sympathies, but whose power is limited by the fact
that she could command, as a rule, only devils and the lowest
orders of spirits. Prospero, on the other hand, is a theurgist,
whose Art is to achieve supremacy over the natural world by
holy magic. The Neo-Platonic mage studies the harmonic
relationship of the elementary, celestial, and intellectual worlds,[21]
and conceives it

no way irrational that it should be possible for us to ascend by the
same degrees through each World to the same very original
world itself, the Maker of all things, and First Cause, from
whence all things are, and proceed . . .[24]

His object is to 'walk to the skie', as Vaughan put it, before
death, by ascending through the created worlds to the condition
of the angels. His Art is supernatural; the spirits he commands
are the dæmons of Neo-Platonism, the criterion of whose
goodness is not the Christian one of adherence to, or defection
from, God, but of immateriality or submersion in matter. He
deals with spirits high in the scale of goodness, and if lesser
spirits ('weak masters') are required, the superior dæmon
controls them on his behalf. He is *divinorum cultor & interpres,*
a studious observer and expounder of divine things', and his
Art is 'the absolute perfection of Natural Philosophy'.[24] Natura
Philosophy includes the arts of astrology, alchemy, and ceremonial magic, to all of which Prospero alludes.[25]

We shall return to the special powers and the learning of
the mage Prospero; the point here is that his Art,* being the
Art of supernatural virtue which belongs to the redeemed
world of civility and learning, is the antithesis of the black
magic of Sycorax.[26] Caliban's deformity is the result of evil
natural magic, and it stands as a natural criterion by which we
measure the world of Art, represented by Prospero's divine

* Always spelled with the capital in the Folio text. This is a recognized method of indicating that it is a technical usage.

magic and the supernaturally sanctioned beauty of Miranda and Ferdinand.

The last thing the 'Names of the Actors' says about Caliban is that he is a slave. We have seen the readiness with which the white man took charge of the New World; Prospero arrived on his island 'to be the lord on 't'. If Aristotle was right in arguing that 'men . . . who are as much inferior to others as the body is to the soul . . . are slaves by nature, and it is advantageous for them always to be under government', and that 'to find our governor we should . . . examine into a man who is most perfectly formed in soul and body . . . for in the depraved and vicious the body seems to rule rather than the soul, on account of their being corrupt and contrary to nature',[27] then the black and mutilated cannibal must be the natural slave of the European gentleman, and, *a fortiori,* the salvage and deformed Caliban of the learned Prospero.

Caliban is, therefore, accurately described in the Folio 'Names of the Actors'. His origins and character are natural in the sense that they do not partake of grace, civility, and art; he is ugly in body, associated with an evil natural magic, and unqualified for rule or nurture. He exists at the simplest level of sensual pain and pleasure, fit for lechery because love is beyond his nature, and a natural slave of demons. He hears music with pleasure, as music can appeal to the beast who lacks reason;[28] and indeed he resembles Aristotle's bestial man. He is a measure of the incredible superiority of the world of Art, but also a measure of its corruption. For the courtiers and their servants include the incontinent Stephano and the malicious Antonio. Caliban scorns the infirmity of purpose exhibited by the first, and knows better than Antonio that it is imprudent to resist grace, for which, he says, he will henceforth seek. Unlike the incontinent man, whose appetites subdue his will, and the malicious man, whose will is perverted to evils ends, 'the bestial man has no sense of right and wrong, and therefore sees no difference between good and evil. His state is less guilty but more hopeless than those of incontinence and malice, since he cannot be improved'.[29] Men can abase their degree below the bestial; and there is possibly a hint, for which there is no support in Aristotle, that the bestial Caliban gains a new spiritual dimension from his glimpse of the 'brave spirits'. Whether or no this is true, he is an extraordinarily powerful and comprehensive type of Nature; an inverted pastoral hero, against whom civility and the Art which improves Nature may be measured.

## ART

1. *Buds of Nobler Race*. The civilized castaways of *The Tempest* are brought into close contact with a representative of Nature uncontrolled by Art. How do they differ from Caliban, and how is this difference expressed?

It is useful to compare Spenser's treatment of two salvage men in *The Faerie Queene*.[30] The one who carries off Amoret in Book IV is an unamiable personification of greedy lust – 'For he liv'd all on ravin and on rape' (IV vii 5). The full description leaves no doubt that this is the wild man of the entertainments, and that his are the 'natural' activities of lust and cannibalism. The salvage man who treats Serena so gently in the sixth book is quite different; though he cannot speak he shows a tenderness which is, apparently, against his nature. The reason is, that 'he was borne of noble blood' (VI v 2); we do not hear how he came to be languageless and salvage, but we know he owes his gentleness to his gentle birth.

> O what an easie thing is to descry
> The gentle bloud, how ever it be wrapt
> In sad misfortunes foule deformity
> And wretched sorrowes, which have often hapt!
> For howsoever it may grow mis-shapt,
> Like this wyld man being undisciplynd,
> That to all virtue it may seeme unapt,
> Yet will it shew some sparkes of gentle mynd,
> And at the last breake forth in his owne proper kynd.
>
> (VI v 1)

That gentle birth predisposed a man to virtue, even if it was not absolutely necessary to virtue, was part of the lore of

courtesy. *Fortes creantur fortibus* . . . – argument as to the mode
of inheriting, and of cultivating, *nobilitas*, runs through the
history of moral philosophy from Aristotle through Dante to
the Renaissance. It is true that, with evidence to the contrary
continually before their eyes, philosophers could not uniformly
maintain that where there was high birth there was virtue,
taking nobility to mean the *non vile*, 'the perfection of its own
nature in each thing';[31] and in Italy there was a growing tendency
to judge of nobility by actual manners and merit, rather than
by family. As early as the *Convito* the conditions of its development are described as much more complex than the racial
theory of its provenance allows,[32] but more commonplace
thought constantly recurs to the biological analogy; *est in
juvencis, est in equis, patrum Virtus* – as Polixenes conceived
that there were 'buds of nobler race'.

The question is debated in the first book of Castiglione's
*Courtier* by Canossa and Pallavicino.[33] The arguments are
conventional, but they serve to illustrate the theory of natural
nobility which animates Spenser's portrait of the salvage man.
Nature makes the work of greatness easier, and the penalties
of failure heavier, for the high-born; 'because nature in every
thing hath deeply sowed that privie seed, which giveth a
certaine force and propertie of her beginning, unto whatsoever
springeth of it, and maketh it like unto herselfe. As we see by
example . . . in trees, whose slippes and grafts alwaies for the
most part are like unto the stock of the tree they cam from: and
if at any time they grow out of kinde, the fault is in the
husbandman';[34] which is to say, in the individual nobleman – a
fault of nurture, not of nature. Thus Canossa, though not to
the satisfaction of Pallavicino, accounts also for the Antonios of
the world. He allows an important place to education, believing,
with Prospero and against Socrates, that pedagogues could be
found capable of nursing the seed:[35]

Therefore even as in the other artes, so also in the vertues, it
is behofefull to have a teacher, that with lessons and good
exhortations may stirre up and quicken in us those moral vertues,
whereof wee have the seede inclosed and buried in the soule.[36]

If the seed is not there (and here Prospero's experience confirms him) the husbandman loses his labour, and brings forth only 'the briers and darnell of appetites' which he had desired to restrain. Canossa omits all the other factors which might be brought into consideration – 'the complex nature of the seed', 'the disposition of the dominant Heaven' – which Dante two centuries before had attempted to calculate, and takes account only of nature and of nurture. This leaves an opening for Pallavicino's reply, and Castiglione had, of course, to arrange matters to suit his dialectic scheme. But for Spenser moral virtues inhabit the simpler, the ideal, world of romance, and his salvage man differs from his kind in that he has the seèd implanted by nature, though not husbanded by nurture.

There is a striking version of the theory by Edward Phillips, the nephew of Milton. Phillips, in a passage so much above his usual manner that critics have seen in it the hand of his uncle, identifies two forces which distinguish the better part of mankind from the more brutish:

... the first is that *Melior natura* which the Poet speaks of, with which whoever is amply indued, take that Man from his Infancy, throw him into the Desarts of *Arabia*, there let him converse some years with Tygers and Leopards, and at last bring him where civil society & conversation abides, and ye shall see how on a sudden, the scales and dross of his barbarity purging off by degrees, he will start up a Prince or Legislator, or some such illustrious Person: the other is that noble thing call'd *Education*, this is, that Harp of *Orpheus*, that lute of *Amphion*, so elegantly figur'd by the Poets to have wrought such Miracles among irrational and insensible Creatures, which raiseth beauty even out of deformity, order and regularity out of Chaos and confusion, and which, if throughly and rightly prosecuted, would be able to civilize the most savage natures, & root out barbarism and ignorance from off the face of the Earth: those who have either of these qualifications singly may justly be term'd *Men*; those who have both united in a happy conjunction, *more* than *Men*; those who have neither of them in any competent measure ... *less* than *Men* ... [37]

Phillips here takes the view expressed by Dante, Pallavicino, and many others, that the want of nature can be partially supplied by Education, and in this respect differs from those who, like Canossa and, as we shall see, the romance-writers, held more rigidly to the notion of the seed without which all husbandry is not only wasted but even harmful, since it promotes the growth of undesirable weed-like qualities. The unknown poet's *melior natura* provides an excellent label for all the ideas associated with 'buds of nobler race', and his 'Education' enables us to see Prospero's 'nurture' in its proper context. Miranda, as Prospero early informs us, is endowed not only with the *melior natura*, but with education:

> here
> Have I, thy schoolmaster, made thee more profit
> Than other princess' can, that have more time
> For vainer hours, and tutors not so careful.
>
> (1 ii 171–4)

She has both these qualities of nobility 'united in a happy conjunction'. Caliban has neither, and there is in the structure of the play a carefully prepared parallel between the two characters to illustrate this point; Caliban's education was not only useless – on *his* nature, which is nature *tout court*, nurture would never stick – but harmful. He can only abuse the gift of speech; and by cultivating him Prospero brings forth in him 'the briers and darnell of appetites' – lust for Miranda, discontent at his inferior position, ambition, intemperance of all kinds, including a disposition to enslave himself to the bottle of Stephano. And there is in his 'vile race' that 'which *good* natures Could not abide to be with' (1 ii 361–2, my italics); in other words there is a repugnance between the raw, unreclaimed nature which he represents, and the courtier-stock with which he has to deal, endowed as it is with grace, and nurtured in refinement through the centuries, in the world of Art.[38]

11. *Prospero's Art*. At the risk of introducing 'distincts' where there is no 'division' it may be said that Prospero's Art has two functions in *The Tempest*. The first is simple; as a mage he exercises the supernatural powers of the holy adept. His Art

is here the disciplined exercise of virtuous knowledge, a 'translation of merit into power',[39] the achievement of 'an intellect pure and conjoined with the powers of the gods, without which we shall never happily ascend to the scrutiny of secret things, and to the power of wonderfull workings'.[40] This Art is contrasted with the natural power of Sycorax to exploit for evil purposes the universal sympathies (see above, pp. 180–1). It is a technique for liberating the soul from the passions, from nature; the practical application of a discipline of which the primary requirements are learning and temperance, and of which the mode is contemplation. When Prospero achieves this necessary control over himself and nature he achieves his ends (reflected in the restoration of harmony at the human and political levels) and has no more need of the instrument, 'rough magic'.[41]

The second function is symbolic. Prospero's Art controls Nature; it requires of the artist virtue and temperance if his experiment is to succeed; and it thus stands for the world of the better natures and its qualities. This is the world which is closed to Caliban (and Comus); the world of mind and the possibilities of liberating the soul, not the world of sense, whether that be represented as coarsely natural or charmingly voluptuous.[42] Art is not only a beneficent magic in contrast to an evil one; it is the ordination of civility, the control of appetite, the transformation of nature by breeding and learning; it is even, in a sense, the means of Grace.

Prospero is, therefore, the representative of Art, as Caliban is of Nature. As a mage he controls nature; as a prince he conquers the passions which had excluded him from his kingdom and overthrown law; as a scholar he repairs his loss of Eden; as a man he learns to temper his passions, an achievement essential to success in any of the other activities.

Prospero describes his efforts to control his own passion in v i 25–7 –

> Though with their high wrongs I am struck to th' quick,
> Yet with my nobler reason 'gainst my fury
> Do I take part.

In an age when 'natural' conduct was fashionably associated with sexual promiscuity, chastity alone could stand as the chief function of temperance, and there is considerable emphasis on this particular restraint in *The Tempest*. The practice of good magic required it;[43] but in this it is again merely the practical application of civility. Prospero twice, and Juno again, warn Ferdinand of the absolute necessity for it, and Ferdinand's ability to make pure beauty 'abate the ardour of his liver'[44] is in the strongest possible contrast to Caliban's straightforward natural lust for it. The unchaste designs of Stephano arouse Prospero's anger also; it is as if he were conducting, with magically purified book and rod,[45] the kind of experiment which depended for its success on the absolute purity of all concerned; and indeed, in so far as his aims were a dynastic marriage and the regeneration of the noble, this was so.

This is characteristic of the way in which the magic of Prospero translates into more general terms. The self-discipline of the magician is the self-discipline of the prince. It was the object of the good ruler to make his people good by his own efforts; and that he might do so it was considered necessary for him to acquire learning, and to rid himself 'of those troublous affections that untemperate mindes feele'.[50] The personal requirements of mage and prince are the same, and Prospero labours to regain a worldly as well as a heavenly power. Like James I in the flattering description, he 'standeth invested with that triplicitie which in great veneration was ascribed to the ancient *Hermes*, the power and fortune of a *King*, the knowledge and illumination of a Priest, and the Learning and universalitie of a Philosopher'.[47]

Learning is a major theme in the play; we learn that Miranda is capable of it and Caliban not, and why this should be so; but we are also given a plan of the place of learning in the dispositions of providence. Prospero, like Adam, fell from his kingdom by an inordinate thirst for knowledge; but learning is a great aid to virtue, the road by which we may love and imitate God, and 'repair the ruins of our first parents',[48] and by its means he is enabled to return. The solicitude which accompanied

Adam and Eve when 'the world was all before them' went also
with Prospero and Miranda when they set out in their 'rotten
carcass of a butt'.

> By foul play, as thou say'st, were we heav'd thence,
> But blessedly holp hither.                    (I ii 62–3)

They came ashore 'by Providence divine'; and Gonzalo leaves
us in no doubt that Prospero's fault, like Adam's, was a happy
one:

> Was Milan thrust from Milan, that his issue
> Should become kings of Naples? O rejoice
> Beyond a common joy! . . .                    (v i 205–7)

He had achieved the great object of Learning, and regained a
richer heritage.[49] But he is not learned in only this rather
abstract sense; he is the learned prince. Like Boethius, he had
been a natural philosopher, and had learnt from Philosophy
that 'to hate the wicked were against reason'. He clearly shared
the view that 'no wise man had rather live in banishment, poverty,
and ignominy, than prosper in his own country . . . For in this
manner is the office of wisdom performed with more credit
and renown, where the governors' happiness is participated by
the people about them.' And Philosophy, though ambiguously,
taught both Boethius and Prospero 'the way by which thou
mayest return to thy country'.[50]

There is nothing remarkable about Prospero's ambition to
regain his own kingdom and strengthen his house by a royal
marriage. To be studious and contemplative, but also to be
able to translate knowledge into power in the active life, was
the object of his discipline; the Renaissance venerated Scipio
for his demonstration of this truth, and Marvell's Horatian
Ode speaks of Cromwell in the same terms.

> The chiefe Use then in man of that he knowes,
> Is his paines taking for the good of all . . .
> Yet *Some seeke knowledge, merely but to know,*
> And idle Curiositie that is . . .[51]

Prospero is not at all paradoxical in presenting himself at the climax as he was 'sometime Milan'. Yet he does not intend merely to look after his worldly affairs; every third thought is to be his grave. 'The end of the active or doing life ought to be the beholding; as of war, peace, and as of paines, rest.'[52] The active and contemplative lives are complementary.

In all respects, then, Prospero expresses the qualities of the world of Art, of the *non vile*. These qualities become evident in the organized contrasts between his world and the world of the vile; between the worlds of Art and Nature . . .

## NOTES

1. *Essays in the History of Ideas* (1948) p. 238. Lovejoy calls Shakespeare's source 'the locus classicus of primitivism in modern literature'. See also M. T. Hodgen, 'Montaigne and Shakespeare again', in *Huntington Library Quarterly*, XVI (1952–3) 23–42.

2. *Montaigne's Essays*, transl. John Florio (1892 ed.) I 219.

3. For the early history of the idea, see A. Lovejoy and G. Boas, *Primitivism in Antiquity* (1935); Democritus alludes to it (ibid. pp. 207–8) and it is commonplace in Renaissance literary criticism (e.g., *The Arte of English Poesie*, ed. Willcock and Walker (1936) p. 304 – the gardener does what 'nature of her selfe would never have done: as to make the single gillifloure double'). One view, that Art is an agent of Nature, and necessary to the development of created nature – the view of Polixenes – is set over against the other, that Art (meaning anything that interferes with Nature) can only corrupt, which is the view of Perdita, of the Mower in Marvell's 'Mower against Gardens' and of Montaigne in this essay.

4. R. R. Cawley, *The Voyagers and Elizabethan Drama* (1938) pp. 346 ff.

5. Beaumont and Fletcher, *Four Plays in One* (Cambridge, 1905–12) X 360.

6. George Sandys, *Ovids Metamorphoses Englished* (1632) p. 477.

7. G. Chinard, *L'Exotisme américain dans la littérature française au XVIe siècle* (1911) p. 4.

8. Samuel Purchas, *Purchas his Pilgrimes* (1625) I (1906 ed.).

9. Cawley, *PMLA* XLI 714 ff.

10. Cawley, *Voyagers*, p. 193. See also Jonson's *Staple of News*, in *Works*, ed. Herford and Simpson, V 245.

11. Chinard, op. cit. p. 118.

12. Arthur Golding, *The XV Bookes of P. Ovidius Naso, entytuled Metamorphosis* (1567), *Epistle,* lines 55–62.

13. E. C. Knowlton in his 'Nature and Shakespeare' (*PMLA* LI (1936) 719 ff.), argues that Shakespeare attributes to Perdita in *The Winter's Tale* 'a kind of rightness', but that his own view was probably that of Polixenes.

14. E. K. Chambers favours the derivation from *cauliban,* a Romany word meaning 'blackness' (*William Shakespeare* (1930) I 494). There are also the Chalybeates, savage cannibals of the ancient world, whom Virgil mentions twice, and whom Pliny situates near the Coraxi.

15. It is discussed by R. Withington, *English Pageantry* (1918) I 72 ff., and by E. Welsford, *The Court Masque* (1927) p. 6. Possibly the practice of abandoning children in forests had something to do with it; some of the survivors, perhaps subnormal to begin with, might have led a bestial life in the woods. Linnaeus classified such survivors as a distinct species, *homo ferus.* Conceivably the Γοριλλα observed by Hanno the Carthaginian has some part in the tradition.

16. Pictorially the wodehouse, or wodewose, flourished in the thirteenth and fourteenth centuries (R. van Marle, *Iconographie de l'Art Profane* (1931) I 183–91). The earliest recorded dramatic specimen is in a Paduan entertainment of 1208 – *magnus Ludus de quodam homine salvatico* (P. Neri, in *Giornale Storico della Letteratura Italiana,* I ix 49; cited by L. Edwards, 'The Historical and Legendary Background of the Wodehouse and Peacock Feast Motif in the Walsokne and Braunche Brasses', in *Monumental Brass Society Transactions,* VIII part vii 300–11). Then they occur with great frequency. In England, there is a wild man in the Christmas entertainment of Edward III in 1347, and they are common in Tudor entertainments, such as the progresses and receptions of Elizabeth. (See J. Nichol, *Royal Progresses* (1823) *passim.*)

17. L. Edwards, loc. cit. This idea persisted into the eighteenth century; Lovejoy quotes a poem which includes the lines, 'De l'homme aux animaux rapprochant la distance, Voyez l'Homme des Bois lier leur existence' (*The Great Chain of Being* (1936) p. 236).

18. *Troilus and Cressida* III iii 265.

19. The closest resemblance is in a beast reported by dos Sanctos in 1597, which had the 'eares of a Dog, armes like a Man without haire, and at the elbows great Finnes like a fish', which the native assistants had believed to be 'the sonne of the Devill'. (Quoted by J. E. Hankins, 'Caliban the Bestial Man', in *PMLA* LXII (1947) 794.)

20. W. C. Curry, *Shakespeare's Philosophical Patterns* (1936) pp. 148–55.

21. Some of the classical *loci* are: Virgil, *Eclogue* VIII, Horace,

*Epode* v, Lucan, *Pharsalia*, 1; Ovid, *Met.* VII 199–207; Seneca, *Medea*, 755–66. These witches had a share in the development of the witches of Renaissance literature. Lyly's *Endimion* has a witch, Dipsa, who says she can 'darken the Sunne by my skil, and remoove the Moone out of her course'. This traditional power is mentioned in the Faust books, and by Reginald Scot.

22. For detailed discussion of these topics, see R. H. West's invaluable *The Invisible World* (1939), the fullest treatment of the supernatural in Elizabethan drama; and Hardin Craig, *The Enchanted Glass* (1936) chap. 1.

23. Cornelius Agrippa, *Occult Philosophy*, transl. J. F. (1651) I i.

24. Agrippa, op. cit. III xl.

25. e.g. I ii 181–4; v i 1, and the many allusions to ceremonial magic – book, rod, cloak of invisibility, which are the instruments of the 'rougher magic' which the mage at a later stage renounces, as Prospero does before confronting Alonso.

26. This highly important distinction is lost if Prospero is called a black magician, as he often is. The arguments against this view are conclusive but there is no space for them here; they can be deduced from the works of West and Curry. It has been objected that Shakespeare could not have presented at the Court of James I a play openly alluding to a system of magic to which the King was notoriously opposed. But James was well accustomed to such treatment; he himself was often presented as a beneficent magician, and he took pleasure in Jonson's *Masque of Queens*, a brilliant iceberg whose hidden part is a craggy mass of occult learning. He no more took exception to this than he did to the presentation of pagan gods, whom he theoretically regarded as devils, because he understood the equation between a fiction of beneficent magic and the sacred power he himself professed as an actual king.

27. *Politics*, 1254 a–b.

28. Cf. Horace, *De Arte Poetica*, lines 391–2: Silvestres homines sacer interpresque deorum / caedibus et victu foedo deterruit Orpheus.

29. See the valuable essay of J. E. Hankins in *PMLA* LXII.

30. The Nature–Art Debate is a leading motive in Spenser; its most complete study is that of R. H. Pierce in *Journal of English and Germanic Philology*, XLIV. A. Thaler (*Shakespeare Association Bulletin*, x) compares with Caliban the son of Hag (*The Faerie Queene* III vii) who lusts after Florimell. J. A. S. McPeek (*Philological Quarterly*, XXV) adds that the beast sent after Florimell is freckled and doglike.

31. *Il Convito. The Banquet* of Dante Alighieri, trans. E. P. Sayer (1887) p. 226. See the curtain-lecture in Chaucer's *Wife of Bath's Tale*.

32. Ibid., see e.g. p. 241. Dante devotes the fourth and last extant

section of the work to this subject. In the earlier *De Monarchia* he allowed more force to heredity. For a short survey of the changing theory see Burckhardt, *The Civilization of the Renaissance in Italy* (1944 English ed.) pp. 217 ff.

33. The same theme, with many variations, is regularly treated in later works on courtesy and the education of princes and nobles. See e.g. *ΗΡΩ-ΠΑΙΔΕΙΑ*, or *The Institution of a Young Noble Man*, by James Cleland (1607), esp IV 7. Peacham (*Compleat Gentleman*, 1622 +) defines nobility as 'the Honour of blood', 'it selfe essential and absolute'. He treats also of the loss of it through vice, and of the irrepressible appearance of nobility in children (ed. Gordon (1906) pp. 2, 3, 9, 14).

34. *The Courtier* (1528), trans. Hoby (1561), 1928 ed. (Everyman) p. 31.

35. This expression occurs so frequently in discussions of this sort that it will perhaps be useful to remind the reader that it had far more force than the modern idea of analogy would allow it, and also that the word 'seed' was also used as symbolizing the element of divine law implanted at birth in the human breast. This connotation is present in *Convito*, IV.

36. Castiglione, *The Courtier*.

37. Preface to *Theatrum Poetarum* (1675) in *Critical Essays of the Seventeenth Century*, ed. J. E. Spingarn (1908) III 257. See also Peacham, op. cit., where learning is treated as an essential adjunct to birth – the gentleman is to be not merely εὐγενής but also πολυμαθής. De la Primaudaye, *Academie Francoise* (1585 +), a widely read book, has a chapter on the subject (XVI) called *De la nature et de la Nourriture*. Bacon uses the phrase *melior natura* in 'Of Atheism'.

38. 'Nature' and its compounds are used in a wide range of meanings in *The Tempest*, as they always are in literature. I have shown how it is used in connexion with Caliban (his 'vile race' opposed to the race *non vile* – the stock etymology of *nobile*) and there is also some play on the idea that this nature is 'monstrous' – i.e. un-natural – a paradox which involves the concept of another and higher nature. 'Lord, that a monster should be such a natural' (III ii 30–1) where the pun depends upon the colloquial 'natural' ( = 'idiot'). Miranda puts the paradox the other way round when she sees Ferdinand, and thinks he is a spirit, 'For nothing natural I ever saw so *noble*' (I ii 421–2), where the *Melior natura* is contrasted with the *vile* she recognized in Caliban. There is here of course a strong admixture of 'natural' meaning 'not supernatural'. This meaning recurs in the last Act, when Alonso, hearing that the ship is safe, says, 'These are not natural events' (V i 227) where we think at once that they are due to Prospero's Art. In V i 157 'natural breath' is of course simply 'human'

breath, though the reading 'These words/Are natural breath' (*The Tempest*, ed. Sir Arthur Quiller-Couch and J. D. Wilson (New Shakespeare Series: 1921)) modifies it slightly. There are three other meanings (though it should be pointed out that this schematization inevitably entails over-simplification): Antonio, who is of noble race, and should have the better nature, exhibits 'an evil nature' (I ii 93) in his ambition. This is a disposition to do evil which can inhere in good stock for reasons given below. He is called 'unnatural' (v i 79) by Prospero as he forgives him; the primary meaning here is 'un-fraternal, neglecting the ties of blood', but there is also the sense of 'degenerate, a betrayer of his race and of the better nature'. See also v i 78–9. Finally, *natura naturans* occurs in a form we have learned to recognize, in Gonzalo's 'all things in common nature should produce' and 'nature should bring forth of it own kind . . .' (i.e. without culture) II i 155, 158–9.

39. West, *The Invisible World*, pp. 41–5.

40. Agrippa, op. cit. III, iii.

41. *The Tempest*, severe and refined as it is, is still a development of folk-tales in which magicians and their agents have not a precise status in academic demonology. Hence Prospero shows certain unschematic resemblances to the simple magicians of Italian popular comedy and Ayrer's *Die Schöne Sidea*, and Ariel is not the unalloyed Platonic dæmon of *Comus*. Nice distinctions are, however, impossible here.

42. Despite the attention given to verbal echoes of *The Tempest* in *Comus*, the deep indebtedness of Milton to the play has not been understood. Shakespeare is of course less formally allegorical, but the play is almost as important to Milton as *The Faerie Queene*.

43. Cf. Jonson's comic use of this law in *The Alchemist*.

44. IV i 56. C. Leech, in his *Shakespeare's Tragedies* (1950), finds the repetition of Prospero's warning 'impertinent' and thinks it 'cannot be understood other than pathologically'; this is the starting-point, as I understand it, of his demonstration that '*The Tempest* gave the fullest and most ordered expression of the Puritan impulse in Shakespeare'.

45. The book, so highly valued by Prospero and Caliban, as well as the rod, occur in all demonology, popular and learned; they were required to be of virginal purity.

46. Castiglione, *The Courtier*, p. 277.

47. Cleland, *The Institution of a Young Man* (1612) II i.

48. Milton, *Of Education*, in *Prose Works*, ed. Hughes, p. 31.

49. For a somewhat similar reading, though different in detail, see N. Coghill, 'The Basis of Shakespearian Comedy', *Essays and Studies* (1950) pp. 1–28.

50. The *Consolation of Philosophy*, IV Prose 5, V Prose 1 (Loeb ed. pp. 335, 365).

51. Fulke Greville, *A Treatie of Humane Learning* (1603–5) st. 144–5; ed. G. Bullough (1938) I 190.

52. Castiglione, op. cit. p. 280. See also Bacon, *Advancement of Learning* (World's Classics ed.) pp. 11–12, 15–16, 42. The theme is a humanist commonplace.

*John P. Cutts*

## MUSIC AND THE SUPERNATURAL IN *THE TEMPEST* (1958)

THE music of the spheres is not referred to specifically as such in *The Tempest,* but the whole play is conceived as taking part on an island that resounds continually to music in the air, which is, I believe, equivalent to music of the spheres. The island governed by the benevolent power of Prospero is in itself a type of the golden-age island, where no ill is ultimately allowed, where strife and friction are allayed and everything is to be wrapped in a serene air of celestial harmony.* The terrible discord of the storm with its tempestuous noise of thunder and its fearful flash of lightning at the very beginning of the play is indicative of the discord that has been perpetrated in the microcosmos. Prospero and Miranda have been deposed from their lawful state and the deposers are now brought to Prospero's island. By music's power he is able to resolve his problems one by one and harmony is restored.

First Ferdinand is to be secured as a husband for Miranda, so that the succession to the Dukedom of Milan from which he had been deposed by his brother may be secured to Prospero again by the marriage of his opponent's son and his daughter. Ferdinand is accordingly shipwrecked on a different part of the island from his father Alonso, Duke of Naples, who had assisted Prospero's brother Antonio in effecting Prospero's deposition. Ferdinand is immediately led by music:

* It is the lawful musical counterpart of the Sirens. They promised freedom from strife in the general lure of the pleasures of the golden age, but their fundamental aim was lust and destruction. Prospero's island magic promises freedom from strife and the benefits of peace and content, but it is basically aimed at restoring Prospero to his rightful position.

*Enter Ferdinand & Ariel, inuisible playing & singing.*

*Ariel.* Song. *Come vnto these yellow sands,*
   *and then take hands:*
   *Curtsied when you haue, and kist*
   *the wild waues whist:*
   *Foote it featly heere, and there, and sweete Sprights*
   *beare the burthen.*  Burthen dispersedly.
   *Harke, harke, bowgh wawgh: the watch-Dogges*
   *barke, bowgh-wawgh.*
*Ar.*  *Harke, hark, I heare, the straine of strutting*
   *Chanticlere cry cockadidle-dowe.*[1] (Sig.A3)

It is not impossible to see in this song a counterpart of the
Sirens' invitation to the wearied mariners to 'Steer hither your
winged pines'.[2] Ariel who sings the song has promised, as they
did, peace and calm after the storm. The line 'the wild waues
whist' has caused editors undue trouble. Of course, as Kermode,
the most recent editor, points out, it is Ariel's music that has
allayed the tempest, but the deeper significance of the return to
order and harmony seems to have escaped attention. It seems to
me that the legend of Circe and her island with the Sirens is
being used as the basis of the plot's construction here, and that
its evil aspect has been replaced by the benevolent power of
Prospero. The sensual Sirens have given place to the 'ayrie
spirit', the celestial spirit, Ariel, working obedient to the divine
will as represented by Prospero. The island has all the magical
charm of Circe's island: strangers from afar have been lured to
it and Prospero provides a magical banquet and charms his
visitors by music's powers, so that they are no longer able to
obey their own reasoning-powers.

Ferdinand's comments on hearing the invitation song indicate
that the music which allayed the storm is now drawing him
almost against his will farther into the island by its power:

*Fer.* Where shold this Musick be? I' th aire, or th' earth?
  It sounds no more: and sure it waytes vpon
  Some God* o th' Iland, sitting on a banke,
  Weeping againe the King my Fathers wracke.

\* The music is celestial in Ferdinand's estimation.

This Musicke crept by me vpon the waters
Allaying both their fury, and my passion
With it's sweet ayre: thence I haue follow'd it
(Or it hath drawne me rather) but 'tis gone.
No, it begins againe.

*Ariell.* Song. *Full fadom fiue thy Father lies,*
*Of his bones are Corrall made:*
*Those are pearles that were his eies,*
*Nothing of him that doth fade,*
*But doth suffer a Sea-change*
*Into something rich, & strange.*
*Sea-Nimphs hourly ring his knell.*
                        Burthen:                     ding dong.
*Harke now I heare them, ding-dong bell.*[3]

*Fer.*   The Ditty do's remember my drown'd father,
This is no mortall busines, nor no sound
That the earth owes.* I heare it now aboue me.
                                               (Sig.A3)

It seems to me that we have here the basic pattern of the
approach to a Circean situation. The music has the power of
Circean enchantment, guiding Ferdinand to Prospero's cave. It
breaks off and begins again to suggest to Ferdinand a sense of
direction and leads him to Miranda:

*Fer.*   Most sure the Goddesse
On whom these ayres attend.              (Sig.A3)

The essential difference is that Miranda, with whom Ferdinand
now associates the music, is not Circe, lusting for wanton love.
Her immediate love for Ferdinand is completely lawful. Prospero
notices the love enchantment with great satisfaction and attributes
it to Ariel's musical power:

*Pro.*   It goes on I see
As my soule prompts it: Spirit, fine spirit, Ile free
thee
Within two dayes for this . . .
                              . . . At the first sight

* Ferdinand associates the music with the immortal Gods reigning
on high.

> They haue chang'd eyes: Delicate *Ariel,*
> Ile set thee free for this

But he is loth to let the love match be so easily made and decides
to put Ferdinand through a series of rigorous tests. Circe on the
other hand placed no impediments in the way of wanton love.
When Ferdinand draws his sword to show opposition he is
charmed from moving, there being no strife allowed to exist on
the island, causing discord to the prevailing harmony.

It is significant that only Ferdinand, who is innocent of any
crime against Prospero and the gods, and Gonzalo, who was
Prospero's friend at the time of the deposition and did all in his
power to help Prospero and Miranda, hear the island's celestial
music. Gonzalo is quickly lulled to sleep by Ariel's 'solemn
Musicke' and sometime afterwards Alonso complains of the
heavy climate and is gradually lost in slumber. Alonso has begun
to feel a sense of repentance and sorrow, mainly caused by the
belief that his son, Ferdinand, is drowned. Antonio and Sebastian
are wide awake; the island's music has no power over them
because their minds are untuned to its harmony and they have
murder in their heart. Their discordant position is made worse
by contrast with the monster Caliban. He is all grossness of the
flesh as opposed to the spirit, and yet even he can hear the
island's music when he is asleep and sober and not engendering
hate of Prospero.

It is Ariel's music, working through Gonzalo, that prevents
the drawn swords of Sebastian and Antonio from striking death
blows at Alonso and Gonzalo:

> *Enter Ariell with Musicke and Song.*
>
> *Ariel.*   My Master through his Art foresees the danger
>        That you (his friend) are in, and sends me forth
>        (For else his proiect dies) to keepe them liuing.
>
>                 *Sings in Gonzaloes eare.*
>
> *While you here do snoaring lie,*
> *Open-ey'd Conspiracie*
> *His time doth take:*                    (Sig.A4ᵛ)
> *If of Life you keepe a care,*

> *Shake off slumber and beware.*
> *Awake, awake.*
>
> . . .
>
> Gon.  Vpon mine honour, Sir, I heard a humming.
> (And that a strange one too) which did awake me:
> I shak'd you Sir, and cride:          (Sig.A5)

Caliban's first entry is to a 'noyse of Thunder' indicative of
the hate that is now welling up in his mind. As soon as he is
associated with the drunken Stephano, who enters singing a
scurvy tune, a bawdy sea shanty, which is in open contrast to
Ariel's heavenly music, Caliban is an entirely discordant note:

> *Enter Stephano singing.*
>
> Ste.  *I shall no more to sea to sea, here shall I dye ashore.*
> This is a very scuruy tune to sing at a mans
> Funerall:* well, here's my comfort.          *Drinkes.*
> Sings.  *The Master, the Swabber, the Boate-swaine & I;*
> *The Gunner, and his Mate*
> *Lou'd Mall, Meg, and Marrian, and Margerie,*
> *But none of vs car'd for Kate.*
> *For she had a tongue with a tang,*
> *Would cry to a Sailor goe hang:*
> *She lou'd not the sauour of Tar nor of Pitch,*
> *Yet a Tailor might scratch her where ere she did itch.*
> *Then to Sea Boyes, and let her goe hang.*
> This is a scuruy tune too:
> But here's my comfort.          *drinks.*   (Sig.A5)

Caliban under the influence of drink takes to singing something that has the ring of nursery rhyme prattle about it, again
in open contrast to Ariel's heavenly music:

> *Caliban Sings drunkenly.*
>
> Farewell Master; farewell, farewell.†
> Tri.  A howling Monster: a drunken Monster.
> Cal.  *No more dams I'le make for fish,*
> *Nor fetch in firing, at requiring,*
> *Nor scrape trenchering, nor wash dish,*

---

* The contrast with Ariel's song 'Full fadom fiue' is implicit.
† Caliban in abandoning Prospero also abandons the island's music.

> Ban' ban' Cacalyban
> Has a new Master, get a new Man.*

While Caliban, Stephano and Trinculo are hatching their plot for taking over the island, an action which could only bring chaos rushing in again, Ariel interjects contradictory statements into their dialogue. He even provides the tune of their catch on a tabor and pipe when Stephano has forgotten the first tune he taught Caliban:

*Cal.*    Will you troule the Catch
         You taught me but whileare?
*Ste.*    At thy request Monster, I will do reason,
         Any reason: Come on *Trinculo*, let vs sing.

*Sings.*
*Flout 'em, and cout 'em: and skowt 'em, and flout 'em,*
*Thought is free.*

*Cal.*    That's not the tune.

*Ariell plaies the tune on a Tabor and Pipe.*

*Ste.*    What is this same?
*Trin.*   This is the tune of our Catch, plaid by the picture
         of a No-body.

The music in the air strikes awe into Stephano and Trinculo; the former thinks the power evil, the latter retributive:

*Ste.*    If thou beest a man, shew thy selfe in thy likenesse:
         If thou beest a diuell, take't as thou list.
*Tri.*    O forgiue me my sinnes.
*Ste.*    He that dies payes all debts: I defie thee;
         Mercy vpon vs.

Caliban assures them that there is nothing to be afraid of, and in a most revealing passage indicates that the island's music has considerable power over him, or rather had before he set Prospero at defiance and thus alienated himself from the island's

---

* I fail to understand how editors have missed the nursery rhyme prattle of this. Caliban in his drunken state would seem to me to be adapting the nursery rhyme 'Johnny shall have a new master', mentally substituting a diminutive of his own name for 'Johnny'.

harmony. The passage is an epitome of the part played by music in the island:

Cal.   Be not affeard, the Isle is full of noyses,
      Sounds, and sweet aires, that giue delight and hurt
         not:
      Sometimes a thousand twangling Instruments
      Will hum about mine eares; and sometime voices,
      That if I then had wak'd after long sleepe,
      Will make me sleepe againe, and then in dreaming,
      The clouds methought would open, and shew riches
      Ready to drop vpon me, that when I wak'd
      I cri'de to dreame againe.

Ste.   This will proue a braue kingdome to me,
      Where I shall haue my Musicke for nothing.

Cal.   When *Prospero* is destroy'd

Ariel leads the discontents away by the sound of his music suggesting the direction they should take, and thus delays their plan of strife:

Trin.   The sound is going away,
      Let's follow it, and after do our worke.

Ste.   Leade Monster,
      Wee'l follow: I would I could see this Taborer,
      He layes it on.             (Sig.A6ᵛ)

It is again Ariel and his fellow-spirits who intervene at the moment Antonio and Sebastian are planning a second time to murder Alonso and Gonzalo. A magical banquet is produced which is very reminiscent of the Circean banquet, but turned to purely benevolent use:

     *Solemne and strange Musicke: and Prosper on the top*
     *(inuisible:) Enter seuerall strange shapes, bringing in*
     *a Banket; and dance about it with gentle actions of*
     *salutations, and inuiting the King, &c. to eate, they*
     *depart.*

Seb.   I say to night: no more.
Al.    What harmony is this? my good friends, harke.
Gon.  Maruellous sweet Musicke.

>  *Alo.*   Giue vs kind keepers, heavens: what were these?
>                                                    (Sig.B)

The situation is meant, I believe, to be compared with the
Caliban, Trinculo and Stephano scene which it immediately
follows. All three in their intoxicated state are too grossly
burdened in the flesh to be at harmony with the heavenly music.
Similarly Antonio and Sebastian, who both have murder in their
hearts, are out of tune with the island's harmony and merely
consider the spirits bringing in the banquet in terms of geographical phenomena, Sebastian calling them 'liuing *Drolerie*'
and Antonio commenting upon them as the kind of creatures
travellers reported seeing in strange lands. Gonzalo and Alonso
by complete contrast find much to admire in the spirits, considering them favourably by contrast with human beings. Prospero
interrupts at this juncture to point out the symbolical interpretation of the banquet spirits in terms which are reminiscent of the
Circean transformation of human beings into gross animals
more nearly representing their bestial natures. Again, however,
the legend is turned for good; it is not the strange spirits that
are bestial in this sense, for they are perfectly in tune with the
island's harmony; it is Antonio and Sebastian who are the
symbolical beasts:

>  *Gon.*   (For certes, these are people of the Island),
>           Who though they are of monstrous shape, yet note
>           Their manners are more gentle, kinde, then of
>           Our humaine generation you shall finde
>           Many, nay almost any.
>  *Pro.*   Honest Lord:
>           Thou hast said well: for some of you there present;
>           Are worse then diuels.
>  *Al.*    I cannot too much muse
>           Such shapes, such gesture, and such sound
>                expressing
>           (Although they want the vse of tongue) a kinde
>           Of excellent dumbe discourse.          (Sig.B)

Sebastian and Antonio are worse than devils; they are frightful
discords in the island's harmony. When the spirits 'vanish

strangely' all that Sebastian is concerned to remark is that it is

> No matter, since
> They haue left their Viands behinde; for wee haue
>     stomacks.
> Wilt please you taste of what is here?

His comment reduces the consideration of the strange spirits and their participation in the island's harmony to their practical convenience of providing earthly necessities. Similarly Stephano, who defied the unseen taborer, was only concerned to remark that he would be able to have his music for nothing – an expression which is full of irony since he expects to have the same music when Prospero is no longer in power. The discordant beings on the island, Sebastian, Antonio, Trinculo, Stephano and Caliban are all portrayed as earthly minded, of the earth earthy, in complete contrast to the heavenly aspect of the island and the powers ruling it.

Ariel in his next entry adopts the symbolic guise of the Harpy, 'a fabulous monster, rapacious and filthy, having a woman's face and body and a bird's wings and claws',[4] acting as a minister of vengeance. The idea of vengeance is further emphasized by the tantalizing position in which the wrecked travellers find themselves; just as they are about to taste the banquet it is whisked away, and by the sound of thunder and the flash of lightning an indication is given of divine wrath:

> *Thunder and Lightning. Enter Ariell (like a Harpey)*
> *claps his wings vpon the Table, and with a quient*
> *deuice the Banquet vanishes.*[5]

Ariel's pronouncement, which follows immediately on this disappearance of the banquet is, in this connection, a crucial passage since it sums up the ideas that I have so far put forward:

> *Ar.*   You are three* men of sinne, whom destiny
>         That hath to instrument this lower world,
>         And what is in't; the neuer surfeited Sea,

* Alonso is associated with Antonio and Sebastian for his crime in supporting Antonio's expulsion of Prospero from his rightful dukedom.

> Hath caus'd to belch vp you; and on this Island,
> Where man doth not inhabit, you 'mongst men,
> Being most vnfit to liue: I haue made you mad;
> And euen with such like valour, men hang, and
>     drowne
> Their proper selues.

The guilty men make as if to use their swords, but are reminded by Ariel that he and his spirits are as invulnerable as the air. The final pronouncement explains the whole play's plot in terms of discord needing to be resolved into harmony, of sin into grace, of retribution into reconciliation:

> But remember
> (For that's my businesse to you) that you three
> From *Millaine* did suppland good *Prospero*,
> Expos'd vnto the Sea (which hath requit it)
> Him, and his innocent childe: for which foule deed,
> The Powres, delaying (not forgetting) haue
> Incens'd the Seas, and Shores; yea all the Creatures
> Against your peace:

> (Sig.B)

The masque is built into the general fabric of the idea that music symbolizes the harmony of macrocosmos and microcosmos alike; it is a straightforward portrayal of music's function in blessing an intended marriage union, with the gods descending to confirm that blessing, which as the instigators of harmony they have the right to confer. The extraordinary thing is that never again in Jacobean King's Men drama was the masque used simply and solely for a straightforward presentation of the gods' blessing on a marriage union. The masque in Fletcher's hands was used to create surprise and to build up an emotional atmosphere which was to be shattered almost immediately in a 'reversal'.

The idea of the initial discord perpetrated in the microcosmos in which a ruler, the divine representative of macrocosmos harmony has been deposed, has been followed by signs of the gods' wrath, thunder, lightning and tempests. Discord in man's actions is paralleled with discord in the heavens. Harmony can

only be restored when the results of man's actions have been
turned into harmonious good. The discord into harmony is
worked out not by political machinations, not by *coups de grâce*,
not by murder and revenge, but by the island's harmony, by
the appeal to the harmony of right order, the music of the
spheres in which man is united to the divine will for creation.
The cure beginning to work first in Alonso's mind is expressed
in musical terms:

> *Al.*  O, it is monstrous: monstrous:
> Me thought the billowes spoke, and told me of it,
> The windes did sing it to me: and the Thunder
> (That deepe and dreadfull Organ-Pipe) pronounc'd
> The name of *Prosper*: it did base my Trespasse,[6]
>                                       (Sig.B)

and thence onwards the return to harmony is a steady progress.
They, like Ferdinand, are now confined to work out their
resolution to harmony in their own heart and mind. Ariel
reports that they are repentant and

> Brim full of sorrow, and dismay: but chiefly
> Him that you term'd Sir, the good old Lord
>   *Gonzallo*,
> His teares runs downe his beard like winters drops
> From eaues of reeds:                              (Sig.B2ʸ)

The final resolution to harmony is worked out by Prospero's
charm. This is, as all editors agree, Shakespeare's adaptation of
Medea's charm in Ovid's *Metamorphoses*. As Kermode so aptly
points out in referring to all the discussion relative to this, 'only
those elements which are consistent with "white magic" are
taken over for Prospero'. This, I find, is in general accord with
the theme I have been propounding. Through Ariel Prospero
turns the Siren and Circe legends from lust and destruction to
lawful love and safety, turns the Circean banquet from its
legendary deprivation of reason to the beginning of the reign
of right reason again, and turns Medea's charm from black
magic into white. The evil aspect of all these old legends adapted
from Ovid that have music associated with them has been
replaced by a benevolent intention.

The charm brings about the final receptive state in which the shipwrecked travellers can receive the news of Prospero's survival, and in which the final resolution to harmony is possible. All good things of creation are called upon to work for Prospero's good:

> *Pro.*  Ye Elues of hils, brooks, stāding lakes & groues,
> And ye, that on the sands with printlesse foote
> Doe chafe the ebbing-*Neptune*,\* and doe flie him
> When he comes backe: you demy-Puppets, that
> By Moone-shine doe the greene sowre Ringlets
>     make,
> Whereof the Ewe not bites: and you, whose pastime
> Is to make midnight-Mushrumps, that reioyce
> To heare the solemne Curfewe, by whose ayde
> (Weake Masters though ye be) I haue bedymn'd
> The Noone-tide Sun, call'd forth the mutenous
>     windes,
> And twixt the greene Sea, and the azur'd vault
> Set roaring warre: To the dread ratling Thunder
> Haue I giuen fire, and rifted *Ioues*† stowt Oke
> With his owne Bolt; The strong bas'd promontorie
> Haue I made shake,[7] and by the spurs pluckt vp
> The Pyne, and Cedar. Graues at my command
> Haue wak'd their sleepers, op'd, and let 'em forth
> By my so potent Art.[8] But this rough Magicke
> I heere abiure: and when I haue requir'd
> Some heauenly Musicke (which euen now I do)
> To worke mine end vpon their Sences, that
> This Ayrie-charme is for, I'le breake my staffe,
> Bury it certaine fadomes in the earth,
> And deeper then did euer Plummet sound
> Ile drowne my booke.
>                                 *Solemne musicke.*

\* The ebb and flow of the tides in their regular motion partaking of the celestial harmony is the thought here. Compare *Comus*, where the seas are described as taking part in the cosmic dance.

† Prospero assumed Jove's power to create thunder and disturbance in the macrocosmos.

Immediately there follows the transfixion of the charm on the travellers:

> *Here enters* Ariel *before: Then* Alonso *with franticke gesture, attended by* Gonzalo. Sebastian *and* Anthonio *in like manner attended by* Adrian *and* Francisco: *They all enter the circle which* Prospero *had made, and here stand charm'd: which* Prosper *obseruing, speakes.*
>
> A solemne Ayre, and the best comforter,
> To an vnsetled fancie, Cure thy braines
> (Nw vselesse) boile within thy skull: there stand
> For you are Spell-stopt.                    (Sig.B2ᵛ)

Music finally settles the unhinged fancy of the traveller's minds, and the relation of the story of Prospero's survival and of the subsequent course of events, the survival of Ferdinand, and his attachment to Miranda, make the play's final return to harmony.

Preparations are now uppermost for the return to Milan and for the rightful ruler to be installed in all amity. The island's music, signifying the harmony from which the banishment from Milan in the first place had been a serious cosmic aberration, and signifying the harmony to which all discord, strife, disunion and evil intentions have been resolved, is finally dismissed in Ariel's paean of sheer joy at release for his service to Prospero:

> *Ariell sings, and helps to attire him.*
>
> *Where the Bee sucks, there suck I,*
> *In a Cowslips bell, I lie,*
> *There I cowch when Owles doe crie,*
> *On the Batts backe I doe flie*
> *after Sommer merrily.*
> *Merrily, merrily, shall I liue now,*
> *Vnder the blossom that hangs on the Bow.*  (Sig. B3)

Ariel's last task is to produce the travellers' ship intact,* and to drive in the last discordant element, which has resolved itself to a certain extent by the return to sobriety from intoxication:

---

* The storm had only been symbolical and, I believe, only in the terms in which I have expressed it as indicating a disturbance in the cosmic harmony.

> *Cal.*                  I'le be wise hereafter,
> And seeke for grace:* what a thrice double Asse
> Was I to take this drunkard for a god?
> And worship this dull foole?
>
>                                         (Sig.B3ᵛ)

The intoxicated Caliban, Trinculo and Stephano had been led
by Ariel's music until they had been safely disposed of in the
'filthy mantled pool', symbolic of their own bestiality:⁹

> *Ar.*                  I beate my Tabor,
> At which like vnback't colts they prickt their eares,
> Aduanc'd their eye-lids, lifted vp their noses
> As they smelt musicke, so I charm'd their eares
> That Calfe-like, they my lowing follow'd, through
> Tooth'd briars, sharpe firzes, pricking gosse, &
>       thorns,
> Which entred their fraile shins: at last I left them
> I' th' filthy mantled poole beyond your Cell,
> There dancing vp to th' chins, that the fowle Lake
> Ore-stunck their feet.                  (Sig.B2)

The glistening apparel which they had stolen from Prospero and
in which they had clothed their bestiality indicates the contrast
between the lordly masquing attire which is put on to disguise
their rude antimasquing nature underneath. The antimasque of
spirits in the shape of dogs and hounds, which hunts them about
is also, I feel, an indication of their bestiality.

I have discussed the function of music in *The Tempest* at
considerable length because I feel it has been so little understood
and very much underestimated. No other play in the whole of
the Jacobean King's Men repertory, with perhaps the exception
of *The Mad Lover*, portrays such an extensive and unified
treatment of music.

---

* Grace is used here not only in the sense of pardon, or favour, but
in the sense of absolution for sin. Caliban has now returned to the
state in which the island's music can make him want to sleep again
and dream of bliss, and after waking cry to dream again.

# NOTES

1. The text of the song given here is exactly as it stands in the Folio. It is a most unsatisfactory text. The question of which lines constitute the burthen is a very vexed one. Editors have suggested a variety of solutions, most of which are summarized by Frank Kermode in *The Tempest* (New Arden ed.: 1954) p. 34 n. 383. I cannot agree with Kermode's own arrangement. It seems to me quite clear that ftrea the song's instruction in line 5 to the 'sweet Sprights' to bear the burthen, all that follows constitutes the burthen until Ariel takes up the singing again. The printers seem to have been generally unconcerned to print refrains carefully; compare the refrains in the 'Willow' song and in the two songs 'Come follow me (you Country-Lasses)' and 'You shall haue Crowns of Roses' from *The Maid in the Mill*.

2. The Sirens' song in William Browne's *Masque of the Inner Temple* (1614/15).

3. Cf. John P. Cutts, 'Robert Johnson: King's Musician in His Majesty's Public Entertainment', in *Music & Letters*, xxxvi 2 (April 1955) 110–25, for a discussion of the actual music extant.

4. *NED* definition. The harpies were cousins of the Sirens. Ariel has already acted the part of the Sirens in an entirely benevolent way: his assumption of that of the Harpy is quite simply in the classical manner.

5. Compare the disappearance of the banquet in *Paradise Regained*, II 402,

> Both table and provision vanished quite,
> With sound of harpies' wings and talons heard;
> Only th' importune Tempter still remained.

The source of both passages is *Aeneid* II.

6. Compare the stanza in *The Faerie Queene* II 12, in which Nature's musical sounds are called upon to enhance the magical appeal of Acrasia's island. Here again we notice the traditional usage for wantonness is being turned for lawful use.

7. The ideas are similar to those expressed in the well-known speech on degree by Ulysses in *Troilus and Cressida*. When degree is disturbed, when the harmony in macrocosmos and microcosmos alike is rifted, then chaos floods in and mountains are toppled, promontories uprooted.

8. Kermode's remark on this is most apt: 'There seems to be no occasion for this; all the other magic feats Prospero has performed, save this one. The function of the speech is not, of course, informative;

although Prospero refers to his recent tempest, its object is the general one of using every possible resource to enforce the potency of his powers immediately before he abjures them.' The thought occurs in Golding's translation of Ovid's *Metamorphoses*: 'I call up dead men from their graves', but its relevance to *The Tempest* is hard to determine otherwise than along the lines suggested by Kermode. Coming last, as it does in Prospero's speech, it may well represent the implication of the utmost potency of Prospero's art.

9. Compare Pyrochles in *The Faerie Queene* II, who plunged headlong into the idle lake, symbolical of the disease of the soul consequent on riot and wantonness. The music which Caliban, Trinculo and Stephano hear now, of course, is not Ariel's celestial music but his tabor and pipe.

*Frank Davidson*

## THE TEMPEST:
## AN INTERPRETATION (1963)

### I

TWENTIETH-CENTURY critics have left us a great variety of sometimes conflicting views on the meaning of Shakespeare's *The Tempest*. They have for the most part, however, been acute in their observations and have, even in their disagreements, bequeathed us a wealth of penetrating comment and points of view on a labyrinthine piece of dramatic art. Some, more objective than others in their approach, have been disturbed by interpretations which seem to have no basis within the framework of the play itself. E. E. Stoll, for example, wearied, it seems, by the insistence that Shakespeare was dramatizing, in a part of *The Tempest* at least, events of his own life, or writing an allegory, contends that the critic should be a 'judge, who does not explore his own consciousness, but determines the author's meaning or intention' from what the play actually says.[1]

This discussion will attempt to restate and examine briefly meanings ascribed to *The Tempest* by several of these critics of renown of the present century and to follow with an interpretation of the play based on philosophical and psychological thinking of the Tudor era and justified, I hope, by the work itself.

### II

For E. K. Chambers *The Tempest* is a 'dream' or 'fairy tale', the protagonists of which are 'imagined beings, taken partly from folk-belief, and partly from literature, to be the symbols of forces dimly perceived by the poet as ruling that life, which is itself, after all, in another degree, but such stuff as dreams are

made on'.[2] In his consideration of Prospero's dissolution of the
hymeneal revels enacted for Ferdinand and Miranda, he follows
Ulrici, Dowden, and others, interpreting the action as Shakespeare's farewell to the stage (p. 309). Sir Arthur Quiller-Couch
finds in *The Tempest* a subject which, he remarks, constantly
engaged Shakespeare's 'mind towards the close of his life:
*Reconciliation*, with pardon and atonement for the sins or
mistakes of one generation in the young love of the children and
in their promise. This is the true theme of *Pericles, Cymbeline,
The Winter's Tale, The Tempest*, successively'.[3] Stoll agrees
with Chambers that the play is a fairy tale, a 'sort of glorious
fairy-tale', he calls it, 'precious not . . . because of the structure
or situations, but because of the characters, the poetry and the
rich and dreamy spirit which for the most part informs it'
(p. 699). He is conscious of a 'tendency to reverie' in the play,
of a 'change in his [Shakespeare's] imagery', of outlines that
'tend to become vast, vague and wavering, as in a dream'
(p. 724), and of some profound thought on 'the end, not only
of man's work but of Nature's, and of life as a dream, and death
as a sleep' (p. 726). He is at total variance with Chambers
with reference to any biographical interpretation. Hardin Craig,
like Stoll, looks at the play objectively but stresses more than
do the other critics the fact that it is stage drama. In support
of his view he directs attention to some significant facts un-
mentioned by Stoll: that 'Prospero has committed error, has
suffered wrongs, has striven against them, even has some
struggles, often overlooked, on the island'.[4] *The Tempest*, he
says, represents 'Man moving toward the realization of the
greatest Renaissance ideal', having 'grown on the one side into
a competent man of action, and on the other into a man of self-
command' (p. 351). G. B. Harrison follows the lead of Chambers
and Stoll in viewing the play as a fairy tale and that of Quiller-
Couch in assigning as theme, 'reconciliation; wrongs committed
in one generation . . . set right in the happiness of the next.'[5]
Donald Stauffer interprets the play as one of 'moral ideas',
which 'grow from age and experience and self-discipline and
resignation, almost from disillusion'.[6] Prospero's 'nobler reason'

is for him 'no scientific rationality, but an ethical control over passion' (p. 304). Northrop Frye rules out allegory and argues that *The Tempest* is about a 'dissolving society' and a 'new kind of social order'[7] that moves 'not out of the world, but from an ordinary to a renewed and ennobled vision of nature' (p. 19). Prospero, he explains, 'takes the society of Alonso's ship, immerses it in magic, and then sends it back to the world, its original ranks restored, but given a new wisdom . . .' (p. 18). He touches on the biographical theory and sees possibilities in it without subscribing to it (pp. 22–23). Frye's is a beautiful piece of exposition, persuasive and charmingly lucid. Mark Van Doren warns the reader that '*The Tempest* is a composition about which we had better not be too knowing';[8] that 'it seems to order itself in terms of meanings' which are not 'self-evident', but which are subject to a variety of interpretations, even contradictory ones, and of which even 'the wildest is more or less plausible' (p. 259). He accepts the 'reconciliation' theme mentioned by Quiller-Couch and Harrison but associates with it a theme of 'separation' (p. 260). He touches upon the biographical theory but lends it no credence (pp. 266–7).

Any of the preceding views, except perhaps the biographical, may be to an extent justified by the lines of the play. Three, however, those of Frye, Stauffer, and Craig, provide some very pertinent observations not included in the others. Frye almost induces belief in his theme of a new society. He finds arguments for it in the compassion of Prospero, in the reconcilation of implacable enemies through the marriage of their children, and in the fact that most of the characters find themselves, 'when no man was his own'. Prospero, however, is so much the center of the action from beginning to end, he so dwarfs the other characters, that the social aspect dwelt upon by Frye is but vaguely defined. Stauffer is aware not only of moral ideas in the play, but of moral ideas which are the outgrowth of 'age, experience, self-discipline, resignation, almost disillusion' and which anticipate '*ethical control over passion*' (italics added). Craig particularizes more than does Stauffer the experience, the self-discipline, and their results. For him, as we have noticed,

'Prospero has committed error, has suffered wrongs, and has struggled against them, even has some struggles, often overlooked, on the island' and under the discipline imposed by these conflicts, has moved toward '*the realization of the greatest Renaissance ideal*' (italics added).

### III

In content as well as in period *The Tempest* is, as Craig implies Renaissance drama. It reflects such inherited classical theories and faiths and philosophies of sixteenth-century Western Europe as natural differentiation in degree and in duties of rulers and subjects ('specialty of rule' Ulysses called it in *Troilus and Cressida*); zeal for learning; the relative importance of speculative and practical living and a morality and psychology based upon convictions about the rationality, the passionate nature, and the free will of man.

Although Craig does not identify the 'error' with which he charges Prospero, there can be hardly a doubt that he has in mind the cause of Prospero's failure as a Duke, a type of error of which the Renaissance took cognizance. As Frye correctly observes, Prospero 'appears to have been a remarkably incompetent ruler of Milan' (p. 20). The obsession or passion with which Shakespeare endowed him would, for an Elizabethan, have made him so, for he devoted himself to speculative studies, 'neglecting worldly ends, all dedicated / To closeness' (1 ii 89–90), and by this immoderate inclination contributed to the defection of his brother, the loss of his dukedom, the exile of himself and Miranda, and the conflict that enmeshed him after he was forced by circumstance to care for himself and his daughter on a practically uninhabited island. 'The government', he tells Miranda, while acquainting her with his former situation as Duke,

> I cast upon my brother,
> And to my state grew stranger, being transported
> And rapt in secret studies . . .
> I, thus neglecting worldly ends, all dedicated

> To closeness and the bettering of my mind . . .
>                          in my false brother
> Awaked an evil nature . . .
>                          Me, poor man, my library
> Was dukedom large enough.
>
>                          (I ii 75–110)

His error is evident in his words. His lack of any practical
interest in the affairs of his people, his passion for a meditative
and private life, and his delegating the actual operation of
governing to a kinsman, as did Lear (in itself a perversion of
nature), would have proved an almost insurmountable barrier
for any sixteenth-century European ruler.[9]

Study was, however, though insufficient in itself, an asset for
the gentleman of the time, and for princesses as well, as Henry
VIII demonstrated, and Prospero, too; for instruction in the
liberal sciences would, says Sir Thomas Elyot, 'prepare the
mynde and make it apte to receive vertue'. But, Elyot goes on
to say, the governor should be 'neyther by study withdrawen
from affaires of the publike weale, nor by any busyness utterly
pluckyd from Philosophy and any other noble doctrines'.[10]
John Lyly voices a similar thought, pointing out that there is
an active life 'which is about ciuill function and administration
of the common weale', and a speculative, 'which is continuall
meditation and studie. . . . If this actiue life be without philo-
sophie, it is an idle life, or at the least a life euill imployed which
is worse: if the contemplatiue lyfe be seperated from the Actiue,
it is vnprofitable'.[11] Prospero's error helps to explain the presence
of Ariel and Caliban in the play and to prepare for the climax.

On the island, to which Providence has guided him, Prospero,
the scholar, dedicated to closeness, is forced to employ that
function of the rational soul which, to this time, he has neglected
– the active. Through the kindness of Gonzalo, he still has his
books and he still uses them, but he must divide his time now
between speculative and practical concerns. He discovers two
inhabitants on the island, Ariel, whom he releases from imprisonment, a delicate spirit, brave, adaptable to a variety of visible
forms as well as to invisibility, freedom-loving, accommodated

to any of the four elements, and Caliban, a creature of earth,
offspring of a witch and the devil, whom he attempts to instruct
in the manners of human life. The former, Prospero detains as
servant in spite of protest; the latter, subsequent to his kind
treatment and its ingratitude, he shuts in a cavern and assigns
menial tasks – a rebellious slave. Neither of these beings is
human. Ariel, who, it must be remembered, acts only on
Prospero's bidding, can, under his direction, perform rationally
(I ii 207–8) but lacks human affection (v i 19); Caliban is without
reason and acts from instinct. But both act. Chambers speaks of
Ariel, as from one point of view, 'the agent and minister of an
inscrutable Providence' (p. 310), which Ariel demonstrates
himself to be (III iii 60–75), with his adeptness at working with
sensory objects – seas, shores, creatures, winds – through which
according to him, Providence operates to maintain order and
justice in the world. Stoll treats Ariel and Caliban in considerable
detail. Somewhat contemptuous of those critics who have a
'taste for an inner meaning, biographical or symbolical', he
likens Ariel to Puck 'in the enjoyment of his own performances
and of his effects on mortals' and speaks of him as 'more
ethereal . . . than the fairies', representing '*a power of nature,* like
wind or water, *harnessed for a time to man's service* [italics added]
and delighting in it, yet ever ready to break loose' (p. 701).
Caliban is for Stoll 'a mooncalf' (p. 700), 'the perfect brute'
(p. 713), who 'fits perfectly into the dramatic scheme as the
creature of earth – both a parallel and a contrast with the spirit
of the air . . .' (p. 711). The two, he significantly remarks,
constitute a 'state of nature – Prospero and Miranda as human
figures coming in between' (p. 711). Stoll lays great stress upon
his point that these two figures are 'not single abstractions
personified, but many-sided conceptions, incarnated', 'develop-
ments out of popular superstitious conceptions, which are
concrete' (p. 700), both closely associated with nature (p. 716).
Of their growth in the poet's mind, he explains that

there was of course a guiding thread of thought, or a germinal
idea – the spirit of the air in the one case, the spawn of the earth
in the other – but that worked darkly under cover. Guided by

touch and instinct, the poet, when consciously active at all, was
intent upon the life and shape of the imagined creature, not on a
meaning within it. (Or rather upon both, for this meaning – this
germinal idea – is simple and inherent, not arbitrary and external
. . . and the creature and its meaning are one.) (p. 719).

One may gladly accept all this and then, making an additional
observation, point out a 'guiding thread of thought, or germinal
idea' in each of these non-human creatures that is different in
some respects from those that have been suggested and more in
keeping with Prospero's necessity, in his isolation, to be practical
as well as informed. His volitions, it may be noted, are transformed to deeds by Ariel and Caliban on his requests and
demands. The 'germinal idea' for each of the two figures seems
to have been drawn from the psychology well known to the
period.[12]

Briefly, one basic concept in Elizabethan psychology was that
man possesses three souls – a vegetative, which he has in common
with plants and the lower animals and whose functions are
nourishment, growth, and reproduction; a sensible, which he
shares with lower animals and whose chief function is, through
affections and passions, to stimulate beast or man to activity;
and a rational, which is peculiar to man and whose chief functions
are to know, to speculate, and to will.[13]

As the sensible soul, seat of the passions, was the one most
closely associated with motion, it naturally became the agent of
Prospero's activity, and at two levels: the basically physical or
vegetal: and the mental and spiritual. Castiglione defines man's
position with reference to these levels and points out two types
of man's government of the active agents at the two levels,
suggesting in terms of body, desire, soul, and reason, a relationship such as in *The Tempest* exists between Prospero and Caliban
on the one hand and between Prospero and Ariel on the other,
the former that of master and slave, the latter that of prince
and subject according to laws.[14]

Significant to any satisfactory interpretation of Caliban
perhaps are this basic psychological concept of the souls and
their functions; the necessity Prospero is under, after he reaches
the island, to act: and his two admissions concerning his relations

with Caliban: first, that he and Miranda have subjected themselves in a measure to Caliban, have come to depend upon him
for building fires, fetching wood, and performing other menial
services that profit them (I ii 311–13), and second, that he
acknowledges 'this thing of darkness' his (v i 275–6). It would
seem that Shakespeare, in Prospero's concession of dependence
on and ownership of the creature, is suggesting that the 'germinal
idea' for Caliban is the brute body, responding to sensory and
sensual instincts and desires, and operating at the subsistence
and reproductive level of life; that, in contrast, the 'germinal
idea' for Ariel is the spirit of the sensible soul, acting, though
dissentingly at times, in the elemental world of nature under the
instruction of a rational soul to the attainment of personal and
universal justice. In other words, Caliban and Ariel are attributes
of Prospero, practical aspects of himself of which he was hardly
conscious during his strictly speculative years. Each would be
free; that was the rational soul's dilemma. Caliban speaks of a
time when he was his 'own king' (I i 342). His attempted rape
of Miranda is representative of the flesh's natural procreative
urge, an instinct whose lustful, insidious propensities Prospero
has not been conscious of in himself until after his banishment
(cf. Stauffer, p. 105) and which he finds 'abhorrent', 'capable of
all ill', and amenable to 'stripes . . . not kindness'.[15] The rational
soul's necessitated employment of the vegetative for practical
ends has given Prospero a peep at the 'unweeded garden / That
grows to seed'; at that dark aspect of nature to which the
bastard Edmund pledged himself in 'Thou, Nature, art my
goddess'.[16]

   With reference to such an interpretation of Caliban and Ariel
as I have attempted here, there may be pertinency in Francis
Bacon's observation:

For the sensible soul – the soul of brutes – must clearly be
regarded as a corporeal substance, attenuated and made invisible
by heat; a breath . . . compounded of the natures of flame and
air, having the softness of air to receive impressions, and the
vigour of fire to propagate its action; . . . clothed with the body,

and in perfect animals residing chiefly in the head, running
along the nerves, and refreshed and repaired by the spirituous
blood of the arteries. . . . [T]his soul is in the brutes the principal
soul, the body of the brute being its instrument whereas in man
it is itself only the instrument of the rational soul, and may be
more fitly termed not soul, but spirit.[17]

Professor Stoll, persevering and right as he is against a critic's
reading his own impressions into *The Tempest* or any other
literary work, does recognize that Shakespeare could 'forget
himself to the point of . . . entering into the soul of a phenomenon
of nature' (p. 705) and giving it reality.

IV

I have observed above that *The Tempest* is Renaissance drama in
that it reflects among other characteristics of the time, some of
the closely related political, ethical, and psychological views.
I have stated one of the basic principles featured in that psychology – old as Plato and new as Spenser – and have tried to show
its applicability to an identification of Ariel and Caliban. Another
basic belief, likewise significant to an interpretation of the play
and incorporated in many of the sixteenth-century works on
moral philosophy, is, that for man's attainment of the highest
good in life, the *summum bonum*, obedience to natural order is
essential. Just as

> The heavens themselves, the planets, and this centre
> Observe degree, priority, and place,
> Insisture, course, proportion, season, form,
> Office and custom, in all line of order . . .
>
> (*Troil.* 1 iii 85–8)

so man, for his felicity, must 'observe degree, priority, and
place' of subject and ruler, of child and parent, of youth and
age, of passion and reason.[18]

Perversions of natural order such as Ulysses sets forth in
*Troilus and Cressida* (1 iii 101–24) develop into a pattern in *The
Tempest*, bringing complications and distress. Twelve years

before the opening incident of the action Antonio, brother and
subject of Prospero, had, with the aid of Alonso, King of Naples,
seized power in the dukedom of Prospero and set him and his
baby daughter adrift upon the sea in the rotten carcass of a tub.
Prospero speaks of Antonio as an 'unnatural' brother. The first
incident of the play ties in with this recollected earlier one and
reveals the contemptuous behavior, during a shipwreck ('degree
being vizarded') of sailors toward a king's councillor and
toward the king himself. In rapid succession then come the
demands of a servant, Ariel, for his freedom from his master;
the defiance of a master by a slave, who claims ownership of the
island on which they live; the plotting of Antonio and King
Alonso's brother, Sebastian, to assassinate the king and seize
Naples (a duplication in many respects of the conspiracy that
unseated Prospero); Miranda's taking issue with her father
concerning a lover; and the fomenting of a conspiracy by
Caliban and two drunken sailors against Prospero. All these
revolts, save that of Ariel, who can act under the direction of
reason (I ii 206–8), originate in uncontrolled passions: ambitious
desire, anger, hatred, youthful love, cupidity.

Passions were not looked upon as evil in themselves by
Elizabethans, except among the stoics; they were, however,
when out of control, considered dangerous to both body and
mind.[19] One of man's greatest conflicts was, at least in theory,
that between his reason and his passions, and this conflict,
according to Francis Bacon,[20] became a theme even better
adapted to artistic than to philosophical treatment. It is basic to
the struggle in the second book of *The Faerie Queene,* where,
up to the close of canto v, Sir Guyon contends against Furor,
and, through the remainder of the book, against Acrasia or
concupiscible desire. Shakespeare makes the passions an active
force in his tragedies,[21] and in *The Tempest* he employs them
as chief contender against Prospero.

The lines of *The Tempest* are interlaced with the diction of the
contemporary psychology in its treatment of the reason and the
passions. There are words, phrases, clauses that speak of the
restraint of this enemy: 'be patient'; 'Be collected'; 'music crept

by me upon the waters, / Allaying both their fury and my passion'; 'The white cold virgin snow upon my heart / Abates the ardor of my liver'. Many expressions reflect the effects of the uncontrolled passions: 'I'm out of patience'; 'being transported / And rapt'; 'beating my mind'; 'amazement'; 'infect his reason'; 'a fever of the mad'; 'tricks of desperation'; 'immitigable rage'; 'At the first sight / They have changed eyes'; 'My spirits, as in a dream, are all bound up'; 'madness'; 'Their great guilt . . . / Now 'gins to bite the spirits'; 'I have made you mad'; 'ecstasy'; 'anger so distempered'; 'vexed'; 'my beating mind'; 'a madness held me'; 'they devour their reason'. Other passages indicate a return to a normal state of mind after the working of a passion: 'their rising senses / Begin to chase the ignorant fumes that mantle / Their clearer reason'; 'Their understanding / Begins to swell, and the approaching tide / Will shortly fill the reasonable shore / That now lies foul and muddy'; 'their senses I'll restore'.

Even the title of the play is not so much concerned with the sea storm Prospero raises as with the passions he stirs in his guests and in himself, passions that in his twelve years of isolation may have shown calm at the surface but which now, as he faces his foes, mount high again. In the books of philosophy and psychology of the day a not unusual symbol for the passions is a tempest.[22]

Incidents of the play as well as the diction and the title speak of the passions. Prospero lectures Ferdinand on continence in love after the lovers, with his consent, have plighted troth, and predicts dire calamities if his exhortation goes unheeded (IV i 14–24; 50–4). The scene is echoed in the wedding masque (IV i 96–7) when Iris speaks of the 'vows . . . no bedright shall be paid / Till Hymen's torch be lighted'.[23] Both Stoll and Fry are perplexed by Prospero's seemingly unnecessary admonition. Stoll associates it with a 'measure of ugliness and horror, cynicism and grossness' to be found in the late comedies of Shakespeare, and asks, 'Why should he [Prospero] warn Ferdinand, about to be left for a moment with Miranda, not to break her virgin-knot, and then, the next moment, harp on the subject again?' (p. 723). Frye attributes Prospero's moments

of anger to the 'nervous strain of dealing with such characters'
as those about him and states that 'in his fussing over protecting
Miranda from the obviously honorable lover, there is a touch
of the busybody' (p; 20). Elizabethan psychology would have
supported neither of the critics, as it leaves no doubt about the
danger of concupiscible pleasures.[24] When Prospero warns
Ferdinand, 'Do not give dalliance / Too much the rein' (IV i
51-2), he is not speaking grossly and is not a busybody.

Passions of grief and remorse are vigorously presented in
III iii of *The Tempest*. Ariel appears to Alonso, Sebastian, and
Gonzalo as a harpy, reminds the first three of their sins, informs
them that he has made them mad, proclaims himself and his
aids ministers of fate, and warns that

> The powers, delaying not forgetting, have
> Incensed the seas and stones – yea, all the creatures
> Against your peace.                      (III iii 73–5)

Alonso, grieving the disappearance of his son, whom he has
given up for dead (III ii 7–10), imagines that he hears the
billows, the winds, the thunder accusing him of the evil he has
done Prospero (III iii 95–102) and reminding him that because
of his misdeeds he now suffers the loss of his son. Sebastian
and Antonio are in a frenzy. Gonzalo, seeing that 'All three of
them are desperate', requests that someone with suppler joints
than his, 'follow them swiftly, / And hinder them from what this
ecstasy / May now provoke them to' (III iii 107–9). Shakespeare
had used the passions of grief and anger very effectively as a
cause of Lear's madness and, in *The Tempest*, shortly before
Gonzalo beseeches someone to follow the desperate trio, has
Prospero, aware of what has occurred, reflect:

> And these mine enemies are all knit up
> In their distractions.                      (III iii 89–90)

v

Prospero, as has been noted, while informing Miranda of his
past, assumed some of the blame for his disaster, attributing it
in part to his immoderate zeal for speculative learning to the

neglect of his active duties as a ruler. Linked with his intemperate behavior was a self-pride, which characterizes him through most of the play: 'Prospero the prime Duke', he boasts to his daughter, 'being so reputed / In dignity, and for the liberal arts / Without a parallel' (I ii 72–4). His sensitivity displays itself in his susceptibility to feelings of resentment, anger, and revenge. In the wrongs done him by his brother and in the challenges to his authority by Ariel and by Caliban, he is hurt most by their ingratitude; in each instance he lays great stress upon his own kindnesses to these betrayers of his trust and tenderness (I ii 67–70, 93–7, 257–9, 261–3, 345–7, 353–8), and on each occasion gives way to anger, just as he does when his daughter, attempting to argue a point with him about her lover, draws the quick, sharp rebuke, 'my foot, my tutor?' (I ii 469) and the more vehement reproof, 'one more word / Shall make me chide thee, if not hate thee' (I ii 475–6). To Ferdinand he appears 'crabbed' and 'composed of harshness' (III i 8–9). When he suddenly remembers that Caliban and the sailors are moving against him, his passion is such as to alarm Ferdinand and Miranda. To the former's observation, 'Your father's in some passion / That works him strongly', the latter replies that 'till this day' she has not seen him 'touched with anger so distempered' (IV i 143–5). Prospero, noting their concern, confesses vexation, and requests, 'Bear with my weakness, my old brain is troubled. / Be not disturbed with my infirmity' (IV i 159–60). He will take a turn or two, he says, 'to still my beating mind'.

The revenge motif in *The Tempest* has never had the attention it deserves. Stoll attributes the scenes involving Prospero's anger to 'the poverty of the plot', and observes that 'No obstacles opposing his omnipotence from without, one must be raised up within' (p. 723). Stoll seems unaware of the tension building up from the *protasis* of the second scene of the play to the moment when this man who, as scholar, had been 'transported and rapt in secret studies' must make a momentous decision. 'The drama', says Stoll 'is indeed seldom performed: there is too little suspense, and the conjuring tricks pall upon us' (p. 705). Craig comes nearer the mark in his assertion quoted above that 'Prospero . . . even has some struggles, often overlooked, on the island'. Miss Campbell takes cognizance of the vengeance motif but only to point out how Shakespeare transformed to comedy an impending tragedy of revenge.[25] Frye seems to be quite conscious of the dark strain in the play but lets it pass with the observation that 'Like Hamlet, Prospero delays revenge and sets up a dramatic action to catch the conscience of a king . . .' (p. 15). It should be noted that the revenge motif carries into the secondary action as Caliban urges Stephano to avenge the wrongs Prospero has done him (III ii 61–2). Desire for vengeance has apparently lain dormant in Prospero through the years of his banishment, and now, with the sudden advent of his foes, the great wrong of twelve years before is stirringly present again, arousing the passions and stimulating the will to action. Tensions begin building in the first act, when Prospero insists that his daughter be alert to the situation they face. 'The hour's now come', he says; 'The very minute bids thee ope thine ear. / Obey, and be attentive' (I ii 36–8). After outlining for her the significant events of the unfortunate past, he comes again 'to the present business / Which now's upon's, without the which this story Were most impertinent' (I ii 136–8). He must seize upon the moment or his 'fortunes / Will ever after droop' (I ii 83–4). The suspense intensifies in Act III when Prospero announces concerning his enemies, 'They now are in my power', and mounts to a climax at the close of Act IV:

> At this hour
> Lie at my mercy all mine enemies.
> Shortly shall all my labours end. . . .

VI

*The Tempest* is not mere spectacle or story of a magician's supernatural dominance of men and spirits.[26] Nor does it lack suspense. The conflict that makes drama is present in Prospero, and its resolution comes, not so much of physical, as of moral and mental travail. The two functions of the rational soul,

H

speculative and practical: at last fuse. The former has prepared
'the mynde and [made] it apte to receive vertue'; the latter wills
and acts virtuously. 'Degree' is preserved; reason, the distinctive
attribute of man, triumphs over passion. When Ariel, who lacks
human sympathy but who recognizes suffering when he sees
it, reports the sorrowful plight of Gonzalo and the penitence
and grief of Alonso, the 'enemy . . . inveterate', Prospero meets
the challenge. 'Shall not myself', he asks,

> One of their kind, that relish all as sharply,
> Passion as they, be kindlier moved than thou art?
> Though with their high wrongs I am struck to the quick,
> Yet with my nobler reason 'gainst my fury
> Do I take part. The rarer action is
> In virtue than in vengeance.                    (v i 22–8)

So the conflict ends. Prospero has achieved virtue, and the virtue
seems to be *magnanimity*, 'the wonderful effects' of which,
'appear principally in three points', the second of which is
'dutie towards enemies, against whom generositie will in no
wise suffer a man to practise or consent to any wickednesse. . . .'[27]

A note has sounded throughout the play, however, of a force
superior to and within whose compass man's reason and virtue
operate. At the end of the first scene, when death seems
imminent to members of the court party, Gonzalo exclaims,
'The wills above be done!' Near the close of the play he gives
credit to the 'gods' for having brought him and his party to the
island, and with his comment raises the question whether all
the events of the past twelve years have not been parts of a
Providential plan. Between these two pronouncements Prospero
makes acknowledgment to 'Providence divine' for having
brought him and his daughter safely ashore, Ariel associates the
'powers' with the maintenance of justice in the world, and
Ferdinand lays claim to Miranda through 'immortal Providence'.
Relative to this 'Providence' with its continuity and greatness,
man, even with his reason, 'is such stuff / As dreams are made
on, and [his] little life / Is rounded with a sleep'.[28]

Another repetitive note in the play is freedom. The word

'liberty' accompanies Ariel's first appearance, and the last command he receives opens the final line of the drama, 'Be free'. Just before his release, however, Prospero requests he set Caliban and his companions free. Ferdinand can find liberty even in confinement if, from his prison, he may see Miranda daily, and he compares his willingness to be her husband to that of bondage to be free. The freedom of Ariel and Caliban, as we might expect, follows closely Prospero's liberating himself from the passion that has ridden him and his finding his true self in the rule of reason. The relations of the servant and of the slave to Prospero change with this event; they are no longer in revolt. Caliban's sense of values, for instance, is transformed to such a degree that he can exclaim, 'How fine my master is!' and wonder at his own asininity of a moment before in mistaking Stephano for a god. In brief, master, servant, and slave, each finds his freedom in the degree or specialty of rule that nature assigns him.

Frye thinks that Prospero shows little promise of being a better Duke after his return to Milan than he was before leaving it (p. 20). This view comes perhaps of the statement made by Prospero near the close of the drama, 'Every third thought shall be my grave', as if he plans to be again the purely meditative man. The implication of Frye's thinking is that Prospero has learned from his long experience little of lasting worth for a ruler. We must remember, however, that he will re-occupy Milan through conquest;[29] he has conquered himself and his political foes. His prospective meditation is certainly not unusual for his day or for his immediate situation. Having proved the power of reason concerning a passion closely aligned with life, he can now exercise that power to promote serenity of mind in the contemplation of death, a subject which seems to have haunted Elizabethan thought.[30] Frye's prediction is not so well based as Craig's: that Prospero, having achieved virtue and restored himself to power, will, upon his return to Milan, attend to practical affairs of state without abandoning study and meditation; '. . . the Renaissance', he says, 'put no premium on ignorance' (p. 351).

# NOTES

1. E. E. Stoll, 'The Tempest', in *PMLA* XLVII (1932) 703.
2. E. K. Chambers, *Shakespeare: A Survey* (A Dramabook: New York, n.d.) p. 304.
3. *The Tempest*, in *The Works of Shakespeare*, ed. Sir Arthur Quiller-Couch and John Dover Wilson (1921) p. 1.
4. Hardin Craig, *An Interpretation of Shakespeare* (New York, n.d.) p. 343.
5. G. B. Harrison, *Six Plays of Shakespeare* (New York, n.d.) p. 214. Quotations from *The Tempest* are from this edition.
6. Donald Stauffer, *Shakespeare's World of Images* (New York, 1949) p. 310.
7. Northrop Frye (ed.), *The Tempest* (Pelican Shakespeare: Baltimore, 1959).
8. *A Midsummer Night's Dream, As You Like It, Twelfth Night, The Tempest* (Pocket Library: New York, n.d.) p. 260.
9. See Ruth Kelso, *The Doctrine of the English Gentleman in the Sixteenth Century* (University of Illinois Studies in Language and Literature, XIV: 1929), and Peter de la Primaudaye, *The French Academie* (1594), quoted by Lily Bess Campbell in *Shakespeare's Tragic Heroes: Slaves of Passion* (New York [1930]) p. 93.
10. Sir Thomas Elyot, *The Boke Named the Governour* (Everyman ed.) pp. 278–9.
11. John Lyly, *Euphues: The Anatomy of Wit* (Arber Reprints: Westminster, 1904) p. 142. Cf. E. M. W. Tillyard, *Shakespeare's Last Plays* (1958) p. 49.
12. Elizabethan psychology remains a fact to be reckoned with by any student of Shakespeare's plays. Edward Dowden was a pioneer in this field of study with his chapter on the subject in his *Essays, Modern and Elizabethan* (1910). A year earlier P. A. Robin had written on a particular aspect of that psychology in 'The Old Physiological Doctrine of the Spirits', in *Englische Studien*, XL (1910) 332–50. In the middle and later 1920s it was attracting the attention of such scholars as Murray Bundy, 'Shakespeare and Elizabethan Psychology', in *Journal of English and Germanic Philology*, XXIII (1924) 516–49; Hardin Craig, 'The Ethics of King Lear', in *Philological Quarterly*, IV (1925), 97–109, and 'Shakespeare's Depiction of the Passions', in *PQ* IV (1925) 289–301; George T. Buckley, 'The Indebtedness of Sir John Davies' *Nosce Teipsum* to Philip Mornay's *Trueness of the Christian Religion*', in *Modern Philology*, XXV (1927) 67–78; and Ruth L. Anderson, *Elizabethan Psychology and Shake-*

*speare's Plays* (Univ. of Iowa Humanistic Studies, III no. 4: 1927), and 'A French Source for John Davies of Hereford's System of Psychology', in *PQ* VI (1927) 57–66. In 1930 Lily Bess Campbell's *Shakespeare's Tragic Heroes: Slaves of Passion* appeared, a detailed study of Elizabethan psychology as it figures in Shakespeare's tragedies.

13. Cf. *Nicomachean Ethics* (Everyman ed.) p. 12; *Batman upon Bartholemew* (1582) book III, chap. 7; and Robert Allott, *Wits Theatre of the little World* (1599), pp. 37–8. The three souls are symbolized in *The Faerie Queene* in the tripartite structure of the House of Alma. Sir Toby Belch seems to have known the lore and would have Sir Andrew join him in a 'catch that will draw three souls out of one weaver' (*Twelfth Night* II iii 61–2).

14. Castiglione, *The Book of the Courtier* (Everyman ed.) p. 275.

15. Georges Poulet, in his *Studies in Human Time* (Baltimore, n.d.) p. 65, has a single reference to *The Tempest*, and that comes in his discussion of the three dreams of Descartes on the night of 10 November 1619. He indicates the similarity to *The Tempest* of the third dream, but not of the first, in which Descartes' experience with the animal aspect of his body is much like that of Prospero's with Caliban (p. 61). John Vyvyan (*The Shakespearean Ethic* (1959) p. 181) identifies Caliban with the unregenerate self of Prospero.

16. Cf. Frye, *The Tempest*, p. 17, and Nelson Sherwin Bushnell, 'Natural Supernaturalism in *The Tempest*', in *PMLA* XLVII (1932) p. 691.

17. *The Philosophical Works of Francis Bacon*, ed. John M. Robertson (1905) p. 494.

18. Cf. *Lear* IV iii 15–17, Richard Hooker's *The Laws of Ecclesiastical Polity* (Morley's Universal Library: n.d.) p. 66; and *Gorboduc*, in *Early English Classical Tragedies*, ed. John W. Cunliffe (Oxford, 1912) I ii 203–9 and 220–3.

19. Cf. Francis Meres, *Wits Commonwealth. The second part. A Treasurie, etc.* (1634) p. 345, and Peter de la Primaudaye, *The French Academie*, trans. T. B[owes] (1586) p. 309.

20. Bacon, *Philosophical Works*, p. 574.

21. Lily Bess Campbell, *Shakespeare's Tragic Heroes* (1930).

22. See *Of the Diseases of the Mind and the Body. A Discourse Written Originally in the Greek by Plutarchus Chaeronensis* ... (1651), reprinted in *The Works of Henry Vaughan*, ed. L. C. Martin (1915) I 113. See, too, Richard Barckley, *The Felicitie of Man, or His Summum Bonum* (1631) pp. 675–6, *The French Academie*, pp. 191–2, and *Wits Commonwealth*, p. 315.

23. A reminiscence perhaps of *The Aeneid* similar to those likenesses pointed out by Frye (*The Tempest*, p. 23). In the love affair of Aeneas

and Dido, Juno, encouraged by Venus, will, in her strategy against
her rival, 'join them in lasting marriage . . . / With Hymen present in
person' (*The Aeneid*, trans. C. Day Lewis (New York, 1953) IV 56–
127).

24. See *The Republic of Plato* (Everyman ed.) p. 300; *The Nicomachean Ethics* (Everyman ed.) pp. 164–5; *The Boke Named the
Governour*, p. 250 and *The Faerie Queene*, in which Spenser gives
five cantos of book II to the irascible passions and seven to the
concupiscible, introducing the sixth canto with an observation on the
subject. Tillyard thinks that Elizabethans would have sympathized
with Prospero's anxiety (*Shakespeare's Last Play*, p. 56).

25. Campbell, *Shakespeare's Tragic Heroes*, p. 24.

26. Explanations of Prospero's magic vary. Stoll and Frye take the
reader back to the white magic of Shakespeare's time (Stoll, pp. 703–4;
Frye, p. 20), though Frye warns that 'we distort the play if we think
of Prospero as supernatural' (p. 19), a view with which Craig is in
accord (p. 352). Nelson Sherman Bushnell, in his 'Natural Supernaturalism in *The Tempest*' (*PMLA* XLVII (1932) 693), argues that
in this play Shakespeare has turned away from his earlier practice of
introducing undiluted supernaturalism to present the supernatural
naturally as a valid and 'valuable factor in man's experience, an
essential part in the scheme of things'. To reach his conclusion,
however, he moves forward two centuries from Shakespeare and finds
an explanation in the thinking of Coleridge, Wordsworth, and Carlyle.
Bushnell insists upon one matter: that in 'all the claims of supernatural power made by Prospero or in his behalf . . . the pretended
spells are almost always wrought through the agency of familiar
forms of external nature, and are almost always described in terms of
everyday physical experience' (p. 688).

I venture another explanation. Prospero, to sustain himself and
Miranda on the island, drew upon his learning, his imagination, and
his newly discovered ability (represented in Ariel) to convert thoughts
and imaginative concepts to concrete form and deed. In order to
heighten his effects he adopted the extraneous devices of what Bacon
(*Philosophical Works*, p. 110) calls 'a palliation of a great part of
Ceremonial Magic. For it may be pretended that Ceremonies, Characters, and Charms, do work not by a tacit or sacramental contract with
evil spirits, but serve only to strengthen the imagination of him that
useth it; as images are said by the Roman church to fix the cogitations
and raise the devotions of them that pray before them'. Just before
the marriage revels, Prospero spoke of this coming event as a 'trick'
and requested Ariel, 'Go bring the rabble [Juno, Ceres, Iris and
others], / O'er whom I give thee power . . . for I must / Bestow upon
the eyes of this young couple / Some vanity of mine art' (IV i 37–41).

After he has put himself on the side of the 'nobler reason', he is ready to 'abjure' his 'rough magic', break his staff, and drown his book (v i 50–7). He insists that what he has done has not been supernatural.

27. Primaudaye, *The French Academie*, p. 289. Vyvyan (*The Shakespearean Ethic*, pp. 170–1) speaks of Prospero as a 'rising soul' whose elevation is determined by two tests concerning which Prospero makes his own decisions: (1) care and affection for a daughter (whom Vyvyan identifies as 'Love in the allegorical and archetypal sense'), who in turn aids in his ascension; and (2) a humane response to Ariel's account of the distracted enemies. Vyvyan does not, however, take into account the father's harshness toward his daughter when she crosses him, nor does he differentiate the significance of the tests, the first of which involves natural affection; the second, the 'nobler reason' of man with reference to, among others, an inveterate enemy and an 'unnatural' brother.

28. In *The French Academie*, p. 15, is a quite similar thought, which the author credits to Pindarus.

29. Lewis D. Einstein (*Tudor Ideals* (1921) p. 9) points out that in the Tudor age forceful ability as a ruler took precedence over even hereditary right.

30. Contemporary contemplation of death is excellently illustrated in the advice given Claudio by Duke Vincentio (*Measure for Measure* III i 5–41), in which the argument is similar to that in Montaigne's 'That To Learn To Philosophize Is To Learn to Die' (*The Essays of Montaigne* (1927) I 75–90). Such contemplation is plentiful, too, in the dirges, epitaphs and laments and lyrics of the day.

*Rose Abdelnour Zimbardo*

# FORM AND DISORDER IN
# *THE TEMPEST* (1963)

WHEN one is travelling through that wild terrain of criticism relating to Shakespeare's last plays, there is very little upon which to rely. One is faced with a thousand questions – Are the plays myth, romance, or an elaborate working out of the tragic pattern? Were they written because the poet wished to return to the forms he had used in youth, because he was bored, or because he was pandering to the tastes of a new audience? Is *The Tempest* a pastoral drama, a dramatic rendition of masque and anti-masque, or a religious parable? To each question there is a most ingeniously contrived reply. But, however sharply the critics disagree in their interpretations of *The Tempest*, there are two points upon which they stand together almost to a man. The first is that the last plays must be considered together; as Tillyard puts it, *The Tempest* 'gains much in lucidity when supported by the others'. The second point of agreement is that all of the last plays are concerned with the theme of regeneration, and that *The Tempest* realizes this theme most perfectly. It is upon these two points, I think, that the critics are most completely in error. *The Tempest* does not gain in being considered as part of a thematic whole that includes the others, rather its meaning becomes obscured in such a context. And the first error of tying the plays together leads inevitably to the second; it is always after a recapitulation of Thaisa's resurrection from the sea and Hermione's revival from the dead that the critics make an unjustifiable extension of the regeneration theory to include *The Tempest*. It is their unshaken belief that regeneration is the theme of the play that makes them slide over the key speech,

Our revels now are ended: these our actors –

As I foretold you – were all spirits and
Are melted into air, into thin air;
And like the baseless fabric of this vision
The cloud-capped towers, the gorgeous palaces,
The solemn temples, the great globe itself
Yea, all which it inherit, shall dissolve
And like this insubstantial pageant faded
Leave not a rack behind; we are such stuff
As dreams are made on, and our little life
Is rounded with a sleep.

This speech and the epilogue sound the keynote, but it is a note that jars with the triumphant harmony that the last plays are thought to express.

The meaning of *The Tempest* can best be approached if we contrast it with the other late plays. The most immediately perceptible difference between *The Tempest* and the romances is structural. Almost all critics of the play remark upon the closeness with which Shakespeare adheres to classical formulae in this work, a method both contrary to the poet's usual practice and almost inimical to the traditional structure of romance. For example, the unities of time, place, and action are preserved. Exposition of past action and the presentation of all the characters (except Stephano and Trinculo) occur before the end of the first act. The second act introduces the disturbance that must be resolved by the end of the play. In the third act the turbulence is intensified according to the formula for epitasis. The fourth act continues the epitasis with the threatened revolt of Caliban, but it also prepares for the comic ending with the union of the lovers. The peculiar insistence of the poet upon the classical structure becomes obvious at this point. As Kermode notes, 'The apparently unnecessary perturbation at the thought of Caliban may be a point at which an oddly pedantic concern for classical structure causes it to force its way through the surface of the play'.[2] The function of the disruption of the masque by the thought of Caliban will be treated later on, but one must agree with Kermode that here as well as elsewhere in the play, the rigorous formality of the structure forces itself

upon the reader's attention. It is a fact impossible to ignore that
Shakespeare deliberately constructed the play in accordance
with neo-Terentian rules. But why, one is led to ask, did he
choose so formal a structure in dealing with the extravagant
materials of romance? Clifford Leech, in his article on the
structure of the last plays has an interesting idea that may shed
light on this strange paradox. The last plays, he says, deal not
with single, limited incidents, as the comedies and tragedies,
for example, do. Rather, they deal with situations that follow
upon one another in haphazard concurrence with the flux that
is the governing pattern in actual life. That is, in the last plays
the beginnings and endings of the plays are not inevitable, but
are arbitrarily set, so that we could imagine the characters
having more adventures after the ending of the play. In *The
Tempest*, because of the controlling magic of Prospero, the
flux is arrested, but it remains as part of the undercurrent of the
play, 'in contra-puntal relationship to the act-structure'.[3] This
idea, when it is pursued, can lead us to the heart of the play, for
the theme of *The Tempest* is not regeneration through suffering,
but the eternal conflict between order and chaos, the attempt of
art to impose form upon the formless and chaotic, and the
limitations of art in this endeavor.

In proving this hypothesis, it might be well to begin with an
examination of the character of Prospero and the relation of
the other characters to him. Prospero is not, as Tillyard would
have him, a king who has made a tragic mistake and then
repented it, nor is he Wilson Knight's superman, nor Churton
Collins' idea of God. It would be going too far to say, with
D. G. James, that Prospero is a poet and Ariel his imagination;
but without falling into an allegorical interpretation we can
safely say that Prospero is an artist of a kind. He uses music,
the very symbol of order, in creating his effects, he attempts to
manipulate the other characters to the end of creating or pre-
serving order and form. We can say that for Prospero, as for
the poet who is creating the play, all time is present and all the
action fore-known to and controlled by him. However, to
counterbalance this image, which by itself might well cause a

critic to mistake him for God, Prospero is also at times irascible, at times a bit ridiculous, and always under necessity to combat those forces of disorder which he cannot control. We might outline his role in this way: Prospero at the beginning of the play is in a position in which he can take his enemies (who represent disordered mankind, since they are usurpers) out of the flux of life – which is emphasized by their voyage from a marriage feast back to the affairs of state. His enemies are Antonio and Sebastian, the center of the forces of disorder, and Alonso and Ferdinand, who will be permanently influenced by their experience; with them is Gonzalo, who already stands on the side of the forces of order. Prospero will place the travellers on an enchanted island which he controls almost completely through order and harmony – I say almost because he cannot wholly bring Caliban, the incarnation of chaos, into his system of order. He takes Alonso, Antonio, and Co. out of the flux of life and into a kind of permanence, a change which Ariel describes:

> Full fadom five thy father lies
> Of his bones are coral made
> Those are pearls that were his eyes
> Nothing of him that doth fade
> But doth suffer a sea-change
> Into something rich and strange.

The process is not one of regeneration into something more nobly human, and despite the interest of the Twentieth Century in Frazer's *Golden Bough*, there is nothing here that suggests fertility, rather the human and impermanent is transfixed into a rich permanence, but a lifeless one. Potentially corruptible bones and eyes become incorruptible coral and pearls; form and richness are fixed upon what was changing and subject to decay. Prospero takes the travellers out of the world of change and places them on his enchanted island, which is permeated with an ordering harmony. Caliban describes the effect of the harmony upon him,

> Sometimes a thousand twangling instruments
> Will hum about mine ears, and sometimes voices

That if I waked after long sleep
Will make me sleep again, and then in dreaming
The clouds methought would open and show riches
Ready to drop upon me, that when I wak'd
I cried to dream again.

This harmony first renders the animate inanimate and then reveals riches. Prospero will subject the travellers to the ordering influence of his art. Upon some of them he will impose an order that (we suppose) will stay with them even after they have returned to the world of change, some of them will be influenced only for the moment, as Caliban in the passage quoted, because they are agents of disorder. But in the end, all of them, even Prospero once he has abandoned his art, will have to return to the world of mutability.

I have said that Prospero is an artist who controls through his art. There is no suspense in the play because Prospero can control future as well as present action. His foreknowledge enables him to control all that occurs within the confines of the play. Kermode says that '. . . the qualities of the poor isle which gave [the characters] new birth, which purged Alonso's guilt and taught the princely skill to submit his fury to his reason, are the main theme of the play' (p. xxx). But the qualities of the isle have nothing to do with Prospero's art. In the exposition he tells us that he brought his art with him to the island, that Sycorax, the very mother of chaos, had employed the qualities of the island before Prospero's art brought them under the control of form and order. Nor can we believe that Prospero has yet to bring his fury under the control of reason. If he really had to wait for Ariel to persuade him to mercy, would he have arranged the union of his daughter with Ferdinand? Prospero has already brought order to himself and his island before the play opens. In the play he will take disordered men out of the world and place them under a control that has already been established. There is no real conflict in Prospero's world and therefore no suspense. The play is not one in which the theme evolves, it is rather displayed. The characters who are, as Pettet suggests,[4] more than half pasteboard, are lined up as representatives of order or disorder. Open conflict between the two forces never really occurs, but we are shown the ways in which chaos is always threatening to overflow the boundaries which form has set upon it. And finally we are shown by Prospero the nature and limitations of his art.

We must first discuss the forces of order and the forces of chaos as they are lined up in the scheme of the play. Prospero, of course, is the center of order, but Ferdinand and Miranda, under his tutelage, become agents of order, and Gonzalo represents an order of his own which exists even before he is manipulated by Prospero. It is significant that the images of an orderer and creator are applied to Gonzalo as well as to Prospero. For instance, in the scene where we first encounter Gonzalo, Antonio and Sebastian are mocking him thus,

> *Ant.* His words are more than the miraculous harp
> *Seb.* He hath raised the wall and houses too.
> *Ant.* What impossible matter will he make easy next?
> *Seb.* I think he will carry this island home in his pocket and give it to his son for an apple.
> *Ant.* And sowing kernels of it in the sea, will bring forth more apples.
> *Gon.* [having pondered] Aye.

Gonzalo, who we are told in the exposition was the one man who aided the exiled Prospero, is described by the men who mock him as a builder, a planter of seeds. It is true that he is a comic character; much of what he says is ridiculous. But the desire for order in a world governed by change is, to an extent, ridiculous. Prospero lives on an enchanted island where his word is law. Gonzalo lives in a world of mutability, governed by agents of disorder, like Antonio. His dream of order in such a world is bound to seem ridiculous. It is significant, however, that Gonzalo is made to long for the return of a golden age.

> . . . treason, felony,
> Sword, pike, knife, gun or need of any engine
> Would I not have; but Nature should bring forth
> Of its own kind all foison, all abundance
> To feed my innocent people.

Preposterous as it is, his account of an ideal kingdom makes its point. His fantasy is, at least, constructive; the chaffing of Antonio and Sebastian, destructive. There are two tests provided in the play that distinguish the advocates of order from the agents of disorder: obedience to laws governing political order, and obedience to laws governing personal, emotional order.

The emphasis that Prospero puts upon chastity and the sanctity of marriage has been interpreted as an indication that this play is a kind of elaborate fertility rite, or that a new, more mature love relationship is being considered here. But the love of Ferdinand and Miranda, as love, is unimportant. The lovers hardly come alive as characters, there is little actual wooing involved, and since we know from the beginning that Prospero approves of the match, suspense plays no part in our reaction to the love affair. But why should Prospero impose the rather meaningless task of log-carrying upon Ferdinand, and why should he be so insistent in urging the lovers to be chaste until the marriage ceremony is performed? Surely in comedy or romance the audience takes for granted that the lovers will be chaste until the wedding day. If there were to be some conflict involved, some reason to suspect that they would break, or at least be tempted to break, their promise to Prospero, this would be sufficient reason for the emphasis that he puts upon their vow of chastity. But Ferdinand and Miranda are so obviously chaste, so obviously obedient, that one questions why the issue should be raised at all. The answer is that ceremony, vows, all attempts to train human behavior to order are important. Ferdinand is made to carry logs, not because log-carrying is necessary, but because he must submit himself to the discipline of a test to win Miranda. He must submit will and pride to order, and when he does, Prospero gives him Miranda as 'thine own acquisition / Worthily purchased'. Chastity before marriage is necessary because it is part of the formal code to which human beings must submit that life may be meaningfully ordered. Ferdinand vows chastity in the hope of gaining 'quiet days, fair issue and long life', a good and orderly existence, not wildly romantic love. He promises not 'to take the edge off the [wedding] day's celebration'. The emphasis is not upon love, nor upon fertility, but upon order, ritual, ceremony.

However, the emphasis is not achieved through action (Ferdinand's trial is purposely made the dull chore of carrying logs) but through contrast. If Gonzalo, Ferdinand and Miranda, with Prospero in the fore, are the creators of and submitters to a system of order, Antonio and Sebastian, Stephano and Trinculo, with Caliban in the center, are creators of disorder. Again the two qualities that distinguish them as agents of chaos are sexual intemperance and the refusal to submit to political authority. Since Caliban is the very incarnation of chaos and an active creator of disorder (as Prospero is of order) it may be well to consider him first. Kermode has said that Caliban is the natural man, unqualified for nurture and existing on the simplest level of sensual pain and pleasure. But Caliban is not just nature stripped of grace and civility, he is unnatural; he is not simply unformed nature, he is deformed. He is not only incapable of receiving form, but he is also potentially able and eager to extend his own disordered nature. To begin with, Caliban is not a pastoral figure, a natural inhabitant of the island. He is not a man at all, but is 'legged like a man and his fins like arms', he is an unnatural half-man, half-fish. His very birth was inhuman, for his mother was Sycorax, a witch, and his father was the devil; he is, therefore, the offspring of active malignancy. G. Wilson Knight has said that Caliban is part of Prospero's nature, basing his arguments upon the speech at the end of the play wherein Prospero owns Caliban his. But Caliban is not part of Prospero, he comprises that element of the disordered that Prospero's art cannot reach, and Prospero claims him as a deficiency or limitation of his art. Caliban is actively opposed to Prospero's order. Prospero cannot enchant him into goodness, he controls him with agues and pinches. Caliban is a 'lying slave / Whom stripes may move not kindness'. At times he can be enchanted by the harmony of the island, but only for brief moments. Prospero's order must be constantly enforced and preserved against the ever-threatening encroachment of Caliban's disorder. It is significant that it is those very bulwarks

of order, temperance and obedience, those qualities which
Prospero so insistently exacts from Miranda and Ferdinand,
which Caliban's disordered nature resists. In the first scene in
which the monster appears we learn that his past response to
the ordering influence of Prospero has been an attempt to
ravish Miranda. His thwarted design is the desire to 'people
... this isle with Calibans', almost a symbol of chaos threatening
to overwhelm order. The idea recurs when Caliban promises
Stephano that Miranda 'will bring thee forth brave brood'. Just
as Ferdinand's obedience to order promises to reward him, after
due ceremony and in proper time, with 'fair issue', so Caliban's
rebellion against order threatens to people the isle with monsters
or drunken usurpers. This brings us to the second manifestation
of Caliban's disordered nature, rebellion. G. Wilson Knight's
description is apt. Caliban, he says, 'symbolizes all brainless
revolution such as Jack Cade's in *2 Henry VI*, and the absurdity
of the mob mentality in *Julius Caesar* and *Coriolanus*'.[5] The
whole scene with Stephano and Trinculo is an exquisite parody
of the power-quest theme. Stephano's attempts at high diction,
'by this hand I will supplant some of thy teeth', and 'the poor
monster's my subject and he shall not suffer indignity', are
delightfully comic. But there is a serious undertone throughout.
Caliban's mistaking a drunken churl for a god, the alacrity
with which he would exchange worth for worthlessness,

> A plague upon the tyrant that I serve!
> I'll bear him no more sticks, but follow thee
> Thou wondrous man.

But more important is the unrelenting malignancy of Caliban.
Stephano and Trinculo are clowns who are drunken and silly;
they can be diverted from their usurpation by the sight of a few
glittering garments, but Caliban's is an active evil. He prods
them to their task constantly with, 'When Prospero's destroyed',
and 'Let's alone and do the murther first'. His will is set upon
the destruction of order and goodness even when he has almost
nothing to gain from his revolt, for he is, after all, merely
exchanging one master for another. He has promised the same

service to Stephano that he had begrudged Prospero, 'I'll pluck thee berries / I'll fish for thee, and get thee wood enough'. His expected freedom is illusory for he has already pledged himself to slavery. His desire then is for the destruction of order and the creation of chaos.

Just as Gonzalo represents Prospero's kind of order as it appears in the world outside of the enchanted island, so Antonio represents Caliban's kind of disorder as it appears in life. Antonio, like Caliban, promotes evil for its own sake. He has nothing to gain from the usurpation by Sebastian of Alonso's throne, yet he prods Sebastian into rebellion and attempted murder for the sake of disrupting order. G. Wilson Knight finds countless verbal and imagistic echoes of *Macbeth* in the scheming of Antonio with Sebastian. This scene, by recalling the tragedies and histories, achieves a seriousness of tone that is rather startling in the atmosphere of the enchanted island. The serious undercurrent that runs through the Caliban-Stephano-Trinculo scenes here breaks the comic surface, and evil for its own sake, the urge of disorder to extend itself, stands fully revealed. Of course, Prospero's magic can control this manifestation of disorder; Ariel wakes Alonso, and all the travellers are put under a spell; but this control is only temporary. As Wilson Knight says, '. . . poetic honesty leaves Antonio's final reformation doubtful' (p. 213).

This brings us to the final question considered by the theme, the limitations of art in imposing order upon chaos. Prospero is a great artist, as we have said, but he is not to be confused with God. He has limitations. In the first place, he is mortal. His great art is a power which is not constant but which is assumed and which must finally be abandoned. Prospero's humanness is revealed to us at the very beginning of the play in two different scenes. The first is that in which he is revealing his past history to an almost completely inattentive Miranda. 'Dost thou attend me?' he asks. 'Thou attend'st not', he gently chides. 'I pray thee, mark me', he insists. A slight diminution from the great magician to dear old Daddy occurs here. But in the scene with Ariel where the mighty magician threatens the wisp of a spirit,

'If thou murmur'st, I will rend an oak / And peg thee in his knotty entrails till / Thou hast howl'd away twelve winters', Prospero earns the name that many critics have bestowed upon him of a crusty and irascible old pedant.

But though the artist is proved a man, that does not answer the question of the limitations of his art. What, we must ask ourselves, does Prospero's art finally accomplish? It has established an ordered future for Ferdinand and Miranda; it has wrought a permanent change upon Alonso; but it has not been able to touch the deeply disordered natures of Antonio and Sebastian and it had never been able to fix form upon Caliban. Prospero's art then can order what is amenable to order, but it can only affect temporarily that which is fundamentally chaotic. W. H. Auden seems to have recognized this problem of the inadequacy of Prospero's art. At the end of *The Mirror and the Sea* he has a stanza which is Antonio's;

> Your all is partial, Prospero
> My will is all my own
> Your need to love shall never know
> Me! I am I, Antonio
> By choice myself alone.

The will, the refusal to submit to order, is at the center of the evil that cannot be reached by Prospero's art.

Prospero is himself aware of the limitations of his art. The masque which has been the jumping-off place for so many of the theories that would describe the play as a fertility celebration, is, we are told by Prospero, only the enactment of his wishes for the blessing of an ordered life upon Ferdinand and Miranda. He describes the figures in the masque as,

> Spirits which by mine art
> I have from their confines called to enact
> My present fancies.

The masque reveals Prospero's desire for order and goodness, but his wish cannot be realized unless those upon whom he wishes this blessing themselves desire it. The masque is simply the projection of Prospero's imagination; it shows its frailty by dissolving when the great artist thinks of something else. The stage directions are quite explicit at this point. 'They join with the nymphs in a graceful dance, toward the end whereof Prospero starts suddenly and speaks, after which to a strange hollow and confused noise, they heavily vanish'. Prospero tells us that they are airy nothing, and as they vanish, he warns, all the endeavors of men at creation, palaces, cloud-capped towers, solemn temples are doomed to fade away. It is significant too that it is the recollection of Caliban, the threat of disorder and the coming of chaos, that drives the masque into thin air. The ordering influence of art can throw up only temporary bulwarks against change, disorder and decay. Prospero is fated, at last, to abandon his art and his enchanted island and to return to being a mere man in a world of change, facing final decay:

> Now my charms are all o'erthrown
> And what strength I have's my own
> Which is most faint . . .

> . . . Now I want
> Spirits to enforce, art to enchant
> And my ending is despair
> Unless I be reliev'd by prayer . . .

Only in a world of art, an enchanted island, or the play itself, does order arrest mutability and control disorder; but art must at last be abandoned, and then nothing is left mankind but to sue for grace.

## NOTES

1. E. M. W. Tillyard, *Shakespeare's Last Plays* (1954) p. 49.
2. Frank Kermode, Introduction to *The Tempest* (New Arden ed.: 1954) p. lxxv.
3. Clifford Leech, 'The Structure of the Last Plays', in *Shakespeare Survey*, 11 (1958), p. 27.
4. E. C. Pettet, *Shakespeare and the Romance Tradition* (New York, 1949).
5. G. Wilson Knight, *The Crown of Life* (1947) p. 211.

# Jan Kott

## PROSPERO'S STAFF (1964)

*The Tempest* has two endings: a quiet evening on the island, when Prospero forgives his enemies and the story returns to the point of departure; and Prospero's tragic monologue, spoken directly to the audience, a monologue out of time. But *The Tempest* also possesses two prologues. The first of these is the dramatic one; it takes place on the ship, which is set on fire by lightning and tossed on the rocks by the wind. The other prologue consists of Prospero's account of how he had lost his dukedom and came to live on the uninhabited island; it narrates the previous history of the *dramatis personae*.

On the surface, the first prologue – like Prospero's closing monologue – seems unnecessary. It takes place out of the island and only provides, as it were, a frame. But it serves a double dramatic purpose. It shows a real tempest, as distinguished from the inner storm, from the madness which will overcome the characters in view of the audience. It is only after the physical and material tempest has been depicted that the morality will be performed. All that happens on the island will be a play within a play, a performance produced by Prospero.

But this dramatic prologue has one other purpose. It is a direct exposition of one of the great Shakespearian theses, a violent confrontation of nature with the social order. The ship carries a king. What is royal might and majesty when confronted with raging elements? Nothing. Shakespeare repeats Panurge's famous invocation from the fourth book of *Gargantua and Pantagruel*, but how much more sharply and strongly he does it.

> *Gonzalo.* Nay, good, be patient.
> *Boatswain.* When the sea is. Hence! What cares these roarers for the name of king? To cabin: silence! Trouble us not.

*Gonzalo.* Good, yet remember whom thou hast aboard.

*Boatswain.* None that I more love than myself. You are a counsellor; if you can command these elements to silence, and work the peace of the present, we will not hand a rope more; use your authority: if you cannot, give thanks you have lived so long . . .

(1 i)

This in a nutshell, and in a condensed form, is the theme of *King Lear*.

In the prologue to *The Tempest*, the deprivation of majesty's sacred character – so characteristic of the Renaissance – is realized once more. Faced with the roaring sea, a boatswain means more than a king.

Now for Prospero's account, which is the other prologue to *The Tempest*. It is a long account and seems to include some undigested elements of an old play from which Shakespeare has probably taken the plot. It is of no importance. Prospero's story takes up one of the main, basic – almost obsessional – Shakespearian themes: that of a good and a bad ruler, of the usurper who deprives the legal prince of his throne. This is Shakespeare's view of history, eternal history, its perpetual, unchanging mechanism. It is repeated in the Histories and in the Tragedies – in *Hamlet* and *Macbeth* – even in the comedies, for this theme is present in *Measure for Measure* and in *As You Like It*. Only in the Roman tragedies, although the mechanism of history and of the struggle for power remains the same, are the *dramatis personae* different; they include the senate and the people, the patricians, tribunes and army generals.

In Prospero's narrative the framework of feudal history is bare, purged of all allegory and chance, almost deprived of names and character; it is abstract like a formula. Prospero's account is a summary of Machiavelli's treatise, *The Prince*.

> . . . the liberal arts,
> . . . being all my study,
> The government I cast upon my brother,
> And to my state grew stranger . . .
> . . . Thy false uncle –

Being once perfected how to grant suits,
How to deny them, who t'advance, and who
To trash for over-topping, new created
The creatures that were mine . . .
                    . . . set all hearts i'the state
To what tune pleas'd his ear; that now he was
The ivy which had hid my princely trunk,
And suck'd my verdure out on't.

To have no screen between this part he play'd
And him he play'd it for, he needs will be
Absolute Milan.

                    . . . confederates –
                    . . . . with the King of Naples
To give him annual tribute, do him homage.

                    . . . one midnight
                    . . . did . . . open
The gates of Milan . . .                          (I ii)

Prospero's narrative is a description of a struggle for power,
of violence and conspiracy. But it applies not only to the dukedom of Milan. The same theme will be repeated in the story of
Ariel and Caliban. Shakespeare's theatre is the *Theatrum Mundi*.
Violence, as the principle on which the world is based, will be
shown in cosmic terms. The previous history of Ariel and
Caliban is a repetition of Prospero's history, another illustration
of the same theme. Shakespearian dramas are constructed not on
the principle of unity of action, but on the principle of analogy,
comprising a double, treble, or quadruple plot, which repeats
the same basic theme; they are a system of mirrors, as it were,
both concave and convex, which reflect, magnify and parody
the same situation.[1] The same theme returns in various keys,
in all the registers of Shakespeare's music; it is repeated lyrically
and grotesquely, then pathetically and ironically. The same
situation will be performed on the Shakespearian stage by kings,
then repeated by lovers and aped by clowns. Or is it the kings
who ape the clowns? Kings, lovers, clowns are all actors. Parts
are written and situations given. So much the worse, if the actors

are not suited for their parts and cannot play them properly. For they perform on a stage which depicts the real world, where no-one chooses his or her part, or situation. Situations in Shakespearian theatre are always real, even when interpreted by ghosts and monsters.

Even before the sea-currents took the raft, carrying Miranda and Prospero, to the island, the first act of violence and terror had already taken place. Ariel had been captured by the witch Sycorax and – for refusing to obey her abominable orders – imprisoned in a cloven pine-tree. He suffered, for until then he had been free as air. 'Thou wast a spirit too delicate to act her earthy and abhorr'd commands' – as Prospero will tell him. Prospero liberates Ariel, but only to make him serve, to make him obey his own power. Shakespeare is always in a hurry to state the conflict and situations, abruptly and at once. No sooner has Prospero ended his narrative, and Ariel given his account of the shipwreck, than the conflict breaks out with full force. The prologue is over; action has begun.

*Ariel.* Let me remember thee what thou has promis'd,
    Which is not yet perform'd me.
*Prospero.* How now? moody?
    What is't thou canst demand?
*Ariel.* My liberty.
*Prospero.* Before the time be out? no more!          (I ii)

The theme of force has already been introduced twice. But on the island there is another character of the drama: Caliban. The same theme, the same situation will be repeated for the third time. Only the parts will be reversed and Shakespeare will introduce a new mirror. This time it will be a crooked mirror. Caliban is the offspring of Sycorax's union with the devil. On her death he assumed rule of the island. He was its rightful lord, at least in the feudal sense. Caliban lost his realm, just as Prospero had lost his dukedom. Caliban was overthrown by Prospero, just as Prospero had been overthrown by Antonio. Even before the morality proper is performed, and Prospero's enemies undergo the trial of madness, two acts of feudal history have already been played out on the desert island.

*Caliban.* This island's mine, by Sycorax my mother,
Which thou tak'st from me. When thou camest first,
Thou strok'dst me, and made much of me; wouldst give me
Water with berries in't ...
                           ... I ...

                           ... first was mine own king ...                    (I ii)

Caliban's first revolt still belongs to the antecedents of the
drama. Caliban assaulted Miranda and tried to rape her. His
attempt failed. Caliban was confined to a cave, forced to carry
wood and water, and suffer torture consisting of cramps, aches,
pricks. Shakespeare is a master of literality. Ariel's sufferings are
abstract, and the liberty he seeks is abstract too. It is a rejection
of all forms of dependence. Caliban's sufferings are concrete,
physical, animal. Characters in Shakespearian dramas are never
introduced by chance. The first scene in which Ariel appears
brings a demand for liberty. The first appearance of Caliban
marks a recollection of revolt. It is the entry of a slave. The
cruelty of this scene is wholly deliberate; so is its brutal
materialist quality.

*Prospero.* Thou poisonous slave, got by the devil himself
Upon thy wicked dam, come forth!
*Caliban.* As wicked dew as e'er my mother brush'd
With raven's feather from unwholesome fen,
Drop on you both! a south-west blow on ye,
And blister you all o'er!                                                   (I ii)

The exposition is over. Such are the life-stories of the inhabitants of a desert island, on the rocky shores of which the ship
carrying Prospero's old enemies has been wrecked.

For most commentators the island in *The Tempest* is a utopia,
or a fairy isle. Let us look at it more closely, as it is going
to be the scene of the drama proper. Where does this island
lie, what does it signify, and how has Shakespeare described
it?

From the itinerary of the sea-voyage undertaken by Alonso,
King of Naples, who is returning from Tunis, and from the

story of the witch Sycorax, who had come to the island from Algiers, it follows that Prospero's island should be situated in the Mediterranean. At the cross-roads of both routes lies Malta. Other commentators place the island nearer to Sicily and think it is the rocky Pantelleria. Still others are of the opinion that the island lies near the shore of North Africa and take it to be Lampedusa. But Setebos, whom the witch Sycorax worshipped, was a god of the Patagonian Indians, while Ariel brings Prospero 'dew from the still-vex'd Bermoothes', or Bermuda.

In 1609 the Earl of Southampton sent a large fleet with the men and equipment necessary to colonize Virginia, the first English colony on the North American coast. The expedition raised hopes of fabulous fortunes and fired the imagination. For the first time not only astronomers, but also merchants, bankers and politicians realized that the earth is really round. The world inhabited by man was enlarged to twice its size in the course of a century. The discovery of another hemisphere caused a shock that can only be compared to the landing of an earth-launched rocket on the moon and the photographing of its farther side. Jean Fernel, one of the most eminent people of the new era, a humanist, mathematician and court physician to the King of France, wrote in his *Dialogue* in the year 1530: 'Our times have seen things not even dreamt of by the ancients . . . The Ocean has been crossed thanks to the bravery of our sailors, and new islands have been discovered . . . A new globe has been given us by the mariners of our times'. If new worlds, inhabited by intelligent creatures, have been discovered on earth, why should they not exist in the heavenly spheres as well? This is the conclusion reached by Giordano Bruno; a conclusion for which he was burnt at the stake in 1600, on the charge of heresy. At that time Shakespeare was beginning to write *Hamlet*. *The Tempest* was written eleven years later.

Recent commentators connect the origins of *The Tempest* with the accounts of the English fleet's expedition to Virginia in 1609. The expedition failed. The flag-ship *Sea Adventure*, caught in a storm, was wrecked and the sailors landed on an uninhabited island, forming part of Bermuda. They spent ten

months there; then they built two new ships and eventually
managed to reach Virginia. They called the islands on which
they were thrown by the storm, Devil's Islands. At night they
could hear mysterious howls and noises, which – according to
contemporary accounts – they attributed to demons. It is from
them that Shakespeare may have taken the Boatswain's story of:

> strange and several noises
> Of roaring, shrieking, howling, jingling chains,
> And more diversity of sounds, all horrible.          (v i)

These accounts made the colonists indignant, and the council
of the colonists of Virginia published a pamphlet by William
Barrett declaring that rumours of Bermuda being visited by devils
and evil spirits were false, or at any rate exaggerated, and that
in that 'tragical comedy there is nothing that could discourage
the colonists'.[2] The settlers of Virginia interpreted Shakespeare
more sensibly than some of his most recent commentators.

It has also been found that Prospero fed Caliban with a certain
kind of inedible 'fresh-brook mussels', mentioned in accounts
of the unfortunate expedition. In Ariel setting fire to the ship
('I'ld divide, and burn in many places; on the topmast, the yards,
and bowsprit, would I flame distinctly') some Shakespearian
scholars see the picture of the St. Elmo fires, which so terrified
those who were shipwrecked at the time of the Bermuda disaster.

Shakespeare's fantastic vision was always based on contemporary realities; thanks to them the world he showed in a
condensed form on the stage became even more concrete. But it
was always the whole world. It is useless, therefore, to look
for the longitude and latitude of Prospero's island.

In *The Tempest* there is, doubtless, something of the
atmosphere of long sea-voyages, mysterious desert islands;
but there is also the anxiety and daring of the conclusions
reached by Giordano Bruno. In any event, *The Tempest* is a
long way removed from the naive enthusiasm and childish pride
of the first witnesses of geographical discoveries. The questions
raised by *The Tempest* are philosophical and bitter.

The morality staged by Prospero will last less than four

hours. But the island itself is outside time. There is on it both winter and summer. Prospero bids Ariel 'to run upon the sharp wind of the north, to do . . . business in the veins o'the earth when it is bak'd with frost'. The island has salt and sweet waters, barren and fertile lands, lemon groves and quagmires. It abounds in hazel-nuts, apples are ripe, there are truffles in the forest. The island is inhabited by baboons, hedgehogs, vipers, bats and toads. Jays have their nests here, sea-gulls perch on the rocks. Berries grow here, there are sea-shells of various kinds; feet are hurt by thorns; one hears mastiffs bark and cocks crow.

Commentators on *The Tempest* find on this island the idyllic atmosphere of an Arcadia. No doubt they interpret the play only through bad theatre performances; those with a ballet-dancer and a translucent screen. They see fairy-tale and ballet all the time. Well, one would rather trust those who undergo on this island the trial of madness:

> All torment, trouble, wonder, and amazement,
> Inhabit here: some heavenly power guide us
> Out of this fearful country! (v i)

That is why it is useless to look for Prospero's island even among the white spaces of old maps, where the contours of the land grow indistinct, the ocean blue turns pale and either drawings of fantastic monsters appear, or the inscription: *ubi leones*. Even there the island does not exist. Prospero's island is either the world, or the stage. To the Elizabethans it was all the same; the stage was the world, and the world was the stage.

On Prospero's island, Shakespeare's history of the world is played out, in an abbreviated form. It consists of a struggle for power, murder, revolt and violence. The first two acts of that history had been played out even before the arrival of Alonso's ship. Now Prospero will speed up the action. Twice more will the same history be repeated; as a tragedy, and as a grotesque; then the performance will be over. Prospero's island has nothing in common with the happy isles of Renaissance utopias. It rather reminds us of the islands in the world of the late Gothic. Such worlds were painted by one of the greatest visionaries among painters, precursor of the Baroque and

Surrealism, the mad Hieronymus Bosch. They rise out of a grey sea. They are brown or yellow. They take the form of a cone, reminding one of a volcano, with a flat top. On such hills tiny human figures swarm and writhe like ants. The scenes depict the seven deadly sins and the human passions, above all lechery and murder, drunkenness and gluttony. As well as people there are demons with beautiful, slender angelic female bodies and toads' or dogs' heads. Under the tables shaped like big tortoise-shells, old hags with flabby breasts and children's faces lie embracing half-men, half-insects with long hairy spider-like feet. Tables are set for a common feast, but the jugs and plates assume the shape of insects, birds or frogs. This island is a garden of torment, or a picture of mankind's folly. It is even similar in its shape to the Elizabethan stage. Boats arrive at a quiet harbour at the foot of the mountain. This is the apron-stage. The main scenes take place in large caves and on terraces of the volcanic cone. The flat top of the mountain is empty. There are no actors on the upper stage. No one gives his blessing or sits in judgement over the follies depicted. The island is the scene of the world's cruel tortures. In that world Shakespeare was a witness. But there are no gods in it, and gods are not needed. Men will suffice:

> Our natures do pursue,
> Like rats that ravin down their proper bane,
> A thirsty evil; and when we drink we die.               (I ii)

This quotation from *Measure for Measure* could serve as an inscription to the large canvases by Bosch depicting *The Temptation of St. Anthony* or *The Garden of Pleasure*. Such is Prospero's island. Ariel is its angel and its executioner. That is why when wishing to be seen he assumes in turn the form of a nymph and a harpy. This is the sentence he pronounces on the shipwrecked:

> Destiny, –
> That hath to instrument this lower world
> And what is in't, – the never-surfeited sea
> Hath caus'd to belch up you; and on this island,

Where man doth not inhabit, – you 'mongst men
Being most unfit to live. I have made you mad;
And even with such-like valour men hang and drown
Their proper selves.                                    (III iii)

On Prospero's orders Ariel pursues the shipwrecked, leads
them astray by his music, torments and scatters them. Alonso,
the King of Naples, and the loyal Gonzalo are tired. They fall
asleep with the entire retinue. Only the treacherous Antonio,
and the King's brother, Sebastian, are to keep watch. The story
of the plot aimed at seizing power will repeat itself. But
Shakespeare uses a different mirror. The loss of the dukedom by
Prospero has been told concisely, with a dry precision, as if in a
history text-book; it has been unfolded like a formula, like a
mechanism. This time, action is slowed down and shown in a
typically Shakespearian close up. As in a film. Every second
counts, and we can observe every vibration of the soul, every
gesture. The King and Gonzalo are asleep. The moment is
ripe. It may never happen again:

*Sebastian.* But, for your conscience, –
*Antonio.* Ay, sir; where lies that? if 'twere a kibe,
  'Twould put me to my slipper; but I feel not
  This deity in my bosom: twenty consciences,
  That stand 'twixt me and Milan, candied be they,
  And melt, ere they molest!                           (II i)

Antonio and Sebastian raise their swords. In a moment
murder will be committed. Shakespeare is, indeed, obsessed by
this theme. Only the mirrors change. And every one of these
mirrors is just another commentary on situations that remain
the same. Prospero's island, like Denmark, is a prison. Antonio's
and Sebastian's plot repeats scenes from *King Lear*;

        If that the heavens do not their visible spirits
        Send quickly down to tame these vile offences,
        It will come,
        Humanity must perforce prey on itself,
        Like monsters of the deep.                     (IV ii)

Swords will be put back again, for Ariel is watching. He
is both an agent-provocateur and the stage-manager of the

performance produced by Prospero. Murder does not have to be committed. It is enough that it has been exposed. For it is only a morality that is being performed on the island. Prospero submits the castaways to a trial of madness. But what does this madness mean? Sebastian repeats Antonio's deed of twelve years ago. The island is a stage on which the history of the world is being acted and repeated. History itself is madness. As in *Richard III*:

> Welcome, destruction, blood and massacre!
> I see, as in a map, the end of all.                          (II iv)

Prospero conducts his characters through ultimate, eschatological situations. Sebastian repeats Antonio's attempt to assassinate his brother and gain power. But Antonio had made his attempt in Milan in order to become a real duke. Sebastian wants to murder his king and brother on a desert island. The ship has been tossed on the rocks, and only a handful of survivors are left stranded in a strange land. Sebastian's attempt is in fact a disinterested act, pure folly; like the theft of a sack of gold in a desert, among people condemned to die of thirst. Sebastian's gestures and motives are identical with Antonio's gestures and motives of twelve years ago, following the pattern of a real *coup d'état*. This is the essence of Shakespearian analogy and of the system of ever-changing mirrors. The history of mankind is madness, but in order to expose it, one has to act it out on a desert island.

The first tragic sequence of the scenario devised by Prospero is over. The coup d'état has been performed. But it has been performed by princes. The law of analogy has not yet been exhausted, and another great confrontation awaits us. Actors and their parts are changed again, but the situation remains the same. Shakespeare's world is a unity, and a conglomeration not only of styles. A *coup d'état* is not the privilege of princes only; and it is not just the princes who have a passion for power. A coup d'état has already been shown in *The Tempest* three times through tragic lenses; now it will be performed as a buffoonery. Characters in the Shakespearian theatre are divided into tragic and grotesque. But grotesque in the Shakespearian theatre is not just a gay interlude, intended to entertain the audience after the cruel scenes performed by kings and dukes. Tragic scenes in Shakespeare often have *buffo*, grotesque, or ironic undertones and the *buffo* scenes are often mixed with bitterness, lyricism and cruelty. In his theatre it is the clowns who tell the truth. And not just tell it; they re-enact situations usually reserved for princes. Stephano, the drunkard, and Trinculo, the clown, want power too. Together with Caliban they organize an attempt on Prospero's life. History again repeats itself. But this time it is only a farce. This farce, too, will prove itself tragic. But for the moment it is pure buffoonery:

> Monster, I will kill this man: his daughter and I will
> be king and queen, – save our graces! – and Trinculo
> and thyself shall be viceroys. (III ii)

Prospero's island is a scene symbolizing the real world, not a utopia. Shakespeare explains this clearly when speaking directly to the audience, almost over-emphatically. Gonzalo is the reasoner of the drama. He is loyal and honest, but simple-minded and ridiculous at the same time. The King has not yet fallen asleep. The assassination has not yet been attempted. Gonzalo begins to tell a story of a happy country. He must have read recently the famous chapter on cannibals from Montaigne's *Essays*. He is repeating Montaigne's words. In that happy country work and commerce are unknown, there are no offices and no power:

> *Gonzalo (ending).* No sovereignty, – . . .
> *Antonio.* The latter end of his commonwealth forgets the
>   beginning.
> *Gonzalo.* All things in common nature should produce
>   Without sweat or endeavour: treason, felony,
>   Sword, pike, knife, gun, or need or any engine,
>   Would I not have; but nature should bring forth,
>   Of it own kind, all foison, all abundance,
>   To feed my innocent people. (II i)

Human beings, beautiful and intelligent, live in a state of nature, free from original sin and uncorrupted by civilization.

Nature is good and people are good. Such are the happy isles of the anti-feudal utopias. They were being discovered in the South Seas by the simple friars of the Order of St. Francis who found in them – long before Rousseau – good and noble savages. These 'noble savages' had been written about by Montaigne. But Shakespeare did not believe in 'good savages', just as he did not believe in 'good kings'. When he did look for a Utopia, he located it in the forest of Arden, where Robin Hood had been with his company. But even this utopia had an element of bitterness in it: Jaques did not find his place even there. Shakespeare did not believe in the happy isles. They were too close to the known continents.

*A Midsummer Night's Dream* is a comedy. *The Tempest* was also regarded as a comedy by his contemporaries. The *Dream* is a forerunner of *The Tempest* but written in a lighter vein. The Duke is kind-hearted and understanding. Hermia's father forgives her. Hymen will join three happy couples. Such is the situation in the epilogue. But in the prologue, the father demands the death penalty for his daughter, who has chosen her lover against his will; the lovers flee to the forest. Hermia loves Lysander. Demetrius is passionately in love with Hermia, Helena with Demetrius. The world is cruel and irrational at the same time; it makes a mockery of all feeling. But love itself is irrational, too.

And nature? Nature is represented by the Athenian wood – which is really the forest of Arden. Oberon and Titania live there, but in fact it is the realm of Puck. Puck is not just a country troll. He is also the *commedia dell'arte* Harlequin. But the real Harlequin is the devil. To Shakespeare nature is just as irrational as law and customs. It makes a mockery of feelings, order, conscious decisions.

Some berry juice has been put into a lover's eyes. He wakes, has no eyes for the girl asleep beside him; he runs after another, forgetting the one he has loved. Some more juice and he again forgets everything, even the fact that he has betrayed his girl. For he betrayed her during the night. Night and day have different laws.

Titania is slender, affectionate, lyrical. She wakes in the middle of the night and sees a fool with the head of an ass. That same night she will give everything up for him. She has dreamt about just such a lover, only she never wanted to admit it. In the morning she will want to forget it as soon as possible. Titania, embracing a monster with an ass's head, is close to Bosch's cruel visions. But at the same time there is in her something of the great grotesque of the surrealists. In these dream images of a summer night broken by day's sobriety there is a novel and precursory foretaste of depth-psychology and the subconscious. Madness lasts here throughout the June night. Then the dawn comes. Everybody wakes up thinking they have had strange and awful dreams. They do not want to remember their dreams. They are ashamed of the night. In the grand vision of love's madness Shakespeare is simultaneously a man of the Renaissance and a very modern writer. It is here that one should look for the truly modern Shakespeare: bitter, but very human.

On Prospero's island the laws of the real world apply to an even higher degree than in the forest of Arden. No sooner has Gonzalo finished telling his story and lain down to sleep beside the King than Antonio and Sebastian stand over him, bare swords in hand. A show commences, as cruel as the world; the same world that Hamlet looked upon:

> . . . the whips and scorns of time,
> The oppressor's wrong, the proud man's contumely,
> The pangs of despised love, the law's delay,
> The insolence of office, and the spurns
> That patient merit of the unworthy takes . . .
>
> (*Hamlet* III i)

Ariel has fulfilled Prospero's orders. His enemies have repeated gestures of twelve years ago. Gestures, not deeds. From the first to the final scene they were just a handful of shipwrecked men on a desert island. In such a situation they could only repeat naive gestures. These gestures were madness itself, and this is the essence of the trial through which Prospero leads his actors. They have gone the whole way to the hell raging in their own souls. They have at last seen themselves 'naked like worms'.

This expression taken from Sartre fits here most aptly. Alonso
has realized the purpose of this trial:

> This is as strange a maze as e'er men trod;
> And there is in this business more than nature
> Was ever conduct of . . .                 (v i)

The performance of *The Tempest* and the morality produced
by Prospero is drawing to an end. It is almost six o'clock. The
same clock has counted the inner time of the performance and,
the time of the audience. For it is both actors and spectators
who – in the course of four hours – have gone through the same
tempest. Everybody, in fact.

>                Not a soul
> But felt a fever of the mad, and play'd
> Some tricks of desperation.          (i ii)

On the island, which Shakespearian scholars took to be
Arcadia, the history of the world has once more been performed
and repeated.

## NOTES

1. Analogy as a principle of Shakespeare's dramatic writing has
been referred to by F. Fergusson, *The Idea of a Theatre* (Princeton,
1949); R. Moulton, *Shakespeare as a Dramatic Artist* (Oxford, 1885);
W. Empson, *Some Versions of Pastoral* (1935). Henry James uses the
term 'the central reflector' in connection with *Hamlet*.

2. Quoted by L. Chambrun, *Shakespeare Retrouvé* (1947).

# QUESTIONS

1. How important is music in the play?

2. Coleridge described the play as having 'scenic solemnity'. Justify the appropriateness of this description, by considering the spectacular effects in the play.

3. It has been suggested that since Prospero controls the action of the play, it is lacking in dramatic conflict. Do you agree?

4. What symbolic elements do you see in the play?

5. Consider the different aspects of Time as they are used in the play.

6. What part does the theme of service *versus* freedom play in *The Tempest*?

7. Examine Shakespeare's presentation of villainy in the play: is it possible to distinguish between serious and comic wickedness?

8. Trace the interplay of feelings of wonder and disillusion in *The Tempest*.

9. Examine the patterns of parallelism and contrast in the characterisation of the play.

10. How appropriately does Shakespeare distinguish between the major characters of the play in their styles of speech?

11. Do you agree that the play shows Prospero's limitations as well as his virtues?

12. Compare the reactions of Ferdinand and Miranda to each other as lovers.

13. How far does Shakespeare arouse sympathetic feelings towards Caliban?

14. What is Gonzalo's role in the play?

15. What dramatic purposes do Trinculo and Stephano serve, other than the amusement provided by their clowning?

16. How effective is the opening scene as a beginning to the play. What would be lost if it were omitted?

17. Prospero's lengthy exposition in the second scene of the play has been criticised as a crude technique for giving necessary information to the audience. Can you suggest any means of of defending its effectiveness?

18. Is the Masque of Ceres an integral part of the play, or an interlude in the main action? Justify its presence in the play.

19. Analyse Prospero's speech after the Masque (beginning 'Our revels now are ended'), showing its theatrical effectiveness and relating it to the main themes of the play.

20. Examine the feelings aroused by the last scene of the play.

21. Do you think *The Tempest* appeals simultaneously to sophisticated and naive tastes?

# SELECT BIBLIOGRAPHY

1. *The Tempest*, ed. Frank Kermode (New Arden Shakespeare: Methuen and Harvard University Press 1954).

This is the best modern edition, with an excellent Introduction, and appendices including extracts from the Virginia Company's papers and from Montaigne's essay 'Of the Caniballes'.

2. Enid Welsford, *The Court Masque* (Cambridge University Press and Macmillan 1927).

A standard study of the traditions of the Renaissance masque, illustrated with some fascinating contemporary accounts of examples performed on court occasions.

3. Walter Clyde Curry, *Shakespeare's Philosophical Patterns* (Louisiana State University Press, 1937).

This book includes a discussion of neo-Platonic ideas current in Shakespeare's time about 'white' and 'black' magic, and about the agency of spirits.

4. E. W. Tayler, *Nature and Art in Renaissance Literature* (Columbia University Press, 1964).

The first part of the book gives a general account of these concepts as they were related to each other in European thought from antiquity to the Renaissance; and a later chapter examines Shakespeare's treatment of Nature and Art in *The Winter's Tale*.

5. G. Wilson Knight, *The Shakespearian Tempest* (Oxford University Press, 1932).

An imaginative interpretation of the symbolic use of

music and storm imagery throughout Shakespeare's plays, to dramatise harmony and conflict.

6. E. Law, *Shakespeare's 'Tempest' as originally produced at Court* (Shakespeare Association Pamphlet, 1920).
A historical reconstruction of the stage conditions and methods for the Court performance of November 1611.

7. E. K. Chambers, 'The Integrity of *The Tempest*' in *Shakespearian Gleanings* (Oxford University Press, 1925).
A detailed discussion of textual problems in the play, and a defence of the authority of the First Folio text.

8. G. E. Bentley, 'Shakespeare and the Blackfriars Theatre', in *Shakespeare Survey*, 1 (1948) pp. 38–50.
The article argues that Shakespeare's last romantic plays were written primarily for the indoors theatre at Blackfriars, with its stage machinery and courtly audience.

9. N. Coghill, 'The Basis of Shakespearian Comedy', in *Essays and Studies*, N.S. III (1950) pp. 1–28.
An essay on Shakespeare's debt to medieval conceptions of comedy, with a final section on the 'allegorical impressionism' of *The Tempest*. A shortened and revised version is to be found in *Shakespeare Criticism 1935–1960*, selected by Anne Ridler (World's Classics: O.U.P. 1963).

10. Bernard Knox, '*The Tempest* and the Ancient Comic Tradition', in *English Stage Comedy*, ed. W. K. Wimsatt (English Institute Essays: Columbia University Press, 1954).
This article relates the themes of slavery and freedom in the play to Plautine comic structure.

11. C. J. Sisson, 'The Magic of Prospero', in *Shakespeare Survey*, 11 (1958) pp. 70–7.
This essay shows that magic in *The Tempest* is to be taken seriously and literally, and discusses Prospero's powers in the light of contemporary attitudes to sorcery and alchemy.

12. Don Cameron Allen, 'William Shakespeare: *The Tempest*', *Image and Meaning* (Johns Hopkins Press and Oxford University Press 1960).

A study of some of the play's themes and their background in classical, medieval, and Renaissance literary motifs.

ADDENDUM 1979

Frances A. Yates, *Shakespeare: Last Plays—A New Approach* (Routledge, 1975).

A fascinating attempt to relate the last plays to the court of King James, suggesting that Prospero is Shakespeare's vindication of the magus John Dee in reply to the censure of James.

# NOTES ON CONTRIBUTORS

W. H. AUDEN (1907–73), the best known of the 1930s poets.

REUBEN A. BROWER (d. 1975), was Professor of English at Harvard University. Author of critical works on, among others, Pope and Robert Frost.

JOHN P. CUTTS, American academic, best known for work on Shakespeare and on the seventeenth-century lyric.

FRANK DAVIDSON, Professor Emeritus of English at Indiana University; Shakespeare critic and scholar.

HENRY JAMES (1843–1916), the famous novelist. The Introduction to *The Tempest* published here is one of James's rare excursions into Shakespeare criticism.

FRANK KERMODE, a Fellow of King's College, Cambridge, where he was (1975-82) King Edward VII Professor of English Literature. His works include *Romantic Image*, *The Sense of an Ending*, and important contributions to Shakespeare Studies.

JAN KOTT, author of the much-discussed *Shakespeare Our Contemporary*. He studies Shakespeare in the light of twentieth-century middle-European history, and is particularly concerned with modern theatrical production.

JOHN MIDDLETON MURRY (1889–1957), distinguished author and critic of the early twentieth century, whose numerous books included studies of Swift, Keats and Shakespeare.

E. M. W. TILLYARD (1889–1962), one of the founders of the Cambridge English school, and a distinguished Master of Jesus

College, Cambridge. His numerous books include *Shakespeare's History Plays*, *Shakespeare's Problem Plays*, *Shakespeare's Last Plays*, as well as three books on Milton and a major study of the English epic.

**G. Wilson Knight, Emeritus Professor of English at Leeds. Perhaps the best known and most influential Shakespeare critic since A. C. Bradley. His works include several studies of Shakespeare.**

Rose Abdelnour Zimbardo has taught at City College, New York, and in the State University of New York. Her publications include *Wycherley's Drama* and critical studies on Shakespeare.

# INDEX